For Susan,

May you have trance

forming experiences.

Best Regards,

Carol Kershaw

Library of Congress Cataloging-in-Publication Data
Kershaw, Carol J.
    The couple's hypnotic dance: creating Ericksonian
strategies in marital therapy / Carol J. Kershaw.
        p.   cm.
    Includes bibliographical references and indexes.
    ISBN 0-87630-625-3
    1. Marital psychotherapy.   2. Hypnotism—Therapeutic use.
3. Erickson, Milton H.   I. Title.
    [DNLM: 1. Erickson, Milton H.   2. Hypnosis.   3. Marital Therapy—
methods.   WM K41e]
RC488.5.R49   1991
616.89′156—dc20
DNLM/DLC
for Library of Congress   91-23466
                                                                       CIP

Published by
BRUNNER/MAZEL, INC.
19 Union Square West
New York, New York 10003

MANUFACTURED IN THE UNITED STATES OF AMERICA

10 9 8 7 6 5 4 3 2 1

To Bill, who makes me laugh

Contents

Foreword

This book is about hypnosis, couples, and therapy. To many, such a combination of topics evokes the question, "What's wrong with this picture?" These concepts do not go together in traditional orientations to mental health. Therapists often consider hypnosis as an intrapsychic oriented tool for poking about in memories—possibly with the goal of suppressing a symptom in response to a suggestion or for gaining insight to an historic conflict. On the other hand, many regard couples therapy and family therapy as the opposite end of a continuum where interpersonal dimensions are stressed in the here and now.

Hypnosis, aside from consistently suffering a somewhat peripheral and often suspect role in individual therapy, has remained almost unknown in family therapy. Apart from the work of such mid-century luminaries as R.D. Laing, who pointed out the hypnotic experience of family life, and Eric Berne, who observed that parents hypnotize their children, very little has connected it with family therapy. Generally, most practitioners have associated hypnosis with "deep pathology" and dangerous unknowns.

In fact, the entire field of mental health has focused on labeling and treating individuals as pathological throughout most of its history, and relatively scant attention has been given to acknowledging or utilizing individual health or family dynamics. Only during the last several decades have we witnessed a change in this bias. The larger family and social context is now seen as the backdrop against which (ostensibly) individual pathology is manifested and understandable. Surprisingly, however, even after systemic factors have come under investigation, pathology-oriented labeling continues to be a means for "explaining" individuals within the context of couples and families.

The psychoanalytic oriented family therapy approaches began in the late 1930s with the work of Ackerman and gave rise to the lines along which followed Boszormenyi-Nagy, Bowen, the Philadelphia Child Guidance Clinic, and others. This was but one of three main trends in family therapy. Bateson and his associates, following the conceptualizations of cybernetics and general systems theory in the early 1950s, fostered the interpersonally orientated communication project, the MRI model, and others. Most notable among these were Virginia Satir and the personal growth movement, and Jay Haley's problem-solving approach. Yet a third and quite independent development for family therapy came from a somewhat quieter source who also had considerable influence on the early Bateson team, MRI, Satir, and Haley, because of his unique approach to people and problems. This was, of course, Milton Erickson. Erickson had been seeing couples, families, and individuals, and all the while using hypnosis in his therapy work. Just as Erickson's family work was non-analytic so, too, was his hypnosis work.

In the last few decades, the quiet voice of Milton Erickson has penetrated the mental health field, inspiring many to freshly consider various types of communication, hypnotic and otherwise, within a non-pathological and future-oriented approach to mental health care. Erickson extended current scientific theories of hypnosis to include the common everyday trance, and thus bridged the gap between hypnosis and family therapy suggested by Laing and Berne.

In the following pages, Dr. Carol Kershaw makes salient and timely observations about hypnotic features within the marital dyad. She provides a thorough and practical review of the supporting literature and theoretical underpinnings for these ideas and offers methodological guidelines for practitioners. Her attention to and use of client behavior in a non-pathological and future orientation is the distinguishing mark of Erickson's legacy, but Kershaw also integrates the strengths of competing or contradictory views of hypnosis from other authors.

While primarily focusing upon hypnosis in families, both as a therapeutic intervention and as a naturally occurring component of interpersonal dyads, Kershaw provides both an education in and an overview of hypnosis itself. The education she provides includes a strong focus on the interpersonal context, which is so often underemphasized or ignored entirely in many works detailing aspects of hypnotic technique.

Symptoms are important forms of communication that signal relational processes out of balance or out of control. Symptoms provide unconscious communication about developmental conflicts interfering with here-and-now learning and problem solving. Therefore, Kershaw's perspective involves helping clients retrieve and build their resources in order to facilitate new relational patterns so that symptoms are no longer necessary as a "best choice" to respond to the developmental demands. This exploration furthers our own understanding of expanding traditional uses of individual-focused hypnosis beyond those of relaxation and direct suggestion for symptom removal. Instead, Kershaw's frame includes attention to how what she calls "symptomatic trance" can be utilized to induce a healing trance, complete with alterations in the interpersonal context. The scientific literature on hypnosis as an intervention to facilitate symptom removal with direct suggestion scores a high rate of initial success, especially with anxiety based symptoms. But follow-up studies often reveal that such changes are not lasting or that other "symptoms" are subsequently substituted. When therapists understand the interpersonal-developmental function of symptoms—or what we call the ecosystemic aspects—and work with clients to cocreate new and creative responses to developmental challenges, presenting symptoms are logically abandoned to the past where they had once been adaptive and necessary. It follows that psychosomatic symptoms, as well as marital crisis, are developmental cues that can be seen as opportunities for personal and marital growth.

We especially are attracted to the thorough and respectful way Dr. Kershaw writes about the importance of therapists "shifting lenses." She develops an empathy regarding the individuals and a respect for the well-being of the system as it represents the best choice in their problem solving so far. She defines empathy as basic regard for people and their life struggle that does not include blame. Within this context, she outlines and details useful parameters for assessment of couple dynamics with an awareness of the intrapsychic dynamics that influence interactional events. As therapists grasp system dynamics as well as the developmental knowledge of both the individuals and the coupled dyad, holistic and powerful interventions follow rather naturally. Dr. Kershaw accordingly makes the connection between assessment and tentative treatment plans clear and accountable. The importance of this connection cannot be overstated, especially when departing from traditional hypnosis to an emphasis on indirect approaches. Furthermore, she endorses a highly individualized and specifically tailored treatment plan—yet another hallmark of an Ericksonian approach that values flexibility rather than a rigid model applied arbitrarily to all clients or problem categories. Overall, there is a wealth of ideas presented from which to formulate interventions along with useful guidelines for implementing them.

We especially appreciate Kershaw's metaphor of the interpersonal "dance." As therapists we are also engaged in a "couple's dance." We must balance our position as the expert with an understanding that we don't change anything, but rather cocreate with clients a context in which desired changes can occur. Dr. Kershaw helps readers realize therapy as a dance for stimulating resources and organizing them into coherent packages of behaving and feeling to help people successfully stimulate the self and others en route to developing a healthy marriage and family. She minimizes the therapist's role as each client's self-reliance is enhanced. She offers us a picture of a goal-oriented and strength-oriented therapy. We should expect that this therapy will be briefer than that which focuses on examining pathology and fostering dependence on a so-called "expert" therapist.

Taken in this regard, hypnosis and family therapy are a fabric woven of the same thread. There is nothing wrong with the picture Dr. Kershaw has painted then. Her observations and creativity are consistent with our views and theories of Erickson's work in both areas. We are pleased to see the further clarification of ideas about hypnosis and marriage and family therapy as Dr. Kershaw has laid them out here. This is a book with creativity to inspire readers and scholarship to imbue professionalism—a cotillion for each of us.

CAROL H. LANKTON, M.A., & STEPHEN R. LANKTON, M.S.W.
Gulf Breeze, Florida

Acknowledgments

A book is a project that requires the support of colleagues, family, and friends. First, I want to thank Bill Wade, my husband, to whom this book also belongs. He is one of the finest therapists I know, and he was always there to provide encouragement, emotional support, and wonderful laughter. He offered important editorial comments and participated in the book's conceptualization.

To my stepchildren, Chris, Stephen, and Tiffany Wade, who put up with slow dinners and my distraction, and provided me with wonderful stories about our special experiences together. I love being your stepmother.

To Roxanna Erickson Klein, I owe gratitude and appreciation for her willingness to read early drafts and to correct understandings of her father's concepts. I also treasure her friendship and her way of looking at the world.

To Betty Alice Erickson-Elliott, I thank for consultation and comments on the book. Her infectious sense of humor helped me to deal with the challenges throughout the writing process.

Stephen and Carol Lankton have always been more than supportive of this project. Their teaching and friendship over the years have been special. Bill and I have enjoyed great dinners with them in various parts of the country.

To my Houston editor, Linda Graves, who typed the original manuscript and offered suggestions, personal support, and funny ideas like "fem rage" and "testosterone poisoning." Her husband, Richard, also supported me through the project.

Joseph Zinker and Group 17 have been my extended family during the past 12 years. Thanks for the encouragement and the certainty that I could complete the project. As we grow through the years, I continue to appreciate the value of intimate friends.

To Judy Geer, who lovingly read the manuscript in its early stages and continues to be a dear friend.

To Dale Hill, whose gentle yet firm guidance has been invaluable and endearing to me.

Other colleagues who have supported me in this project include Myer Reid, Don Williamson, Jeff Zeig, Yvonne Dolan, Al Serrano, Carl Whitaker, and many others.

To my mother, father, and grandmother, who laid the foundation for my becoming a professional woman, I thank you.

To Mark Tracten, my publisher, who was willing to take a chance, I have deep appreciation. Natalie Gilman was always a positive influence. To Suzi Tucker, my editor, who worked with me to create the right structure and clarity for the manuscript up to the time of the delivery of her son. I thank you Suzi.

Finally, to my patients, who allowed me to participate in their marital and life journey, I feel a deep sense of respect. Psychotherapy is a process where both patient and therapist touch each other's lives. I have learned much.

Introduction

Every therapist has had the experience of seeing two adults come into the office who begin to fight like three-year-old children. How do we explain this phenomenon? What is it that causes two otherwise pleasant people to begin acting in such argumentative, defensive, and age-regressed ways?

When partners interact, the words they use and the behaviors they display create a kind of hypnotic dance, whereby each person's behavior begins to narrow the attention and focus of the other. This process often triggers painful memories and feelings of intense vulnerability related to other times, perhaps with parents or early caretakers. When the partners attempt to discuss what is troubling them, they become more frightened and vulnerable; they feel and act younger than their years, and they may end up escalating the conflict as a way to obscure the disturbing memory.

As two people interact, trance-like states are mutually stimulated. Trance can be defined as focused attention, a dissociation of thinking, doing, and feeling. Because all hypnosis is self-hypnosis, the interaction itself serves as a catalyst for a hypnotic state to occur in each partner.

Each person's attention becomes narrowed and absorbed, and an interactional sequence begins to take place whereby states of consciousness in each partner produce automatic behaviors that become linked in a pattern of reciprocal sequences. As the patterns develop, they can be experienced as wonderful or horrible.

A pleasant trance-like state might be triggered by the signal to begin sex and the pleasurable automatic behaviors associated with this pattern could be set up. An unpleasant trance-like state accompanied by an horrific behavioral sequence might be triggered by a look, gesture, voice tone, or topic for discussion that is recognized by the couple as the signal for conflict. Even if the patterns are perceived by the couple, they often seem unalterable by a conscious means. More often these patterns remain outside the couple's awareness.

Understanding how marital interaction stimulates positive or negative trance-like states of consciousness in partners, the "hypnotic dance," is useful to both the therapist and the patient. By viewing marital interaction from this perspective, the therapist can more readily and precisely intervene to change the nature of the trance the partners have stimulated in each other. When marital interaction is seen as a type of trance induction, the therapist can begin to understand the subjective nature of each person's experience—why the partners claim that the fights, depressions, pursuits and withdrawals, and the flood of negative feelings seem "just to happen" or are "caused" by the partner and why each partner seems so helpless to alter his or her response cycle.

This book was written as a practical guide to Ericksonian hypnosis in marital therapy and owes much to the works of Milton H. Erickson, M.D.* He was a remarkable clinician whose career and life influenced many fields of study, including psychology, psychiatry, anthropology, nursing, and medicine. The book is particularly designed for clinicians who want a model that elicits marital change in a powerful and respectful way. The goal of the marital psychotherapist is twofold: to alter unproductive, painful, or limiting interactional sequences; and to expand the interactional repertoire of the couple. Interventions can range from depotentiation of a symptom through an alteration in the sequence of behavior by adding or subtracting a behavior between the couple, to altering the internal representation of the spouse, to changing the inner representation of the family of origin, to altering any other element in the ecological context. The ecology of couples includes all of the other systems with which they interact including job, peers,

---

*NOTE: All references to the collected papers of Milton H. Erickson will be denoted as CP followed by the volume number of the document. The bibliography listing is Erickson, M.H., 1980a through 1980d.

community, and recreational activities. Each system includes many other systems. Every element in a system is both part of a whole and a separate entity that has a reciprocal influence. By using hypnosis in marital therapy to impact at any of these levels, the therapist can break up fighting patterns, enlarge impoverished learnings, broaden interpersonal styles, and help retrieve memories of caring.

Erickson evolved his hypnotic approach over his lifetime. In his early career, he primarily used direct hypnosis and referred to hypnosis as sleep (CP III, p. 15). Later, he moved to more indirect work using naturalistic trance, embedded suggestions, metaphor, and symbols to communicate with the unconscious mind (Lankton & Lankton, 1983). He also made a major shift in his thinking from using an external locus of control with the operator or hypnotist being in direct control of the patient, to an internal locus of control, where he encouraged the patient to develop a future-oriented solution to a problem (Klein, R., 1989, personal communication). Erickson believed that using dissociation between the conscious and unconscious minds and joining the reality of the patients in order to utilize their behavior in the creation of a solution was a much more effective approach than his early psychotherapy. This book embraces these assumptions.

A major theme of this book is that people change through a reorganizational process. We are endowed with all of the resources we need to live satisfying lives, although many of them are unconscious. Transformation is not an elimination of any part of ourselves; it is a reorganization of what we already have. We can expand, broaden, and utilize resources that are often unknown or hidden because of our own rigid definitions or categories. We can often overcome difficulties through the use of naturally occurring trance phenomena to elicit our vast inner resources.

A major tenet in this book is that couples mutually stimulate trance through their interactions and that they communicate to each other's unconscious. They anchor or reinforce certain behaviors, attitudes, and emotions at an unconscious level. Anchoring is the process by which sensory elements become associated with certain feelings, behaviors, or events and these experiences are recalled as those elements are triggered. The visual representation of a rose may be associated with a pleasant fragrance and a previous romantic encounter. The harsh prick of a thorn may bring to mind a sad ending to a past relationship. A beautiful melody may have been playing when a couple was in romantic enchantment, and later, the melody triggers the feeling of being in love.

By stimulating a self-induced altered state of consciousness in each partner, couples cocreate complementary patterns of interaction. Each partner self-hypnotizes and enters into co-evolving patterned interchanges that lead to the "hypnotic dance," a mutually created sequence of behaviors and emotions that is stimulated by images and scenes of the best and worst relationships carried from one's family of origin. This "imaged" couple is a symbol of the past, present, and future marriage, both the fantasy and the nightmare versions.

The couple-induced hypnotic state of trance can occur in a variety of ways. This time of inner focus may happen simultaneously with the onset of a symptom, either emotional or physical. It may occur in the complementary and recursive pattern of hypnotic dance between couples. Communication regarding a problem and the attempted solution can serve as a catalyst for trance. Additionally, trance may be triggered by the unconscious suggestions that couples are constantly communicating to each other through embedded suggestions and metaphors in their language. How couples entrance themselves and how the therapist can utilize both the entranced moments and the problem itself to help people experience more satisfaction in their relationships are examined in depth in this book.

An Ericksonian approach employs trance, moments of naturally occurring inner focus, to break dysfunctional patterns and mind sets and to create new learnings. The therapist can disrupt the hypnotic dance and create a counterinduction that leads to a more satisfying experience. Through this process, the patient is helped to give up old symbolic meanings and old solutions that have outlived their usefulness.

Ericksonian psychotherapy accepts and uses the reality of the patient and then expands upon it. When partners complain about each other's behavior, an Ericksonian approach might include accepting how painful things are, how much better the situation would be if the *other* person were to change, and perhaps prescribing the very behaviors about which the couple complains, in a different context, or framing those behaviors in a new light. Alteration of an inner image or idea through a new experience with the psychotherapist or in the patient's world can foster one small change that results in the permutation of an entire life path. The symptom, or old solution when placed in a different context and expanded, can be transformed into a new solution.

Erickson used a pragmatic approach to psychotherapy and found theory incomplete. In fact, he created a theory every time he saw a patient. In a conversation with Jeffrey Zeig (1985), Erickson commented that a therapist needs to understand what patients are trying to say. He believed that theories were formulated and then attempts were made to force patients to fit into them. Erickson might have agreed with T. S. Eliot, who said, "We had the experience, but missed the meaning" (1943). Instead, Erickson suggested that the focus should always be on the patient and the life situation instead of the psychological theory.

Erickson based his pragmatic approach on acute observation. He tried to find unconscious responses to various stimuli. He used to tell his children, "Observe, observe, observe!" (Elliott, Betty Alice E., 1985, personal communication). As therapists, we too must use acute observation to develop ways to unlock chained and rigid behavior between marital partners.

This book is divided into ten chapters. Chapter 1 discusses trance, indirect suggestion, and naturally occurring trance phenomena as they occur in a couple context and how they can be utilized for pattern reorganization and symptom resolution. A review of the basic assumptions of Ericksonian psychotherapy relevant to marital therapy is presented. A bridge between systemic elements and individual dynamics is built for the therapist.

Chapter 2 describes patterned hypnotic interactions that occur in a couple context. Symptoms are redefined as trance inducers and resources that often contain the solution to the problem. Positive and negative trances are described, and the "hypnotic dance" is defined.

In Chapter 3 the couple's construction of reality is portrayed by reviewing how individuals use past experiences to build present and future realities. The perceptual principles that are integral to understanding how realities are created are discussed.

A hypnotic model as a structure from which to do marital therapy is presented in Chapter 4. This model includes: (1) the symptom as the frame for reality through which couples view their relationship, (2) evaluation of the operating belief system, and (3) utilization of the symptom for change. Early experiences in the marriage that are unresolved and unintegrated can lead to symptoms being expressed in the "name" that is given by the partners to the relationship. In large measure, the name may determine what the marriage becomes. For example, the name may be "Marooned on an island," "Water lily on a pond," or "Hurricane Alicia." The particular imagery that the name stimulates between marital partners is examined. How to help couples alter their perceptions of their conflicts to enable them to move toward problem resolution is addressed.

Chapter 5 emphasizes language forms that can be used to create inductions. Hypnotic trance can be stimulated in various ways through the "languageing" that exists between couples. How an Ericksonian approach differs from a more traditional hypnotic approach in inducing trance, how to use a conversational approach to develop a trance induction in a therapy session, and how to use the presenting symptom as a trance inducer, hypothesis builder, and the basis for intervention are demonstrated. Transcript examples are included to illustrate the hypnotic process.

Chapter 6 presents methods for creating a working hypothesis for treatment by assessing the relationship trance dynamics. An assessment questionnaire is presented to assist the marital therapist in creating three different levels of hypotheses: systemic, interpersonal, and intrapersonal. This questionnaire is designed to use the couple's own metaphor for their relationship and perceptions of the partner and self. How to distinguish the couple's dance or the hypnotic interaction, and work with it are described. Uncovering these recursive patterns in the dance is a critical step toward intervention.

Teaching the therapist how to use therapeutic language as a strategy for intervention is the emphasis in Chapter 7. How to build therapeutic metaphors and stories is discussed and examples are given. Protocols that are based on the couple's developmental stage are provided for metaphor construction and are offered as guides for the therapist.

In Chapter 8 strategic trance techniques that may be used with couples are presented. These techniques are based on the particular trance phenomena that the couple may already employ, which is often found in the symptomatic trance they create between them.

The role of trauma in creating the entrancing dance between couples is the focus of Chapter 9. Childhood trauma can lead to problems later in life in terms of negative trance states that are triggered. In this chapter, the effect of childhood trauma on couples is discussed. In alcoholic or abusive homes where repeated traumatic incidents occurred, post-traumatic stress syndrome often develops and is carried into adulthood as a chronic state. Expectations of severe punishment in childhood (Hilgard, 1977) lead many children to escape through dissociation. For protection, an endangered child may become foggy or experience hypnotic dissociation. Childhood trauma, shock, and repression of feelings and memories can lead to a sense of emotional shutdown and overwhelming fear. These feelings and the accompanying hypnotic dissociation are easily triggered. When this state of psychophysiological alert is triggered as an adult, it may manifest itself in marital conflict, psychosomatic illness, depression, "fading out," and severe feelings of shame. Treatment of this syndrome is described using an Ericksonian framework.

In Chapter 10, psychosomatic illnesses that often develop in conjunction with early trauma are considered. Treatment of "contact" allergies as a physical symptom and concomitant systemic and developmental influences are examined. In addition, migraine headache as a physical symptom and as a marital conflict defense mechanism is described.

The marital psychotherapist needs to be able to observe the

couple's hypnotic dance, make some assessment of its dynamics and underlying beliefs, perceive which trance phenomena are being used in the symptomatic trance that develops, and create interventions that utilize the symptoms themselves. When the psychotherapist recognizes the trance that partners stimulate in each other from their interactions, a key can be found to create interventions that are solution-oriented, a language that the couple processes differently, and a sense of hopefulness for the future of the relationship.

Within the dance couples often find a path toward solution and well-being. But the path is always in the dance of the unconscious minds. Once the basic elements of the trance dance between couples and the unconscious are explored in Chapter 1, later chapters guide the psychotherapist in developing useful Ericksonian strategies in marital therapy.

No one better described this unconscious dance than T.S. Eliot in his poem "Burnt Norton":

> At the still point of the turning world. Neither flesh
>   nor fleshness;
> Neither from nor towards: at the still point, there the
>   dance is,
> But neither arrest nor movement. And do not call it fixity.
> Where past and future are gathered. Neither movement
>   from nor towards.
> Neither ascent nor decline. Except for the point, the still
>   point.
> There would be no dance, and there is only the dance.

(Eliot, 1986, p. 177)

The Couple's Hypnotic Dance

Creating Ericksonian Strategies
in Marital Therapy

1

How the Couple's Unconscious Creates a Hypnotic Dance

The couple's dance is the patterned hypnotic interaction of two unconscious minds that provides some common difficulties and potential solutions for that dynamic state we call marriage. For the psychotherapist who works with these interactional patterns, marital hypnosis offers some unique opportunities to develop more precise interventions to assist in creating satisfying relationship processes. Each marital partner often feels caught in a dizzying dialogue where painful and hurtful words are hurled, and hypnotic states of consciousness are stimulated. These states of consciousness and their accompanying behaviors co-create an exquisitely precise dance.

To facilitate a better understanding of this dance, the theoretical framework for the use of hypnotic psychotherapy with couples is first described. Several basic assumptions of an Ericksonian approach are presented as underlying principles for this model of psychological intervention. A variety of elements are examined such as trance, conscious/unconscious mind, trance theory, trance phenomena, and marital trance.

Trance theory is described in this section as encompassing both systemic and psychodynamic models of psychotherapy. It connects three major components: (1) historical family developmental and relational processes, (2) the marital system and structure, and (3) the individual's psychic structure.

The historical family and its dynamics are recorded in the unconscious mind of each individual. These historical processes are captured as internal patterns of brain activity that carry a map for present-day functioning in the marital system. They serve to maintain the individual's psychic structure and to maintain the marital trance, the unique altered reality often stimulated by two people in an intimate relationship.

The second part of this chapter is focused specifically on the marital trance, a partner-stimulated trance. This particular type of interpersonal altered state is described as an idiosyncratic dyadic process that may create positive or negative states and result in conflict-creating or conflict-reducing behavior.

TRANCE

Hypnotic state, trance, or accessing the unconscious are all descriptions of a unique focused awareness in which, according to Erickson, new learning can take place. Because he was opposed to rigid definitions and theories, Erickson used hypotheses and general descriptions. He described trance in several ways: "an artificially enhanced state of suggestibility resembling sleep wherein there appears to be a normal, time-limited, and stimulus-limited dissociation of the 'conscious' from the 'subconscious' elements of psyche" (CP III, p. 8), a "relationship between two people" (CP III, p. 6), "a vital relationship in one person, stimulated by the warmth of another" (Zeig, 1985, p. 63).

Milton Erickson considered the trance state to be "a period of reverie, inattention, or quiet reflection. The face tends to become lifeless and (has) a certain flat ironed-out look. The entire body remains immobile in whatever position it happens to be in and certain reflexes (e.g., swallowing, respiration) may slow down. We have hypothesized that in everyday life consciousness is in a continual state of flux between the general reality orientation and the momentary microdynamics of trance" (Erickson & Rossi, 1981, p. 75). Whenever we focus our attention inward momentarily so that the body looks frozen or the eyes glaze over and bodily processes slow, a natural trance state has occurred. Erickson believed that

> hypnosis is a dissociation of the conscious from the unconscious. The conscious mind is that state of aware-ness where active evaluation and decision-making take place. The unconscious mind is a repository of all of the experiences that you have had within your life. Whereas memory fades on a conscious level, it is stored, at least my dad believed . . . , intact in the un-conscious. The unconscious serves as a protector, and although the conscious mind may not be aware of the influence the unconscious mind is contributing to de-cision-making, both the conscious and unconscious contribute to the actions of the individual. The fun-damental idea of Ericksonian hypnotherapy is that through dissociation problem-resolution could be gen-erated on an unconscious level. Erickson's focus in therapy was to encourage the unconscious to access and utilize unconscious resources and then relearning and reorganization can take place on an unconscious level followed by behavior changes and problem-res-olution on a conscious level. (Roxanna Klein, 1988, personal communication)

It is in this dissociated state that a particular thought process is entertained.

Other individuals have defined trance especially in relation to dissociation theory. Hilgard, for example, defines trance as a "divided consciousness" or dissociation. The conscious mind may be focused on one aspect while the unconscious is attending to something entirely different. Hilgard suggests that two dif-ferent trains of thought can be maintained concurrently. Two people in conversation can at once be listening to each other, planning a reply, and observing feedback so as to change the emphasis in an argument that is unconvincing. Each person may also be planning when and how to end the discussion. A part of a person that may be actively planning a reply may be out of awareness or dissociated from the conscious mind (Hilgard, 1977). Hilgard names this component the "hidden observer."

Other theorists, Daniel Brown and Erika Fromm (1986), define trance as "an altered state of consciousness" that functions to provide "regression in the service of the ego along with increased access to the unconscious" (Fromm, 1980, p. 75). Fromm takes an analytical stance with regard to hypnosis. This definition of an altered state of consciousness (ASC) was developed by Ludwig (1966). He suggested that the ASC could be achieved by psychological, physiological, or chemical means, and that our perception of the world is different in this hypnotic state than in the normal waking state.

Hypnosis is defined by Beahrs (1988) from three perspectives: phenomenal, transactional, and formal/procedural. The phenomenal approach views hypnosis as the process that leads to experiencing alteration in volition, perception and memory, and cognition such as "trance logic," as defined by Orne (1959). The transactional approach is defined by Beahrs as that which includes the patient and hypnotist, the induction, and the hypnotic state of suggestibility. The formal/procedural includes elements from the first two and maintains that the process be ritualized and labeled as "hypnosis."

Beahrs (1982) makes the point that there may be many different kinds of trance state. He cites a conversation that he had with T. X. Barber in which Barber said, "If you are going to talk about 'trance' to begin with, why talk about THE trance? Maybe there are two, three, or even an infinite number of types of trance" (p. 22). This suggestion deserves consideration.

There may be the common everyday trance, the trance state that is elicited in sports, such as the intense concentration required to hit a ball or perform a martial art. There may be a qualitative difference in the trance states that are elicited between marital partners or the ones that occur when children are present. In all of these trance states, according to various theories, dissociation is a central feature.

Trance in this book concurs with the dissociation theories and is defined simply as dissociation of the conscious mind from the unconscious mind. There are several characteristics of trance behavior that include absorption of attention, involuntary behavior in the context of relationship, and biological factors.

For the purposes of this discussion, hypnosis and the conscious and unconscious minds can be defined theoretically. Later in this chapter we can observe how couples' interactions often parallel hypnotic behavior and incorporate trance phenomena in the marital trance. Hypnosis can be defined as that process of creating an altered state of consciousness in which there is a dissociation between the conscious and unconscious minds. It is this dissociation that we call trance: a state of focused attention. The conscious mind is that state of awareness that carries functions for decision making, evaluations, and logical, linear thinking, and maintains a limited number of chunks of information at a time. The unconscious mind is the container of all of the experiences and learnings from the past that researchers (Kandel & Schwartz, 1982) believe reside in patterns of neuronal electric impulses linking many synapses in the brain. The unconscious mind seemingly can integrate sophisticated information without cognitive awareness. The *Brain/Mind Bulletin* of March, 1984, says that the "unconscious mind plays a more primary role in mental life than anyone has previously suspected. Stimuli registered outside awareness have a measurable effect on behavior" (p. 2). Emmanuel Donchin, director of the Laboratory for Cognitive Psychophysiology, University of Illinois, says that "as much as ninety-nine percent of cognitive activity may be nonconscious" (p. 2). The unconscious mind can also respond to likes and dislikes before the conscious mind even knows to what it is responding. Every experience is recorded and organized in a particular pattern and stored in the unconscious mind. These unconscious memories can be retrieved and utilized as resources in the present for problem resolution.

Every experiential learning that we have had can act as a later resource for problem solving. Learning to walk and talk, learning how hunger feels and its signal, learning how to say no and yes to ourselves and to others, learning how to cooperate on a team and how to be an individual—these are among the experiential learnings we gain fairly early and utilize often as adults.

We do not know exactly what hypnotic trance is and there are varying and controversial definitions for it, but a description based on what Erickson believed can be offered. The trance state may be distinguished from the "non-trance" state and can be viewed as being on a continuum of naturally developing trance with several different axes: dissociation, depth of trance, voluntary versus involuntary behavior, low versus high suggestibility, attention, imagination, memory, and trance phenomena. The "non-trance" state can be conceptualized as existing when a person is fully associated into the present and is processing with the conscious mind in a linear, evaluative fashion (see Figure 1.1).

DISSOCIATION

In dissociation there is a disconnection from a fully associated state in the present moment. A person who may be in a slightly dissociated state can have a daydream or fail to notice some activity in the room. As the dissociation develops, depending on the stimulus, various perceptual sensory alterations may occur. There may be a failure to hear something consciously although the unconscious records the sound or any of a variety of perceptual phenomena may be experienced. All of the defense mechanisms that a person might use contain elements of dissociation (these will be discussed in Chapter 6). Finally, the polar end of the dissociation continuum where maximum disconnection exists can be termed multiple personality. This extreme state of dissociation often contains an amnesiac barrier between parts of the self. The organization of these unknown parts can be so fully developed as to maintain completely different states of health. One part or personality might evidence diabetes and another personality not; one self might lack visual acuity whereas another will have perfect vision.

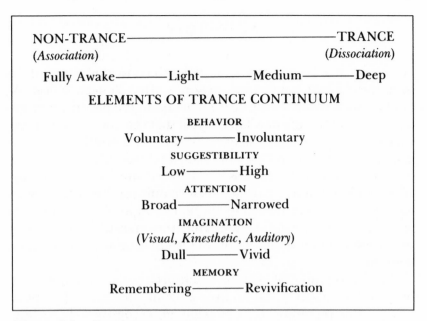

NON-TRANCE————————————————TRANCE
(Association)   *(Dissociation)*

Fully Awake————Light————Medium————Deep

ELEMENTS OF TRANCE CONTINUUM

BEHAVIOR

Voluntary————Involuntary

SUGGESTIBILITY

Low————High

ATTENTION

Broad————Narrowed

IMAGINATION

(Visual, Kinesthetic, Auditory)

Dull————Vivid

MEMORY

Remembering————Revivification

Figure 1.1.   Continuum to trance

DEPTH OF TRANCE

Erickson identified the "common everyday trances" as those that occur daily as our attention is absorbed by a thought, an interesting story, or a daydream. Such light trance states are routine occurrences often marked by such behavior as staring, physical immobility, and inattention to surrounding activity, as well as by changes in respiration. Although they last only a few moments, in a light state of trance, all of the trance phenomena may be observed. At a deeper level of trance, these phenomena are intensified.

For Erickson, the depth of trance needed to deal with a patient's problems depends upon the patient's own personality, the particular problem, and the stage of therapy. In some cases, a light trance is all that is necessary for a difficult problem, whereas in other cases, a deep trance is required even though the problem is relatively mild. The therapist must use clinical judgment in each case, and when one approach does not work, another can be employed (CP IV, p. 29–30).

ATTENTION

Non-trance allows a person to have a broad focus of attention. However, in the trance state, a patient's conscious attention is so absorbed that loud noises may not affect concentration. A loud noise may not even cause a reaction in the patient, though his or her comments may later reveal that the noise was, in fact, registered. Often, there is amnesia for the noise because the conscious mind is so focused on some other stimulus. A patient's conscious mind may be absorbed by an interesting story or curious phenomena of trance dissociation such as a hand levitation or a perceptual change in body weight. Absorption can occur with an engaging look from the therapist, or sudden confusion about a situation, or an idea that captures a person's attention.

An idea or thought may be so absorbing that a patient can become fixated on it and go over it again and again. The purpose of this repetition is to manage an uncomfortable feeling associated with the idea, to avoid a feeling, or to control someone else, which is another way of managing a feeling of fear. This immobility in thinking can occur in obsessional thinking where a thought might be examined in great detail. Erickson's metaphors also fostered this type of absorption—they often were so intriguing that the patient would spend a long time attempting to decipher exactly what he meant.

In the case of a couple relationship, a person can become so stuck on a negative idea about a partner that the internal struggle to resolve anger is painful. This struggle might take the form of ascribing a certain motivation to a partner's behavior that is negative and malicious in intent and then trying to resolve the feelings associated with that particular assumption. The following case illustrates this point.

Jake wanted to know everything Ann did during the day. He always wanted to know where she was going and what she was going to do and with whom. Ann felt invaded and controlled by his intrusive questioning. Even though she was keeping nothing from Jake, her inclination was to be secretive. Jake sensed this evasiveness and understood her self-protectiveness to mean that she was having an affair. He obsessed about the idea, turning it over and over in his mind. One day, when he was particularly tormented, he went to a restaurant to have an early lunch. At the restaurant he hallucinated Ann with someone else and actually "saw" her having lunch with another man. Ann had been actively participating in a community activity on the other side of town at that moment. Even after having evidence of Ann's whereabouts from a printed program she brought home, Jake could not believe her because he "saw" her with his own eyes. Because of some early separation trauma, Jake had expected abandonment some time during the relationship. When Jake began to experience tension as a result of everyday problems, he could not tolerate it. His greatest fear was projected and a negative state was created that led to developing a positive hallucination.

Attention may be absorbed by having the patient relax or by suggesting the patient become more alert. Although trance has traditionally been associated with sleep, it is no longer thought of in this way. Often, absorption of attention accompanies relaxation with suggestions of eye closure and reduced activity. In 1976, E. I. Banyai and Ernest Hilgard developed an active-alert procedure for inducing trance. Subjects rode a bicycle ergometer with their eyes open and while exercising, various suggestions were given concerning feeling more alert and attentive. The results indicated that trance behavior occurred in an alert state, which was demonstrated by the subjects' vacant stares, as if they were focused on a distant object. All of the trance phenomena were experienced in this highly alert focused state, including positive and negative hallucinations, hypnotic dreams, analgesia, hypermnesia, amnesia, and post-hypnotic suggestion.

VOLUNTARY/INVOLUNTARY BEHAVIOR

In the non-trance state, voluntary behavior is most often experienced. People make choices in behavior and respond volitionally. A husband or wife may call a partner and request a forgotten document. The partner can respond by making a conscious choice to answer the request or not. In trance, responses seem to the patient to be avolitional or involuntary.

The indirect suggestion of eye closure by the therapist may be experienced as involuntary eye closure by the patient. The therapist may suggest, "I don't know just when your eyes will begin to feel a certain heaviness or when they will want to close to provide you with more comfort so you can listen to something different." As the patient responds to the suggestion of eye closure, she or he may experience this behavior as avolitional. The response is voluntary, but it has been conditioned to occur under certain circumstances, such as focused awareness.

Behavior can seem involuntary in the context of a relationship. The patient can experience certain trance phenomena that seem as though they are happening without volition. It appears as if the patient is the passive recipient of whatever phenomena the hypnotist elicits. If the therapist asks that the patient see herself sitting "over there" as a youngster of six years old, the cooperative patient in trance can actually see herself as if she were looking at a hologram. The therapist may suggest an arm levitation. To the patient, the arm seems unattached and lifts as if by itself without any conscious choice.

In the example of Jake and Ann, Jake experienced positive hallucination as if it were happening apart from him. Jake was asked to experiment with different hypnotic phenomena in the office without any reference to Jake's fear that Ann was having an affair. It was not until he demonstrated in the office his ability to positively hallucinate Ann walking out the door that he considered how he was constructing reality. At this point we were able to begin psychotherapy with Jake's deeper problem: fear of abandonment. Although it was not necessary for Jake to have achieved insight about this problem for resolution to occur, the combination of a new experience with a new understanding helped him with immediate connections and provided a sense of relief about what was happening to him.

SUGGESTIBILITY

Suggestibility is the willingness to accept, follow, and make another's idea one's own. It is an aspect of both a trance and non-trance state. The act of suggestion can occur in several ways.

Suggestion can occur through verbal, nonverbal, extraverbal, or intraverbal messages. It can be accomplished through any of the sensory channels and include all five senses. Verbal suggestion may be sent via language or human sounds. Nonverbal suggestion can result from gestures, looks, or any body motion. Implication, a powerful force in suggestion, can be considered extraverbal and communicates a message without its being stated openly. Intraverbal suggestion is the implied meaning of the message that occurs through voice modulation or mannerisms of a person (Kroger, 1963, p. 6).

Suggestibility in the non-trance state is a process that can also be examined. Because of the evaluative function of the conscious mind, direct persuasion techniques are needed to influence human behavior such as logical argument, credible sources, and consequences for particular attitudes and behaviors. These communications are judged by the conscious mind according to the individual's own position on an issue and evaluated on the basis of how close or how distant the communication is to the person's own stand. If the communication expresses a position that is close to the individual's own, assimilation will result; i.e., a person will perceive the message as being similar to the one held, will evaluate the message favorably, and will be influenced accordingly. How suggestible the conscious mind is may be determined by how ego-involved the person is in an issue. The less able an individual is to separate the self from an issue, the more the issue becomes an extension of the self. Any communication that supports an idea that stands outside the latitude of acceptance (those ideas that are willingly accepted as true) will have no impact or will be rejected.

If a person holds a strong opinion, any persuasive technique designed to change that opinion may serve only to reinforce the opinion held. The more committed to a position the more ego-involvement, so that any disagreement may be experienced as personal. The person and the position become one. Ego-involvement serves as a filter in how a person judges a message, and an individual will assess the message in terms of personal experiences and beliefs. How suggestible a person is consciously may be determined by how much the communication falls within a range of acceptance, how credible the source of the communication, and how strong the affiliation between the people that are communicating.

Suggestibility is a central feature of hypnosis and the trance state. Trance and trance phenomena are based on the subject's ability to react to suggestions. In fact, a particular behavior that may be suggested for problem resolution and suggestions for reorganization of resources are based on suggestibility (CP IV, pp. 20–21). Because hypnosis was considered by Erickson to be communication with the unconscious, suggestion is a request to the unconscious to reorganize a memory to become a positive resource that may have been forgotten or unknown to the conscious mind. If the subject acts according to the suggestion, it can be deduced that the unconscious has acted in response to the request. When the psychotherapist uses the tool of hypnosis to enhance therapeutic suggestions, a positive response will result in the patient.

IMAGINATION

The act of imagining involves the forming of mental images that have sensory components connected to them. Images affect the sensory processes, and the senses affect the kind of images a person might form. The formation of images will often precede or follow a physical change. Luria (1968) investigated the relationship of imagery and physical response and discovered that one of his patients could increase his heart rate by imagining himself running to catch a train. Luthe and Schultz (1969) used autogenic training, mental imagery, and relaxation in over two thousand studies of physiological effects of mental imagery. Achterberg, Simonton, and Matthews-Simonton (1976) found that the kind and quality of imagery influenced the ability of the cancer patient to manage disease.

In hypnosis, a person's imagination is stimulated to form images that range on a continuum from dull to vivid and that can contain a complex of dimensions: attitudes, affects, and behaviors for past, present, and future experiences. The dimensions of particular attitudes, affects, and behaviors may be represented symbolically in the unconscious mind. These imaginal happenings may include auditory, kinesthetic, and visual components that express the complex of dimensions. These imaginal components and dimensions allow the individual to form a positive future image, alter the present experience, and view the past from a different vantage point.

MEMORY

In hypnosis, memories can be activated through associations and especially through the activity of the limbic system that produces emotions. Seemingly irrelevant details can stimulate critical memories. When driving around an old neighborhood, one may "relive" powerful memories and think about people, places, and things not thought of for some time. Emotions that are attached to perceptions are important for the creating and ordering of memories (Gloor et al., 1982).

Memories act as resources for the individual in that they carry valuable information for a particular learning that was experienced in the past. A family pet that acted as a best friend may have provided many learnings about nurturing, closeness, and warmth. This memory may be activated in terms of what a person was thinking and feeling before and during the interaction with that pet through an association with a friend's pet or through suggestion of the experience using therapeutic metaphor.

Memories can range on a continuum from recalling something that involves the review of an image from a distance to the revivification of a memory where we perceive ourselves to be repeating an old behavior that was thought to have been changed as if it were a reflex action. At the extreme end of the spectrum, full revivification may occur leading us to feel that we have been transported back in time to relive an event exactly as it occurred.

TRANCE PHENOMENA

The various trance phenomena are experiences of the same psychological mechanisms that a person can have in a non-trance state, but to a much greater degree (see Figure 1.2). We can consider amnesia to be an extreme form of forgetting. In trance, we can experience a natural forgetting of an event or a feeling. Couples can have the subjective experience of partner amnesia; that is, the momentary forgetting of a partner and hallucinating the face of a parent. Hallucination and age progression are extreme forms of vivid imagination. Hallucination is the subjective experience of seeing, hearing, smelling, or feeling something that is not actually present in an objective reality. Age progression is the subjective experience of moving forward in time and experiencing ourselves as older in thought and feeling and as more facile in solution generation. Age regression is an extreme form of revivifying memory. In trance, age regression is the subjective experience of returning to an earlier time in our history in thought, feeling, and body experience. Hypermnesia is an extreme form of remembering. Trance can allow an individual to remember in minute detail some aspect of an experience that has long been consciously forgotten. Automatic writing is a greater degree of doodling. In automatic writing, the unconscious may communicate something unknown to the conscious mind. Analgesia/anesthesia is extreme numbing or tingling of extremities. In trance, analgesia or anesthesia can be a subjective experience of little or no feeling.

```
Forgetting————————Amnesia
Vivid Imagination————————Hallucination
Remembering————————Hypermnesia
Doodling————————Automatic Writing
Slight Numbing, Tingling————————Analgesia
Absence of Feeling————————Anesthesia
Revivifying Memory————————Age Regression
Future Imagery————————Age Progression
```

Figure 1.2. Trance phenomena

BIOLOGICAL FACTORS

Normal biological rhythms can alter consciousness and create trance (Rossi, 1986). The normal physiological fluctuations of physical and mental processes we each experience daily lead to shifts in consciousness. Often, before a woman menstruates, her focus is more inward; sometimes accompanied by a drop in energy level and frustration tolerance. Men also experience fluctuations in energy and mood.

In the *Psychobiology of Mind-Body Healing*, Ernest Rossi (1986) describes several natural rhythms that have been identified in the literature. The circadian rhythms are biological cycles that occur every 24 hours and pertain to the sleep-awake cycle. This cycle can be interrupted by stressful life events, such as shifts in the work cycle. An ultradian cycle is a cycle of activity followed by rest that occurs every 90 minutes. It is characterized by REM (rapid eye movement) sleep or dreaming, pupil dilation, change in nasal breathing from one side to another, which is related to hemispheric dominance shift (Werntz, 1981), and penile and clitoral engorgement.

These biological rhythms influence the consciousness and behavior of couples in the area of sexual and hunger appetites, sleep patterns, and so on (Chiba et al., 1977). Rossi (1986) says that "it has been my clinical observation that couples with good relationships tend to integrate spontaneously their circadian and ultradian rhythms and are in synchrony; unhappy couples invariably report conflict and desynchrony on all these rhythms" (p. 217).

BASIC ASSUMPTIONS

Erickson did not adhere to a particular theory of psychotherapy. However, there are a number of basic assumptions from which he operated when working with marital partners. He was not specific about the assumptions. Rather, they have been gleaned from his writings and videotapes and from consultations with several of his children.

1. *Each individual has the resources to deal with present and future*

problems. Erickson believed that people have all the available resources needed to deal with life's problems. It is the perception of and response to the event that makes the event positive or negative. After having to deal with the possibility of his own death many times throughout his life, he discovered that he possessed remarkable natural abilities to manage those difficulties and to overcome conscious limitations, as does everyone. Given this innate ability, there is nothing to fear about tomorrow.

2. *Experience is subjective.* Because our perceptions and reactions bring meaning to what we perceive, the subjective experience of reality can be altered.

Because we bring meaning to what we perceive, that meaning can be changed, and therefore the reality is changed. As the context determines in large part what we perceive, when the context changes, so does reality.

3. *Each person is unique and has many strengths, some of which are unknown to the person.* Erickson believed that each individual is unique and valuable. The resources that are available within, as well as those that exist in the individual's environment, may or may not be known to the individual. Erickson described the unconscious as a repository of memories and life experiences. All of the information is available for problem resolution though the individual may not be aware of it on a conscious level.

4. *Each person has many options for resolving any problem.* It is the role of the therapist to facilitate the retrieval of resources and, thus, help create the change of attitude, behavior, or feeling within the unconscious of the client. It is only on an unconscious level that the extent of change can be anticipated.

There are many learnings already in place, such as knowing how to button a button or to tie a shoe, or the formation of perspective, that can be used for current problems. Thousands of learnings are present in each of us—how to start an argument and how to stop, how to pay attention to a hurt and how to forget it, how to speed up and slow down time, and how to project into the future and take a trip back into the past.

5. *Conflict between partners is contextual.* Specific words ex-

pressed in a particular context may lead to clear communication or to misunderstanding. Irritation can be diminished by renaming the context, for example, changing it into an arena for playful teasing. As long as the context is called safe, it provides an atmosphere for experiential behavior and humor. As a result, partners may laugh about certain areas that were previously painful. However, if one partner disagrees that the context is safe, conflict may occur.

6. *Each partner unwittingly plays a complementary role in any problem that occurs in the relationship.* Although Erickson did not use a systems orientation, his interventions suggest that he was aware of the reciprocity of behavior between marital partners. There are reciprocal perceptions and positions each spouse takes in relation to the other. One spouse who is more introverted and passive will elicit more extraversion and aggressiveness and vice versa.

7. *Trance may result as a consequence of partner interaction.* Partners' interactions may stimulate trance in each other. When this shift of consciousness occurs, the face of a figure from the past may appear on the face of one's partner (partner amnesia), and momentarily a partner may react to the spouse as if he or she were that other person. A verbal or nonverbal piece of behavior may trigger the feeling of being a child. In some psychological theories, this notion is called transference (trance-ference).

8. *Within the problem is the solution.* Erickson believed that often the problem was a metaphor for an underlying difficulty that if understood fully also suggested a solution. Elaborating on this line of thinking, Gilligan (1987, 1988) suggests that "trance phenomena are the same as symptom phenomena." An individual may underutilize or overutilize a particular phenomenon of trance. The answer to the problem can be found within the symptom complex (Gilligan, 1987).

9. *Each individual has a particular learning style for recombining and shifting experience* (Lankton, 1986, p. 32). Someone who almost totally focuses on the negative cannot, when asked, focus on positive aspects. However, that person may be able to differentiate shades of negativity when asked if something is 100

percent negative or if it might be only 80 percent negative. Utilizing rules by which each person functions will create the most useful kind of intervention.

10. *Symptoms occur when people attempt to use the same state of consciousness repetitively, and the needed resources cannot be found for a particular problem.* Erickson said that "psychological problems exist precisely because the conscious mind does not know how to initiate psychological experience and behavior change to the degree that one would like" (Erickson & Rossi, 1979, p. 18). Marital partners often elicit certain states of consciousness from each other that when repeated over time cause difficulty in changing their interactions.

11. *The marital conflict is often metaphorical and reflects a deeper meaning than the content of the issue.* If an argument cannot be resolved at the solution level, some other dynamic is operating. This conflict may reflect a power struggle, an unconscious attempt to resolve a family-of-origin issue, or unresolved anger and disappointment.

12. *Trance phenomena can be viewed as symptoms, resources, and vehicles for the therapist to induce trance with a couple.* Symptomatic trance phenomena occur when a couple is unable to achieve problem resolution and instead remain caught up in a vicious cycle of conflict. The trance phenomena can be helpful resources when utilized appropriately. Beahrs suggests that labeling a patient with a psychiatric term may actually serve to block the therapist from an appropriate intervention. If the therapist can view the problem as a "misused hypnotic skill," the patient can be taught to use the resources within to resolve problems (Beahrs, 1982).

Haley describes Erickson's use of the symptom in the case of a young bride who wanted her husband's relatives to visit less often. She developed an ulcer that incapacitated her. Erickson told the young woman, "You don't really like your relatives. They are a pain the belly every time they come. It ought to be usually developed; they certainly can't expect you to mop up the floor if you vomit when they come" (Haley, 1973, p. 127). She followed his advice and vomited each time her relatives came so they would have to clean up. They stopped coming so often and would leave any time she began to look ill. Erickson commented that, "She needed to be helpless, and in this way she saved up all her pain in the belly for the in-laws' visits and had her satisfaction. . . . It was an awfully good stomach that could throw the relatives out" (Haley, 1973, p. 128). In order to work toward achieving problem resolution, the therapist may use the trance phenomena that the couple employs in a symptomatic trance to induce a healing trance.

BRIDGING DYNAMIC AND SYSTEMIC ELEMENTS

Because of Erickson's atheoretical stance in psychotherapy, he possessed a kind of fluidity and creativity that characterizes a master. He was able to encompass both psychodynamic and systemic theory in his approach to trance work. In fact, he moved beyond theory and sometimes provided wizard-like interventions that often led to dramatic change. More often, he spent a long time with cases and worked arduously. He came at change from a number of perspectives. An individual's psychodynamics as well as the system in which the individual operated were important. Erickson's own philosophy of change was unique: "In psychotherapy you change no one. People change themselves. You create the circumstances under which an individual can respond spontaneously and change. And that's all you do. The rest is up to them" (Zeig, 1985, p. 69; Ritterman, 1985).

Erickson utilized the trance state to influence both intrapsychic and interpsychic dynamics in unique ways. Trance can assist the individual in the creative reorganization of intrapsychic dynamics. At the same time, Erickson could affect the present system. As Nichols says, present relationships tend to reflect real and fantasized past and present relationships (1987, pp. 28–29). He suggests, for example, men who grew up with critical and intrusive mothers may carry a critical inner image of women in general. The adult man may become afraid to displease women and strive to keep them happy at the expense of attending to his own needs. The result may be that the man pushes great anger and resentment underground (Nichols, 1987). If this man marries, he may perceive his wife as a monster when she becomes upset with him. He must "kill" the monster with kindness, passivity, or with some other technique to create distance. Consequently, intrapsychic dynamics influence interactional events.

Erickson viewed trance as an element of the interactional process. The interpersonal process triggers an internal search in the individual. The couple context invites certain internal processes to occur. Erickson believed that an individual's psychodynamics were important. However, he emphasized the interpersonal context as the place where symptoms begin. There are "important signs of developmental problems that are in the process of becoming conscious. What patients cannot yet clearly express in the form of a cognitive or emotional insight will find somatic expression as a body symptom" (Erickson & Rossi, 1979, p. 143). Although he was speaking about physical symptoms here, the same is true of psychological symptoms. Erickson went on to say that symptom resolution may occur by working with a patient's psychodynamic aspects in such a manner that the conscious mind does not know why the body symptom disappears. He adds, "Moreover, the developmental problem that was expressed in the symptom is also resolved in an apparently spontaneous manner" (Erickson & Rossi, 1979, p. 143).

SHIFTING LENSES

Because a particular theory determines in large measure how psychological dynamics are viewed and how the notion of change is perceived, it both limits and expands one's view of the "behaving field." No one theory can say everything there is to say about behavior. Every theory ultimately breaks down because it is merely a description of "reality." Each theory is useful in that it provides a different lens through which to interpret behavior and identify patterns. A systems theory describes patterns of behavior between people. An individual theory regards the internalized images of family, unique defenses a person may have developed, and developmental tasks that need to be accomplished. Thus, being able to view behavior from an integrated approach that includes these different perspectives allows the therapist to obtain a more complete picture. Trance may be used to make a paradigmatic shift from an individual point of view to a systemic position. In trance both intrapsychic and interpsychic dynamics may be addressed simultaneously (Kershaw, 1986). Shifting the particular lenses through which a couple is perceived by the therapist allows movement from one level of organizing data to another. The therapist is able to determine in what developmental stage each individual is operating as well as what dynamics the couple system is utilizing.

By viewing behavior from an integrated, mosaic perspective, both developmental and systemic data can be incorporated into a clearer assessment picture. Understanding what developmental stage an individual may be in is an important component in the understanding of what tasks need to be completed in order to move on to the next stage. Viewed from a developmental stance, the couple can also be examined in light of developmental family tasks that need to be completed. When a therapist grasps the system dynamics as well as the developmental stage for both the individuals and the couple dyad, a more holistic and perhaps more powerful intervention can be made. Learning hypnosis is useful in sharpening the therapist's ability to observe minute behavior and, thus, to move with ease back and forth between hypothesizing about individual dynamics and couple interaction.

We have examined a theoretical framework for the use of hypnosis in marital therapy. Because the interpersonal context often stimulates trance in each partner, the sequences of behavior, attitudes, and feelings that follow can be recognized by the psychotherapist as potential problems and resources. Conscious and unconscious minds have been defined, as well as several basic assumptions outlined that may be used in an Ericksonian approach with couples. Various elements of trance have been discussed as they relate to the marital trance. The couple's hypnotic dance is examined more fully in Chapter 2. Patterned hypnotic interactions and symptomatology formation and meaning are presented for the psychotherapist.

2

Patterned Hypnotic Interactions

The couple's hypnotic dance occurs within the interpersonal context and it contains several components. These interacting elements can be understood from a second-order cybernetic position, in which the symptomatic behavior influences the system to develop around the symptom itself. This chapter examines aspects of symptoms, positive and negative trance states, how partners stimulate trance in each other, and the hypnotic loop.

Both individual dynamics and system dynamics interplay to result in hypnotic interactions. Jurg Willi (1982) has delineated several collusive patterns of behavior between couples. He describes how individual needs and unfinished developmental tasks play a role in the couple system to maintain the particular pattern of the behavioral dance. Other authors (Dicks, 1967; Mittelmann, 1948; & Winch 1958) have also outlined various patterns. Mittelmann (1948) says, "Because of the continuous and intimate nature of marriage, every neurosis in a married person is strongly anchored in the marriage relationship. The presence of a complementary neurotic reaction in the marriage partner is an important aspect of the married patient's neurosis" (p. 491). These collusive patterns reflect the couple's hypnotic dance of complementarity in which two people "fit" together with exquisite accuracy. Examples of these complementary positions are caretaker/patient or earth-mother/infant-son, parent/child, master/slave, and worshipper/idol. Other patterns of hypnotic dance may include dominant mother/withdrawn father, blaming, critical mother/incompetent son (or nurturing mother/loving son), and critical father/rebellious daughter. These roles contain in metaphorical form shared assumptions about the marriage relationship. In some complementary relationships, projective identification is used. One partner may feel anxiety about some issue. As soon as the other partner takes on the feelings, the first partner may stop worrying and even criticize the other for worrying. We tend to elicit particular defenses from others and then defend against them with complementary or symmetrical defenses.

Depending on the assumptions a partner makes about a spouse's behavior and the resultant meanings or interpretations, symmetrical patterns can also be elicited in the couple's dance. Symmetry may be observed in a competition between the two marital partners about who does the same task the best. Couples often use competitive words such as "win/lose" or "better/worse" when describing their interactions. Roles that employ symmetrical positions might include competitive mother/competitive father, rebellious daughter/rebellious son, passive mother/passive father, or cooperative equals.

Additionally, partners often unconsciously select each other to express parts that are denied or split off in themselves. The psychodynamic classic "obsessive/compulsive" man connects with the "hysterical" woman so that she may express his feelings and he may express her intellect. These labels are somewhat simplistic and stereotyped, but a description of the interaction is useful. One psychologist suggests that in a dysfunctional marriage "the woman loses her mind, and the man loses his soul" (Kelly, 1979, personal communication); that is, the woman "deskills" and depends on her husband to make decisions. The husband sacrifices his ability to be a separate human being with legitimate needs. The partners may then criticize those aspects of each other that represent their own split off parts. Thus, one spouse may carry the affect and one the cognitive ability. The woman, for example, may cry her husband's tears while he remains stoic. Or, the husband may carry his wife's anger so she does not have to feel it. One partner may feel much more anxiety than the other and because systems tend to reflect ends of a polarity, the other partner will feel calmer.

The process of projective identification is a powerful dynamic between couples. We can only know our phenomenological world, the world of experience. If the internal representations of those who were in the role of nurturers carry conflicting emotions, they are likely to be projected outwardly. The "evil" father, for example, that is an aspect of the self is the evil father in one person projected outwardly and seen in another. The loving mother in one person may be projected onto a partner in the same way. These roles, of course, may be reversed. Joseph Zinker (1977) comments on this process that

> Projection is a form of escapism. . . . In pathological projection, the impotent person colors the world castrating, the angry person colors it destructive, the cruel person colors it sadistic, the person who fears his homosexuality sees a world of marching faggots. Every person colors the world with his inner life. The disturbed inner life searches for and locates nightmares even if it must hallucinate them. (p. 15)

The calm and emotionally stable person may search for and discover lovely fantasies. Thus, there are these two aspects of projection. First, we retain a certain identification with what we have projected. Second, we elicit from others, particularly our partners, a way of behaving toward us. This is why people often divorce for the same reasons they married.

Often, it is the inner life projected outwardly that may lead the system to run amok. There was a patient who alternated between inappropriate intense anger and seductive childlike behavior. She deflected with practically every interaction so that the other person never quite knew if some action had been agreed upon between them. When confronted with her anger and inappropriate behavior, she either denied feeling or behaving that way. In order to break out of her depression, she would either pick a fight with her ex-husband or go on a spending spree. Each interaction left the other person feeling confused and disoriented. When severely depressed, she would rage at the children and other people in her life. She would complain that people were conspiring against her. She was argumentative and felt easily slighted. Her children treated her with extreme caution and experienced a high level of anxiety themselves. Her oldest son became confused easily, her younger son developed a strong attitude of entitlement and became asthmatic. Her eldest daughter developed an eating disorder, and the youngest seemed easily frightened. Most every attempt by the children's father to remain involved in his children's lives was blocked by this mother. The father found himself having to think and act in strategic ways to bypass her. He would often feel trapped in confusing interactions with her. This experience would parallel past communications with his own mother. Combined with a strong injunction not to hurt his mother from his own father, he struggled with feelings of guilt and shame for leaving this dysfunctional marriage and claiming a life for himself. He found himself attempting to be overly understanding and forgiving because his ex-wife had been an abused child. However, at the same time, he felt just as abused by her as she had been by her parents.

In interaction with her ex-husband, this woman felt victimized by him. She believed that it was necessary to protect the children from someone who should be feared. Any kindness on the part of the father she perceived as obligating her and making her too vulnerable. Her "self" seemed to collapse often, and, in response, she would rage again toward the children or her ex-spouse. To this woman, the world was frightening and unsafe, and she had to be hypervigilant to ward off danger. Finding ways to remain in control was behind every interaction.

Pathological behavior in a system leads to other members in the system reflecting the pathology. In the example above, the father found himself rageful and thinking paranoid thoughts when he was forced to interact with his ex-wife. He reported that this was the only context in which he experienced these feelings. The negative trance, a state of consciousness that is an inward focus on terrible and confusing feelings, was experienced in the interaction and with disorienting communication.

In order to make sense out of a series of confusing interactions, the ability to shift from an individual point of view to a systemic position can be helpful in treatment. From a cybernetic perspective, it is important to distinguish between sequences of family behavior. According to Lynn Hoffman (1985), it is useful to examine "sequences of relationships in a feedback web" to be able to create an intervention. She concludes that "it is the pattern that is the problem not the system" (p. 386).

Each family member's reaction and inter-reaction to a symptom and to each other defines the system. Consequently, the therapist needs to understand how each member is involved in the system. As Hoffman (1985) states, "We can no longer say that it [psychiatric illness] is in the family, nor is it 'in' the [spatially defined] unit. It is 'in' the heads or nervous systems of everyone who has a part in specifying it. The old epistemology implies that the system creates the problem. The new epistemology implies that the problem creates the system. The problem is whatever the original distress consisted of plus whatever the distress on its merry way through the world has managed to stick to itself" (p. 386–387).

As can be seen in the previous example, individual dynamics are an important consideration in understanding a problem. The individual's internal map, which serves to create an interactive network of beliefs, is often the created problematic reality. Early learnings in one's family, personality makeup, and developmental cumulative learnings lead to the development of this internal map. This created perceptual reality often leads to pain and dissatisfaction in relationships when an individual projects the patterns of the internal map onto the behavior of another and looks for an appropriate fit or for that reality to be confirmed.

Often, a collusive pattern is established between couples and within families, and the hypnotic dance moves on its "merry way." Paul Wachtel (1985) describes a similar process in a concept he calls cyclical psychodynamic theory. Wachtel and Wachtel (1986) suggest that this theory emphasizes the role of the unconscious in matters of conflict and defense and serves to maintain a self image. Consequently, "one's hidden 'inner world' in this view is not a realm unto itself, but at once a product, a symbolization, and a cause of the interaction patterns in which the person engages" (Wachtel, 1985, p. 18). Therefore, both interpsychic and intrapsychic dynamics need to be considered when formulating a treatment plan.

This ability to shift lenses allows the therapist to develop empathy regarding the individual and respect for the well-being of the system. If a system or individual perceives that one or the other is not attended to, resistance and protectiveness may be elicited. Resistance can be defined as response to danger, a move toward maintaining the integrity of the family and individual.

Empathy is a basic regard for people and their life struggle. There is no place for blame in psychotherapy. Family therapists have often blamed the parents for the problems of the child. They often journey on an investigative mission to flush out the "culprit" who is responsible for the pathological behavior. The blame may be in the form of subtle nuances that express disdain for the parents. This blame is similar to the attitude that used to be conveyed regarding the mother by individual therapists. The mother was defined as the pathological parent. Now family therapists often include the father in the search for culprit.

A more useful paradigm comes from second-order cybernetics theory where the "problem creates the system." Rather than the parental system being blamed for the presenting problem, the problem, which has multi-etiology, serves as the stimulus to the evolving system. The system organizes around the problem in order to manage the difficulty. As the problem is exacerbated, the system evolves to accommodate the management of it (Kershaw, 1986; Hoffman, 1985). The components of symptomatology shared by couples can now be explored.

SYMPTOMATOLOGY

Each symptom is a valuable form of communication that signals something is wrong. The pain the symptom causes cues the one who bears it that something is out of balance and out of control. Symptoms are frozen sequences of behavior that are repetitive and that communicate the same problem resolution. Spontaneous hypnotic behavior often appears as a symptom (Frankel, 1976). The symptoms have several aspects, including complex of behavior, relational time, altered conceptualization and behavior, ideodynamism, and symbolic meaning.

Symptoms often occur around developmental transitions and form in complex patterns of behaviors. Who says what to whom with what effect, and the reciprocal response create the pattern of behavior involved in a symptom. With a couple, the symptomatic behavior may occur shortly after marriage when the family-of-origin introjects become activated, when the projection process begins, and the couple's hypnotic dance moves on its "merry way." Problems may begin after the birth of a child, a job change, the onset of middle-age, or after the children have left home. Any shift in the family structure or transition that is perceived as difficult may result in symptom formation.

Because of the function they serve, there is usually an investment in the symptomatic behaviors. Defenses almost always serve to manage anxiety, albeit in unproductive ways. Attitudes, behaviors, and feelings are difficult to change by working with the conscious mind in a direct fashion because they have demonstrated some past success in keeping anxiety at bay. The focus of therapy is to alter or disrupt the symptom or the habitual pattern of behavior. Everyone has unrecognized learnings that make problem resolution possible. Utilizing the unconscious as the agent of change can lead to reorganization and resolution of difficulty. Being mindful of relational time is useful in developing a change plan.

In a discussion on pain, Erickson and Rossi (1979) described discomfort as having three components of relational time. Any symptom may contain these time components: memory of past discomfort, present discomfort, and anticipation of future discomfort. Symptoms are usually developed in response to a stressful situation when an individual's defenses cannot manage the circumstance. The symptom serves as a trance inducer in that the pattern of behavior focuses the individual's attention inwardly and narrows the response field or freezes the responses to only one or two.

In the midst of a painful symptom, the couple will experience these three components of relational time. If the pain of the symptom is manageable, the couple may be able to utilize the memory of past discomfort and anticipation of future comfort to find the resolution to the symptom by discovering the resources they utilized to move beyond the symptom in the past. They can then look forward to the future with the awareness that they know the steps out of the present dilemma. For example, asking the couple how they moved from conflict to a peaceful coexistence the previous time may help the partners rediscover a resource they already know how to employ, such as humor, resting, cooling off, or leaving. However, a person in the middle of a symptom loses a sense of time. Time becomes distorted—slowing down, speeding up, or even stopping. Negative feelings may seem to have continued for months when only minutes of objective (or clock time) have passed.

Each symptom often contains some form of trance phenomena and may include amnesia, time distortion, positive or negative hallucination, anesthesia, or hypermnesia. The shared symptomatic trance dance between couples may utilize one or more of the phenomena and be "self-devaluing" (Gilligan, 1987). In research on dissociation (Sanders et al., 1989), findings suggest that dissociation normally occurs with perceived stress.

Another element of a symptom is its ideodynamism. Couples usually experience a problem as being out of their control. It seems to occur without them doing anything in particular. Of course, what the couple does not identify is the mechanism of reciprocal trance induction both partners use.

Erickson believed that symptoms may symbolize a traumatic event, may recreate particular life circumstances, or may be the adaptation to life's circumstance. Additionally, they may both ". . . constitute defenses against, and punishment from, underlying instinctual drives. They may mask underlying schizophrenic reactions or hold suicidal depressions in check" (CP IV, p. 103). Determining the meaning of the symbolic representation is helpful to the patient resolving the underlying psychodynamic conflicts. In fact, symptoms were viewed by Erickson as blocked resources. Heller and Steele (1987) comment that, ". . . all presenting problems and symptoms are really metaphors that contain a story about what the problem really is. It is therefore the responsibility of the therapist to create metaphors that contain a story that contains the (possible) solutions. The metaphor is the message" (p. 30).

Symptoms often contain the solution to the problem. Couples often overutilize or underutilize resources, and this process may develop into symptom formation. As Gilligan (1987, 1988), Frankel (1974), and Horowitz (1983) suggest, phenomenologically, symptoms often are the same as trance phenomena. The complex of symptoms is a rigid sequence of behaviors and immobilized attitudes that are replayed repetitively. The solution is often found in the trance behavior used in the complex itself.

POSITIVE AND NEGATIVE TRANCE STATES

Much of Erickson's work is based on the premise that the conscious mind is limited, and the unconscious is a reservoir of resources. Because of his remarkable ability to observe, which he learned from having to teach himself to walk again after polio, Erickson discovered that what we focus on becomes our frame of reality. In addition, he learned to trust the unconscious to lead him on the most productive path.

Trance may be negative or positive (Araoz, 1985). Gilligan (1987) also describes trance as either self-valuing or self-devaluing. One young woman patient illustrates the negative trance state. She had developed a fear of the night and of dark rooms. In her story of the origins of this fear, she described how her parents kept telling her she could not drive at night. She remembered them saying, "You will be hurt or be killed." This statement caused her to focus inward in a negative manner that she described as having trance-like qualities. They expressed fear that someone might run her off the road or that she would be unable to handle other hazardous situations. However, her parents had allowed one of her friends to drive the car at night. She began to doubt herself and to be cautious to the point of expecting a catastrophe. By reacting to the cautiousness and uncertainty that they had instilled in her, her parents reinforced those characteristics and she responded with intense fear until the young woman became phobic. Each time the woman attempted to act in a competent way, her parents would become anxious. Soon, the fear of driving at night generalized to going outside at night, then the fear was transferred inside the house and generalized to dark rooms. The images her parents created formed a picture of failure. The feeling of fear was associated with these images and it fostered a physiological/psychological response of agitation from the release of adrenaline and other biochemicals. Thus, the negative trance-like state inspired by the client's past experience dominated her present situation. In this example, the sequence of events that stimulated a trance-like experience also proved to be self-devaluing.

Either positive or negative trance states may be created by the ideosyncratic dyadic process. This process produces a specific type of interpersonal altered state. Symptomatic or conflict-reduced relationships result from the interpersonal altered state and positive or negative trances. How these trances are stimulated is explored in the next section.

PARTNER CO-INDUCED TRANCE

Because social interaction can produce trance, couples often entrance each other naturally. One person may say something that triggers a moment of internal focus for the other. The entranced partner then may focus on an association from the past or an association with an emotional overlay. The second partner may respond with a reaction that will elicit another internal focus in the first. Partners often have patterns of interaction that produce naturally occurring inductions. This process is a natural happening in an interpersonal context. The partners are not victims of each other's hypnosis—they cocreate the process.

There are five kinds of cue inductions that occur between marital partners, which stimulate inner imagery: power words, visual experiences, auditory experiences, kinesthetic experiences, and the use of interspersing suggestions.

Power Words

Marital imagery occurs with a verbal induction in which a word or phrase may focus the other partner's attention inward to create a moment of trance. For example, for one female client, the word "cute" stimulated negative imagery. When her husband called her "cute," she heard it as a third-order compliment. "That is kind of what you say when she is kind of homely but has a good personality," she remarked. She associated that word with objectification and, as a result, she became quickly enraged. On the other hand, her husband had a pleasant association with the word. Verbal stimulus by one partner can lead the other to experience a memory that is pictorial, auditory, or one that creates a particular feeling. When these memories are evoked, the individual usually responds to the internal experience and often projects the interpretation of the experience onto the other person. The result is a positive or negative perception of the first partner.

Visual, Auditory, and Kinesthetic Cueing of Induction

Induction can also occur through a look, gesture, touch, or other behavior. Similarly, cues such as the action of one partner may trigger an internal movie, voice, or kinesthetic experience in the other partner. Just a slight touch, a small bit of pressure, may trigger a whole scenario. This kind of process may occur when one partner has been an incest victim, for example. One kind of touch from the partner may place this individual back into the scene of being victimized. If a person has a memory for the feelings but amnesia for the event, then the couple may wrongly assume that the pain lies in the relationship rather than in an historical event. The feelings may be elicited by the induction cue, but the memory of the event is protected through amnesia.

A person may have an amnesia for the event and an amnesia for the feelings. When a partner touches the person in a particular way, this unconsciously reminds that person of the traumatic incident. Dissociation is a common method used to cope with trauma such as rape. After a rape, certain touches may unconsciously trigger the dissociation, which may then lead to difficulty in sexual arousal.

Dissociation can be linked to stimulus generalization. We all create models in our heads to interact with world. We receive feedback that tends to maintain the model we have created. An event in the present can trigger a traumatic memory and associated behavior. The feedback may maintain the behavior, may worsen it, or may work to resolve it. Traumatic events from the past may shape behavior and the behavior shapes the environment in a mutual recursive way. After many years the two become intertwined. Thus, a woman who was traumatized by incest may be unresponsive sexually with her husband. The husband may believe that the problem has to do with some inadequacy on his part. He may have traumatic memories of being rejected and feeling unwanted.

This couple may create a set of feelings that seem to only be related to the relationship. Soon this way of interacting and the resulting feelings may take on a life of their own and the painful feelings become associated with each other. The present events then begin to weigh heavily. In order to unwind the tangled ball of what feeling fits where, it is useful for the therapist to help the patient sort out and recover repressed memories and feelings. A powerful tool for this work is trance.

Often a person will have a feeling that seems unrelated to present events, and that feeling creates a state of confusion. The person may target his or her spouse as the source of pain in order to move out of the state of confusion. This blaming process helps the individual to maintain a feeling of control. Therefore, a husband may react to a particular feeling in a number of ways. He may think that his wife does not love him, or that she is having an affair, for example. This reaction justifies and explains the feeling that is initially disorienting to him. Trance work induces mild confusion. In a safe environment, trance allows the person to experience confusion and to tolerate it. When the person has these feelings, they then become curious phenomena rather than problems. Therefore, effective trance work may result in curiosity over angry feelings rather than focusing on a problem that needs to be solved with the partner. There may, in fact, be an issue that requires resolution, but more than likely the feeling is related to something else. A quick solution that blames the partner may make the situation worse. Rather than seeking psychological amputation such as divorce, it may be more useful to fit the feeling into a more relevant context.

Couple Use of Interspersing Suggestions

Another form of couple induction is the mutual use of interspersing embedded commands. One wife complained that her husband's mode of verbal interaction with her consisted entirely of questions. He would appear to be asking for information, but she felt compelled to do whatever the questions implied. For example, he would ask, "Are you going to pick up clothes at the cleaners?" This sort of question usually would be posed just as she was walking out of the house to go to work. The embedded suggestion in such a question is, "You are going to pick up clothes at the cleaners." The wife's response would be to drop into trance and to have an internal conversation: "Am I going to the cleaners? No. He wants me to though. I do not have the time, but I guess I will anyway." She would feel angry and resentful, and yet, she would stop by the cleaners. Her husband was baffled by her anger and attributed it to a hormonal imbalance. Neither partner realized that a state of negative suggestion was occurring until they came for therapy. I suggested that she time several requests to her husband as he walked out the door. The context soon shifted from one of hurt feelings to one of humor. What once was serious and painful became a delightful game they shared.

Interspersal of suggestions that provoke the development of trance through a mutual induction process can have powerful effects. The embedded message speaks to the unconscious (Erickson, 1966) mind. At one level, a communication is being delivered about one subject; and at another level, a different message is received with instructions regarding specific behaviors. One couple complained that they were too sensitive to one another's moods. The wife constantly inquired of her husband, "Are you going to be mad today?" The suggestion to him was,

"You are going to be mad today." He politely cooperated and became angry.

HYPNOTIC DANCE

Couple interaction can be seen as a kind of hypnotic dance. This hypnotic dance can be pleasant or painful. Depending on the context, a sequence of verbal and nonverbal behavior may occur in an interaction that is repeated frequently and that induces trance in both partners at the same time.

There can be paradoxical communication that creates two opposing messages between partners when rules about the relationship are being defined. The messages that are sent are often requests for help that are then denied and requested again. If a wife says to her husband at dinner, "I'm so tired," the husband may hear the request for help. If he offers to cook dinner, she may say with resignation, "No, that's alright." He continues to hear the request and begins to feel anxiety and anger. His wife may sense his irritation and react with her own anger and resentment. The looped communication is entrancing and often leads to a negative experience (Haley, 1963). As a way to resolve the paradoxical messages that are contradictory at a variety of levels, partners dissociate and become entranced.

As meanings are context bound, a person can be caught in a paradoxical hypnotic loop, and can only escape by moving to a different level of meaning. The character of Yosarian in Joseph Heller's *Catch 22* was caught in a bind in having to fight in the war. As a pilot, if he is sane, then he must fly the airplane in the war. If he flies, he will most likely die; thus, he is insane if he makes that choice. If he is insane, he cannot fly. An insane man cannot make a sane choice to fly for the war effort (Jacobs, 1980). The only ways out of the bind or loop are for the war to end, for Yosarian to die a hero, or for him to escape to a neutral country.

This paradoxical and hypnotic loop may be distinguished in times of stress where the sequence leads to conflict as a way out of the loop. For example, the loop might evolve around a basic rule in the marriage. If we are together, then we can let go of each other. If, however, we are separating (as in just sometimes being apart) then we must hang on to each other. If we hang on to each other, that means we are together. For example, a couple on vacation may decide that they can take two hours alone per day. Anything beyond that may be interpreted as wanting to be apart for good. Therefore, the two people must come back together and tell each other they hated being apart.

Another rule that employs the hypnotic loop might be that if the husband knows best, then he makes the decisions. But if he decides, then he will decide that his wife knows best. If his wife knows best, she will decide that her husband knows best. Examples of this loop abound in everyday life. A husband may tell his wife he wants her to decide on a movie for them to see. She may respond by telling him that she doesn't care, that whatever he wants to do is fine. He may then continue the loop by passing the final decision back to her. This kind of paradox creates a need to discover a new alternative (Jacobs, 1980). This bind might represent fusion between marital partners where distance, in the first example, is a regulator of intimacy and differentiation. When too much emotional distance occurs, anxiety is raised that may cue the beginning of the loop. Therapists often recognize this theme in conflicts: who can do what apart from the other partner and what should be done together. Little flexibility here is a reflection of feelings of insecurity about being separate selves and may represent an impasse in the separation-individuation stage of development.

The second loop again reflects problems in stating a position. If the balance is right and each person has the latitude to make decisions, then sometimes one will know best and sometimes the other will know best. However, if there can be no separateness, then a pseudo-togetherness exists. This theme may be recognized by the therapist as pseudo-mutuality. There is no individuation, and thus, neither person feels a sense of comfort in taking a position. Hostility, anger, and resentment usually underlie this loop because one or both partners yield to doing something unwanted. Under these conditions when negotiating occurs, the partner who seems to have the most power usually assumes that he or she is right and that the yielding partner is in complete agreement and not angry. Thus, the rules and beliefs about one's self and one's partner can fit together in a paradoxical and hypnotic loop that can lead to conflict or satisfaction. Looped communication from marital partners requires both stability and change from each other and the psychotherapist. One way to disrupt the loop is for the therapist to reframe the couple's communication as protection or to use the negative trance that the partners cocreate as a counterinduction to a more positive trance.

Particular couple rituals such as weddings, meals, specialized couple games (known only to the partners), or other activities, such as attending church, may lead to feelings of satisfaction as the couple moves out of the negative loop through the ritual activity. A couple in the midst of a loop can be induced into a pleasant trance that might occur as they attend a wedding and are reminded of the pleasant feelings they had for each other at their own wedding.

During an interaction, partners often engage in a co-induction of trance. Different trance phenomena occur within this process that make the trance a positive or negative experience and may be utilized by the therapist to enable couples to function at a higher level. These phenomena may include age regression, age progression, time distortion, amnesia, partner amnesia, hypermnesia, or dissociation. These phenomena may be problematic, but can be utilized by the therapist for more positive outcomes. In Chapter 8, these trance phenomena are discussed in terms of depotentiating symptoms and problems.

When one marital partner overreacts to the behavior of the spouse, a negative state of trance has likely occurred. The overreacting partner has either regressed to an age when a similar dynamic had occurred, or some signal was given to alert the beginning of the hypnotic paradoxical loop. Thus, the interpersonal system often interacts with the individual dynamics.

Erickson discovered that because couples often entrance each other, a therapeutic approach employing direct communication such as having the couple only use certain words, for example, "I" statements, may not create lasting change. Even though marital partners may learn to speak differently to one another, gestures, looks, tones, or any of a number of other cues may trigger a negative trance and lead to dysfunctional behavior. What is perceived by each partner leads to a particular response. Consequently, a look at perceived reality between partners is presented in the next chapter.

3

How Couples Create
Their World

A few years ago a young social worker requested supervision from me. As a student in a marriage and family graduate program, he struggled with trying to integrate all of the many theories, in addition to learning appropriate diagnosis, and making interventions. He told me that he felt inadequate as a clinician. He deeply yearned to help people change but believed he could not make a difference. Embarrassed and shameful, he not only had difficulty charging an appropriate fee for his services, but at times, he would work for free. The more I encouraged him and emphasized that the process of learning theory and integrating it into a comprehensible paradigm takes time, the more he complained that it was impossible for him. The more positive I would be, the more negative he would respond.

Finally, one day in class I walked up to this student and said, "Rick, I have something for you." I held out my hand and gave him a quarter. I said, "I understand you are interested in a little change." He looked stunned, puzzled, immediately dropped into trance, and became momentarily immobile. Since he was motivated to help people change but felt inadequate and, therefore, uncomfortable about charging for his services, he was interested in a "little change." Within the experience I

created for Rick, he received a psychological shock that drew
a distinction, created a confusion, and shifted his frame of reference for the problem in a way that I could not have done
directly.

The play on words and the shock sent him into trance to do
an inner search for meaning. The next time he came for supervision, he asked, "Dr. Kershaw, just what did you mean by
giving me that quarter?" I responded that he should make his
own meaning out of that experience and allow his unconscious
mind to glean a learning. A few weeks later, Rick began to
struggle less with the process of learning and happened to tell
me he was charging appropriate fees for his services. A few
months passed and he left supervision to continue other studies.
Two years later I saw him at a conference and he asked again,
"Dr. Kershaw, just what did you mean by giving me that
quarter? I have thought of many interpretations." I responded,
"Your unconscious has the ability to have many learnings from
one experience. So you may want to continue reviewing that
experience from time to time to discover what meaning your
unconscious wants you to have now." For Rick, this was an
experience in a generative perceptual shift he will always remember and carry with him. There will be continued learning
generated from this one symbolic experience. Understanding
how symbolic experience works in conjunction with principles
of perception is useful in knowing how reality is constructed.

There are several perceptual principles that are integral to
an understanding of how couples create the reality between
them.

1. Personal constructs create reality.
2. Language creates reality.
3. Culture and sub-culture create reality.
4. Perception is egocentric.
5. Physiology creates reality.
6. Interaction with another partner is based on the internal
   interaction, not on what occurs "outside" the person.
7. Subjective trance states influence the perception of objective reality.

PERSONAL CONSTRUCTS CREATE REALITY

Any distinction we draw or description we create about what we "see" is inadequate. There is always something else that can be said. Further, we are constrained by our basic assumptions and beliefs, particularly as they relate to relationships. Combs and Snygg (1959), in expressing a phenomenological view, state that "all behavior, without exception is completely determined by and pertinent to the phenomenal field of the behaving organism" (p. 40). We can say that our perceptions based on our assumptions create our reality.

A Chilean biologist who has influenced the field of family therapy, Humberto Maturano, says that we cannot distinguish between perceptions and illusions. The observer makes distinctions and uses languaging to change the kinds of distinctions that are made. He says that the observer distinguishes what will be observed. The couple specifies what they listen to and hear. The conscious mind filters what is heard through a particular belief system and may retain rigid categories. When the therapist works with the unconscious, the process is valuable in changing distinctions.

Since it is the frame of the window that determines what is seen, the frame distinguishes a part of the world that comes into focus. If we look through a large picture window, we will necessarily see something different than if we peer through a porthole. The frame of the window is constructed and can be expanded further or contracted. In other words, the frame of the window has a certain quality of plasticity or fluidity.

This concept is well illustrated in a familiar piece of literature. To her amazement, Dorothy in *The Wizard of Oz* discovers just how fluid experience is by what Oz does with the people in Emerald City.

> "Just to amuse myself, and keep the good people busy, I ordered them to build this City, and my Palace, and they did it all willingly and well. Then, I thought, as the country was so green and beautiful, I would call it the Emerald City. And to make the name fit better I

put green spectacles on all the people, so that everything they saw was green." "But isn't everything here
green?" asked Dorothy. "No more than in any other
city" replied Oz. "But when you wear green spectacles,
why of course everything you see looks green to you
... My people have worn green glasses on their eyes
so long that most of them think it really is an Emerald
City, and it certainly is a beautiful place." (p. 149)

The wizard created an illusion, and the character interaction
with that illusion illustrates both how assumptions about the
world actually create the world and how, when reality changes,
it is our perception of reality that changes.

Another example of this concept is the story of Darwin and
his ship *The Beagle*. He was anchored off the coast of a south
sea island and ordered his crew to row to shore and explore
the island. Upon landing, the crewmen were astonished. The
natives on the island could perceive the rowboat, but they could
not see the ship. The natives had no prior experience of sailing
ships, but they had known rowboats. What ships may be anchored just outside our own awareness?

We construct personal reality by what we are taught. Families
who perceive the world as dangerous and something to be
feared teach their children to function out of the same model.
An adult may struggle through life with a view of the world
that is negative and limiting, even if he or she knows rationally
that this world view fosters anxiety and dissatisfaction in life.
If a family perceives the world as fairly benign and believes that
each person can have influence and make decisions about what
direction or path to take, the child will develop a positive future-
oriented world view. It is the therapist's task to help rearrange
a person's world view to one that is more functional. Part of
that process is altering an individual's central model or metaphor, a life belief that may take many forms but be enacted
repetitively. We might say that all of us live in a metaphorical
bubble. One young man who lived in a literal one had a unique
view of the world.

David was a young man born with immunodeficiency syndrome, an inability to defend against viral and bacterial invad-

ers. To protect from infection, he lived his life in a sterile hospital environment. Because of his isolation and lack of normal perceptual experiences, David experienced distortions in depth and distance perspective. He believed that buildings he observed across the street from his hospital room had no backside. It was only after he was able to use the walking bubble developed by NASA to see behind the building that he realized the building was built like a box. He was astonished to learn that the green color in plants comes from the plant itself. Viewing other buildings across the street as smaller, David actually believed that the building was smaller not because it was farther away but because it had been built smaller. He had no notion of perspective; how objects "grow" in size when one walks toward them and "decrease" when one walks away. It was only when he had the walking bubble that he could prove to himself that objects in the distance become larger as he approached them (J. Vogel, 1985, personal communication).

David's view of grass and trees was also fascinating. He believed that they had no roots. It was only after his nurse allowed him to pull a plant from a pot of soil that he realized the plant grew under the soil. David was unable to understand the natural world through television programs or explanations. It was only through the actual experiencing of perceptual phenomena that he could alter his beliefs about the way the world looks, and how humans operate within the body of their own organismic perceptual phenomena. The nurses who worked with David reasoned that "observation of his perceptual development suggests that we unconsciously insert our past experiences as we view space and distance . . . Phenomena must be experienced to be learned" (Murphy, M. & Vogel, J., 1984, unpublished manuscript).

Each partner in a marriage carries a frame or web of constructs to interpret the world of the marital relationship and in particular, the behavior of the other partner. These constructs or beliefs about oneself, life, and one's partner are used to predict the future, bring some order to the present, and categorize the past. We all have personal constructs. They are internal creations or assumptions about what is outside ourselves. These constructs allow observers to look at the world and make interpretations about what they believe is there. George Kelly (1963) says that "all of our present interpretations of the universe are subject to revision or replacement" (p. 43). He suggests that people perceive their worlds through "transparent patterns," which they themselves create and then they attempt ". . . to fit over the realities of which the world is composed" (Kelly, 1963, p. 8).

We anticipate what will happen through the constructs we carry and the shared meanings we experience and then we behave as though we have actually visited the future. Just as H. G. Wells' time traveler was a man ahead of his time in *The Time Machine*, personal constructs and shared meanings create anticipated future reality by marital partners who are ahead of their time.

Reality comes into being for us because we see what we have a need to see. We select those perceptions based on past experiences and project a created world through our body of beliefs onto people and events.

LANGUAGE CREATES REALITY

Language is a symbol system that embodies a culture's experience and interpretation of that experience. It becomes spectacles through which we view reality. In fact, the Sapir-Whorf hypothesis suggests that we tend to take on the presuppositions of the language we learn. What we perceive is determined in large measure by the way language frames or names what is outside of ourselves. Consequently, different languages reflect different meanings, and therefore, different constructions of reality.

However, words construct maps of reality. Alfred Korzybski (1933), creator of the concept of general semantics, cautioned against confusing the map for reality itself. He suggested that theoretically there are two worlds: the world of reality and the world of symbol. Necessarily, there is a gap between these two worlds, and the wider the gap, the more "insane" we are. We might say today that language can only represent phenomenological experience through symbolization. The more wedded we become to the description of reality as being "right" the less sanity can we know.

Each person's view of the world is only a subjective interpretation of an objective reality. Joseph Pearce (1971) suggests that since we create the world with our senses and words, we not only observe but participate in it simultaneously. He says, "Our reality is a semantic creation by our cultural beliefs. What we believe to be true becomes true" (p. 136). Each interpretation is only a description that was created to help us in the world. Sometimes we may forget that the description is only a description and not a complete reality.

Our inner reality is constructed from past experiences, the culture in which we live, and the present and past values to which one holds. In addition, the inner world is a world of images, feelings, sensations, and to understand all of these elements we use thought. We think in symbols as a way to represent experience and communicate in a language, which is always changing and evolving as the community experience evolves.

Language represents a shared way of defining reality, a shared value system, a common way of viewing the world. More than that, language is a way of our knowing our own unconscious. The unconscious is expressed through symbols, and the self is maintained in the experience and expression of those symbols. George Steiner (1975) wrote, "We do not speak to ourselves so much as speak ourselves" (p. 18).

Harry Goolishian and Harlene Anderson of the Galveston Family Institute suggest that human systems are language generating and meaning generating systems. Since we give meaning to actions, the social structure evolves from the meanings we generate among ourselves. The particular problem presented in therapy is in the "meaning" not in the structure of the system. Therapy is, then, a linguistic event that sets a goal of creating new meanings to create new narrative realities. Goolishian and Anderson (1988) says, "Problems are not solved; they are dissolved."

Language can limit the representation of experience. There is often something lost in the translation of an individual's experience through words. For example, a person who is 40 years old now will have a very different experience of that age than someone who was 40 years old 20 years ago. The father was never the child's age because the two worlds are different. We could even say that our parents have lived on a different planet; our children know that to be true about their parents. In order to become more sane, according to Korzybski (1933), what we do with language must be altered. He suggests that three postulates of Aristotelian linear thinking be challenged: law of identity, law of the excluded middle, and law of contradiction.

Law of Identity

This law maintains that a statement such as "Marriage is difficult" equates marriage with difficulty, thereby creating a definition that views the whole of marriage as difficult. The definition does not describe the process of marriage as a dynamic energy between two people. It locks in a concept, forms a negative inner image, and predicts struggle. This definition limits an individual's reality because of the category that is arbitrarily created.

Law of the Excluded Middle

This law suggests a dichotomous reality rather than multi-value orientation. A world where there is only right-wrong, white-black, true-false does not encompass the shades in between. This dichotomous thinking is illustrated by one patient who revealed that her mother taught that a woman should only marry a man if he loves her, not if she loves him. Give this admonition, the daughter needed to rebel against her mother, and she reversed this belief and categorized available men as only those whom she loved. This notion always kept her in pursuit of an impossible goal, an emotionally unavailable man. The world is multi-valued but is often described in only two values. A two-valued orientation makes us "insane" or distorts thinking.

Law of Contradiction

This law emphasizes that an entity cannot possess one characteristic and its opposite at the same time; that one thing cannot possess two characteristics that are mutually exclusive. Water, for example, can be both hot and cold depending on the frame of reference. If someone comes inside from a freezing day and plunges her hand into 40° water, the water will be perceived as warm. However, if the person comes in from a warm summer day, the same water will feel cold. In marriage, one's partner can be both hated and loved. In fact, unless the murderous rage that sometimes exists between couples is acknowledged, the love cannot be fully experienced.

CULTURE AND SUBCULTURE CREATE REALITY

Different cultures experience reality in different ways and necessarily develop different descriptions, Eskimos have evolved many words for the English word "snow." Because Eskimos' livelihoods are dependent on harmonizing with a snowy environment, they have become adept at recognizing various elements and forms of snow. The Hopi Indians have a different concept of time than do we. There is no linear notion of time. There is no past or future, only the present. In fact, their verbs have no tenses, which allows them to live in a continuous present. The language focuses more on one's relationship with nature (Rogers et al., 1977).

The Tahitian language does not have words for depression or grief but it has over 40 words for different levels of anger (Mendelson, 1974). If we did not have the words for depression, perhaps we would not have the phenomenon. Those cultures that do not have words for the concept, do not experience it (Rowe, 1982).

Subcultures, particularly those of men and women, experience different realities and have different descriptions. Women are socialized to be more relationship-oriented and men more goal-oriented (Gilligan, 1982). Unless a man has been sensitized to gender issues, he will be reared to achieve power and set the rules. Women are reared to be caretakers and nurturers. Even if women have been encouraged to have careers, they are reinforced for caretaking behavior. This difference in focus means that men and women experience the world in distinct ways.

Individual family subcultures provide unique descriptions of reality. Each person's family life creates an internalized model of lovers, parents, roles for men and women, as well as the frame of "normality" for family life and a world view.

PERCEPTION IS EGOCENTRIC

All people interact with something outside themselves that they call reality. However, the construction or model developed in our minds about the world is always related to ourselves. It is impossible to move out of the self and observe something objectively.

> Perception is essentially egocentric from every point of view tied to the perceiver's position in relation to the object . . . , it is strictly personal and incommunicable except through the mediation of language or of drawings. . . . The egocentrism is not only limiting but also the source of systematic errors. (Piaget, 1969, p. 285)

There is a certain distortion that occurs when we perceive through our own filters of self, vulnerability, values, fears, fantasies, and dreams. This distortion affects memory and perception of the present and future. In fact, we review negative memory fragments repetitively and they often give us more trouble than if we could always recall the entire memory (1990, Betty Alice E. Elliot, personal communication), Attempting to understand each person's distortion in a couple system is useful in treatment. For example, people tend to believe that whatever they experience is reality. Physicists know otherwise.

The physicist, Fred Alan Wolf, says that "no past event is in existence. Its only record exists in our neural creases" (1984, p. 109). He continues that "Freud claimed that our memories were filled with pasts that we didn't even know existed" (p. 110). In fact, we have many different pasts and, in trance, we can examine them and bring to the present those resources that we need.

PHYSIOLOGY CREATES REALITY

Because of the manner in which our senses are constructed, the world we see, hear, taste, smell, and feel, defines the world as having mass and depth, color, texture, odor, sound, and flavor. This way of "seeing" supposes that events happen to us, and we respond; that events transpire outside of ourselves. The eye can only perceive a limited part of the electromagnetic spectrum. There is also a fascinating phenomenon all human beings experience called the blind spot. This is an area in the retina that is insensitive to light. There actually is a hole in an individual's vision. However, we perceive continuous patterns and space. As Humberto Maturano suggests, "We do not see that we do not see" (Maturano & Varela, 1987, p. 17). Another interesting feature of vision is that the colors we see do not exist outside ourselves. The color does not come from the outside but is dependent on neural activity inside the human being. How we perceive colors is also based on states of neuronal activity that are triggered by perturbations in the environment and are determined by the structure of each person.

Other animals have different visual abilities. The sky hawk has telescopic vision, and from a mile high in the sky can perceive a little field mouse. However, its peripheral vision, is poor. The cat can see quite accurately in the dark, but its vision is thought to be grainy and colorless. The gorilla can see up to six miles away.

Hearing is a function of the human animal as well. Our ears can respond to sound vibrations between twenty cycles per second and twenty thousand. However, the air vibrates higher and lower than the human ear can detect. There are other sounds that some animals hear that we do not. Further, there is a time lapse between the actual hearing of a sound and the moment the sound occurs. Although microseconds pass between the ringing of a phone and the hearing of the ring, they are recorded in our minds as concurrent events. Wolf (1984) believes that "for the real event to register in our consciousness, our 'mind's ear' projects the hearing of the phone ring backward in time toward the actual ringing phone. This projection is unconscious" (pp. 193–194).

In terms of objects looking as though they have mass and depth, quantum physics provides evidence that there is no such thing as solid material. What scientists believe is that there are wavelike probability patterns of interconnections. At the sub-atomic level, everything is connected so that the universe reveals a unity (Capra, 1975). At this sub-atomic level, however, there is only space and patterns.

SUBLIMINAL REALITY

Physical senses receive constant data from others and allow individuals to respond based on their "out of awareness" interpretation. Various emotions cause the blood vessels to contract and expand and can be "seen" or "felt" by astute observers. Although these reactions are picked up on a subliminal level by most people, they may not know at a conscious level what feelings are being expressed. The unconscious mind has the ability to know when another is angry, sexually aroused, physically ill, or a variety of other conditions because of the different temperatures associated with those states. For example, information can be accumulated through the skin by, being able to detect colors from different levels of warmth or vibration. The color of the skin changes with different emotions. There are temperature receptors in the skin that record information about shifts in warmth and coolness and may suggest a new sensory channel of dermo-optical perception (Youtz et al., 1966).

When one of the senses is impaired, others become more attuned to information sorting. Research has been done with blind people who can sense the presence of objects in a room. Hearing acuity improves as well as the ability to sense radiated heat (Marcuse, 1959). What this means is that anyone has this ability. The senses can be heightened through focused attention. T. X. Barber (1984) demonstrated that "enhanced cognitive proficiency" can occur by giving instructions to focus in a particular way. Under normal control is skin temperature, visual acuity, allergic responses, pain, age regression, amnesia, and relaxation.

The olfactory sense is utilized by most people to receive messages about others (Weiner, 1966). Many families can recognize each other by their smell. In fact, there must be an olfactory attraction between marital partners for the bond and attachment to grow. One patient of mine complained that he did not enjoy his wife's genital odors, even when she was freshly bathed. He distanced from her for a number of other reasons and eventually left the relationship. The husband had been aware of his discomfort with her natural smell from the beginning of the relationship but married her anyway because of pressure from his family. As there was no physical cause of the unusual odor, the problem became a metaphor for the difficulties in the relationship.

Therapists can enhance their sensory ability by spending time focusing on one sense. In our training groups, we often have people go to restaurants and attempt to hear conversations across the room, or sort out food smells from people odors. This activity may be socially unacceptable but training in sensory development is useful.

INTERACTION WITH A PARTNER IS BASED ON THE INNER IMAGE

We could say that because we create reality, we also create our partners. The person who is outside us is not exactly the internally perceived person. In fact, if some partners could peer into their spouse's mind and view the movie that was playing, they might not be able to identify themselves. In relationships that are highly conflictual, each partner may carry a representation of the other that would be responded to with "That's not me!" In many ways each partner is a construction and is represented as an image that sometimes embodies the worst and best spouse. Gregory Bateson (1978) suggested that we are meaning generating and creating systems. We cannot create meaning apart from another person. The perception of another person is a projected image from the brain of the first person. The meaning is generated from the interaction of two people. Each marital partner is, in effect, "created" from the interaction.

Each partner has various states that are especially elicited from the other partner. There is a state of consciousness elicited from the marital partner that is unique to this particular relationship in that other individuals may behave similarly but not evoke the same emotional responses. The state of consciousness may shift to an emotional age based on experienced needs and receptivity and availability of the partner. When feeling needy and frightened, one partner may emotionally be quite young for a few moments. When one partner attacks the other, there is a particular state of consciousness that the attacking partner utilizes. Usually, there is a sense of tunnel vision, where visual acuity is altered and only what is directly in view can be seen. Once "in" the state, it is so difficult to move out of it that the person must cycle through it. Sometimes, there is amnesia for what was said while in this state.

SUBJECTIVE TRANCE STATES INFLUENCE THE PERCEPTION OF REALITY

Consciousness changes with activity and normal trance states occur every day. Various trance phenomena influence how an individual experiences the world. Many have had a negative hallucination while driving and not "seen" an approaching car or positively hallucinated a stop sign that is not there. It can seem as though a long time has passed when only several minutes have elapsed, and there is a subjective experience of time distortion. In trance, perception becomes distorted and focus becomes narrowed. This process can create positive or negative results.

SYMBOLIC EXPERIENCE CREATES REALITY

Any experience that disrupts a patterned way of responding, alters consciousness, and represents a universal theme may become a generative symbolic learning. These experiences may range from common to unusual. The experience that Rick had when I gave him the quarter was a symbolic challenge that altered his reality just enough to move him beyond an impasse.

People who have survived terrible accidents or illness have had their reality altered in a more dramatic way. They have been on the edge of death, which may have provided an unusual opportunity to reevaluate and reprioritize. The universal question of "what is the purpose of life" takes on new meaning for these individuals and they often alter their lifestyle and begin to place more emphasis on family and relationships. This powerful shift in focus resulting from a life-changing experience becomes a marker for a different path toward a deeper and richer life.

Symbolic experience utilizes all of the principles of perception and always works to change reality. Before we move on to a different reality, sometimes our assumptions must be shattered by new perceptions. The meaning we bring to these symbolic experiences shapes our personal lives and those of our patients.

THE COUPLE'S CONSTRUCTION OF REALITY

Each partner brings to the relationship an image of and a name for the desired marriage. There may be romantic images or practical ones. Perhaps one partner wants the other to be a companion, lover, friend, harlot, mother, father, child, mechanic, or gourmet cook; someone to repair early wounds; someone with whom one can be intimate; and someone with whom to make contact. These images have names inherent in the images themselves—all-loving Mother, Father Knows Best, the Shepherd. Besides naming the other's role, the relationship itself may be named. When asked what they would "name" their marriage, patients came up with a broad selection: "Third World War," "Honeymoon," the "Good Ship Lollipop," "the Grateful Dead," the "Iris Garden," and "Grace Land." The metaphors are rich with sensory images. Although the name of the relationship may be out of awareness, there is an expectation of a role to be played and a wish for specific care-taking behavior from the partner.

These names are often constructed out of deep inner longings and from unfinished business of childhood. The hope that a spouse will be all the things that neither parent was is kindled in the romantic dreams and fantasies that are stirred in the beginning of a relationship. In those moments where a spouse manages to briefly match the idealized image, the excitement and hope bubbles up that finally we can be fully loved. When a spouse's behavior seems to fit the inner picture, the other partner begins to hope and expect a scenario that is projected on the inner movie screen, that part of the mind that has the ability to replay the past, the present, and future in movie form. What really happens, however, often fails to parallel the fantasized scenario. Until these hopes and longings are resolved, people will often look to the partner to meet certain unrealistic demands. If the names are unrealistic, then conflict is in store.

Part of the obstacle to experiencing happiness in relationships has to do with the quality of contact individuals make. People generally know when they have missed making contact or psychologically penetrating someone. There is a lack, something missing, a sense of being alone and feeling sad for what was missed. Pintauro (1970) understands this feeling well: "Egg shells are sometimes so thin, you may see out of one for a hundred years and never know you were inside." It is useful for the therapist to understand the inner images and names each partner is carrying around about present and past relationships. In order to define each partner's construction of reality, the language each uses is important. In addition, expectations and beliefs about how to resolve conflict, how to express affection, rules about communication, role expectations, and rules about rules are important information for the marital therapist. This information can be gleaned through the process of therapy.

Because we create reality by making meaning out of what and who we experience, we could say that each marital partner is a creation. The perception of the other is made up. Sometimes the description closely resembles the description by the other partner; sometimes it does not. When the descriptions are similar and growth enhancing, the relationship is close and vibrant.

The next chapter presents a model for psychotherapy based on Erickson's assumptions about change and the process of therapy. The model is one this author developed.

4

Model of Psychotherapy with the Hypnotic Dance

The psychotherapist needs to attend to both the process of therapy and the goal to be attained. Those aspects of establishing and maintaining a warm, caring, and respectful relationship with the patient are crucial to eliciting cooperation. Defining a goal for therapy and moving toward it are also important. To accomplish both, a model is presented for working with couples from an Ericksonian perspective.

WORKING WITHIN AN ERICKSONIAN CONTEXT

The overall process of psychotherapy within an Ericksonian framework follows several stages: looking at the dance, understanding the dance, joining the dance, trapping the dance, doing a counter-dance, and retrieving resources. To focus even further, each session could follow specific steps. The following steps are identified in this therapeutic model.

1. Observe the hypnotic dance. Distinguish the reciprocal nature of the problem.
2. Pace the affective reality of the problem for each partner

to establish rapport. Enter into each person's reality momentarily.
3. "Trapping the Attention": Absorb the couple's attention.
4. Identify which hypnotic phenomena are being utilized.
     (If age regression is occurring, determine what age is being elicited by each partner. Partners often become age regressed to their most vulnerable historical times.)
5. Determine the symbolic meaning of the problem.
6. Retrieve or build resources.
7. Utilize the symptom in the intervention.
8. Symbolize the solution.

Observe the Hypnotic Dance

The hypnotic dance that occurs between couples is that sequence of behaviors and feelings that are triggered by each other, have a trance-like quality to them, are ideosyncratic to the couple, reciprocal, and synchronous. When the couple describes the problem from both perspectives, the therapist can begin to discern the sequence that causes difficulty.

Each individual will probably maintain a fairly entrenched position regarding the spouse's behavior that she or he considers to be problematic. From each person's perspective, one's behavior seems reasonable and protective of the individual and the couple relationship. Each distortion will reveal psychodynamic issues or unresolved conflict that one partner is attempting to order, make meaning from, seek some resolution for, but is fearful that the old injury is occurring again without any hope of healing. The phenomenon of "entrainment" can be distinguished in these relationships.

Entrainment is a concept to explain why a synchrony of rhythms develops between any object or being that expends energy through pulsating action. For example, the pendulums of two grandfather clocks will begin to swing in the same direction at the same time if left in a room. Baby chicks will begin to peep in synchrony if sharing the same space. Women who live together often find that their menstrual cycles begin to coincide. Therapists and patients have reported a synchrony in breathing patterns and heart beats (Leonard, 1978). According to William Condon (1975), there are a multitude of subtle synchronous movements between people that are quite similar to a dance. He has captured some of these movements on film. Condon reports, "Communication is much like a dance, with everyone engaged in intricate and shared movements across many subtle dimensions, yet all strangely oblivious that they are doing so . . . There is no discernible lag even at 1/48 second. When there is silence and the speaker begins again, after 1/48 second the listener begins synchronous movements" (p. 43).

Condon and Sander (1974) also studied normal infant reactions to the mother and discovered that the baby and mother create a synchronized movement as they look and listen to each other and move in rhythm. The infant moves its body in coordination with speech patterns. The researchers found that the baby may raise an eyebrow when a speaker takes a breath or move a limb when the speaker emphasizes a syllable. This synchronization seems to be the basis for later emotional relating.

Besides the physical movements, there is the coinduction process at a verbal level. There are interactional sequences that coinduce a positive or negative trance state. These sequences occur repetitively around different content but similar themes.

When the dance stimulates a positive trance state, it is pleasurable. When the dance stimulates a negative trance, it is unsatisfying. Usually the negative trance is activated when one of the partners feels fearful and then attempts to gain security by controlling the other, sometimes through hypnotic implication. When one patient of mine began to tell her husband how she was attempting to become more autonomous, a request he had made of her in therapy, her husband responded with, "You have to decide what you are getting out of the relationship and what you are not, and you can stay when you are enjoying it." This remark raised her anxiety as she heard it as his ambivalence about staying. I suggested that he was avoiding his feelings in response to his wife talking about standing on her own. Although her lack of autonomy had been a complaint of his about her, he was able to identify that he was fearful of her becoming more separate from him.

On another occasion, a wife asked her husband, "Why don't you feel close to the boys?" (a hidden question about his feeling toward her). He became angry and sullen and defended himself by saying, "I am close to them. Sometimes I just don't know what to say." She could only focus on the withdrawal behavior. She could not see the larger context of a man who was reared by a stepfather who did not know how to be both masculine and intimate and who distanced himself when emotions were intense. Because her husband had left her in a sudden departure 12 years earlier and she was never certain he came back because he wanted to be with her, the trauma of that leaving caused her to carry anxiety and expectations that he would leave her again. She became hyper-alert to any distancing behavior on his part. In reaction to her comments regarding his behavior, the husband became hyper-alert to her pursuit and unspoken demand that he move back into closer contact with her. He would begin to feel overly responsible for her feelings and resent the burden of needing to take care of his wife. He would then begin to perceive her as a clinging needy child and distance even more, to which she would respond by demanding to be closer.

In this example, the wife utilized hypermnesia by remembering the husband's previous behavior before he left, and amnesia for the times when he behaved affectionately toward her. She also used age regression when she remembered feeling at that time totally incapable of taking care of herself or her boys. She had even considered suicide. This wife reported feeling three years old when her husband left before. Her husband, on the other hand, would experience age regression when she pressured him to be closer. He also experienced amnesia by perceiving his wife as his overbearing mother from whom he had to get away. This coinduction resulted in a negative trance state for each that led to a narrowed problem focus and concomitant emotional pain.

Negative trance states can occur when the interactions become deadened or attacking. The partners lose the ability to use externally oriented trance dissociation and observe their process more objectively from outside themselves. Solomon

(1989) suggests, "In this state, the 'observing ego' is unavailable for conscious reflection on the process while it is happening. The ego state that attacks or provokes attack is unavailable to reasoning or to other states of consciousness" (p. 90). Instead, the partners become hyperfocused in an internal trance state, lose peripheral vision, and often report losing a sense of self while they "become" a feeling with no body and no mind. Sometimes this trance state can only be broken by dramatic means such as yelling, crying, or violence where anger is used to recover a sense of self through a sudden shift in states of mind.

Besides observing the synchronous movements and interactional process between couples, it is useful to observe ideomotor movements that are unconscious signals in response to communication. These movements may suggest themes usually buried beneath the surface and reveal areas of conflict that may be avoided consciously. Small movements in any of the extremities or of the head may be especially attended to by the psychotherapist. One partner may nod slightly in agreement or disagreement while the other talks. Or a partner might appear to agree with his or her spouse, while a foot shaking anxiously tells another story.

The marital therapist can identify the sequence of behaviors and emotions with couples in observing them interact around feeling-laden issues. The sequence is patterned and ritualized so that each time one partner begins the sequence the other partner follows with the next behavior in the sequence. There is a shared ritualized pattern between partners that can be stimulated in a number of ways and performed unconsciously whether the couple is physically present for the entire sequence or not. Each partner knows the "Choreography" so well that the steps are performed together or apart in imagination with the concomitant feelings. The automatic nature of the hypnotic dance is related to the utilization of hypnotic phenomena in the ritual. The couple's hypnotic dance is dissociated from both partners' conscious awareness. The automatic nature of a behavioral response makes it seem like there is little personal control possible. An individual has many images that develop in the midst of the patterned and automatic response.

Part of identifying the hypnotic dance is distinguishing each partner's images of the worst and best relationship that are stimulated within a couple context. The image of that relationship may fall somewhere along this worst-best continuum. To ask about the "name" of the marriage is useful here. The images that are evoked and the name that is given may reveal the symbolic meaning of the problem. This observational step is important to the direction of therapy.

The therapist is called upon to use keen observational skills to really "see" the hypnotic dance. Erickson was a master at observation and saw each patient with new eyes. Don Juan, the Mexican sorcerer, tells Carlos, his apprentice, "When you see there are no longer familiar features in the world. Everything is new. Everything has never happened before. The world is incredible" (Castaneda, 1971, p. 159). This process is more than objective viewing. The therapist must become part of the "aliveness" that occurs in the office between people. As Franck says in *The Zen of Seeing*, "In seeing, there is an entering into the process of life—of making contact with it—not just observing it uninvolved" (1973, p. 6).

Pace the Affect to Establish Rapport

Each partner's experience seems so real and correct that it is useful to acknowledge the affective reality of the problem for each spouse. This step can be tricky because it must be done without one partner thinking the therapist is siding with the other. Sometimes, because the level of neediness is so great for both partners, the therapist will find it too difficult to support each partner in the presence of the other and will need to see them individually. This problem may occur when one spouse perceives as abandonment any attempt by the therapist to be supportive of the other spouse.

To enter into and accept the reality of each partner is important in establishing rapport and in understanding how the hypnotic dance becomes activated and proceeds through the stages of intensity, explosion, resolution, only to be reactivated.

Trapping the Attention

Erickson was a master at holding the conscious mind's attention while he spoke to the unconscious mind. He used context disarrangement to push people out of seeing the world in the ordinary restrictive way. Carol Lankton (1983) tells the story of a visit to Erickson when, as she was leaving, he threw to her what looked like a heavy piece of rock. When she caught it, it was incredibly light. He remarked with a twinkle in his eye, "Don't take anything for granite."

Trapping the attention in this Ericksonian model refers to (1) disarranging the usual context or depotentiating the conscious mind set, (2) reframing the distortion of both partners' perception of the other's behavior in positive future-oriented terms, and expanding their frame of reality, and (3) focusing on the partners' lack of understanding rather than their resentments. One couple who came to me for therapy were engaged in tremendous conflict. The wife reacted every time her husband came home from work and began asking questions about why things had been done a certain way. She had left the car parked on the street to work in the garage, and he asked why the car was there. Her interpretation of his questions was that he was being critical of her for doing tasks inappropriately. In fact, it was true that he was quite conscientious and obsessive in his worry about perfection, but, at the same time, he also felt pushed outside the family and was clumsy in his attempts to make contact with family members when he came home. Indeed, at one level, he was criticizing her. The wife reported to me, "He just wants to control me," suggesting a malicious motivation. I responded with, "Does he want to control you or is this his way of re-entering the family, clumsy though it may be?" This question trapped her attention through the reframe, and she dropped into trance, creating a receptive moment in which the painful category she had constructed to describe her husband's motivation expanded. At the same time, the husband dropped into trance and began to signal yes with slight ideomotor head movements. This technique of "siding descriptions," a form of reframing, will be discussed further in Chapter 8.

Identify Hypnotic Phenomena

It is useful to identify which hypnotic dissociation phenomena are being utilized by each partner in the dance. Various trance phenomena may be utilized by couples in the hypnotic dance: (1) age regression, (2) age progression, (3) positive and negative hallucination, (4) time distortion, (5) dissociation, (6) analgesia/ anesthesia, (7) amnesia, and (8) hypermnesia.

Age regression may occur as a result of the interaction. If so, the therapist may want to determine what age is being elicited by each partner. Partners become age regressed to their most vulnerable historical time when they had fewer resources to use consciously in problem resolution. Asking what age each partner feels is useful in proceeding with the therapy.

Age progression occurs when one partner rushes forward into the future and lives in imagination the best or worst scenario. Decisions may be formulated in the present based on this "time" travel. One patient of mine so feared that men would leave her that she always arranged to leave the relationship first. Another who feared abandonment reported that she always influenced the situation so that the man would become angry with her and leave. She set this event up in order not to be the one who made the overt decision to leave.

Positive or negative visual or auditory hallucinations may be experienced by marital partners. In the midst of the hypnotic dance, positive hallucination may happen where one partner "sees" the other behave in a particular way or "hears" the other partner make a particular statement when neither occurred. Often an inner movie is activated that may incorporate some very intense emotions. Negative hallucination can certainly abound when partners do not hear or see what has occurred. One of the most profound examples of negative hallucination is one partner's not seeing evidence of an affair by the other partner.

Time distortion may occur in the hypnotic dance where if the dance is pleasant, time seems to pass quickly. On the other hand, if the dance is conflictual, time seems to slow down and negative feelings seem to be unending.

Dissociation may be experienced in a variety of ways. Any of the other trance phenomena are forms of dissociation. However, it should be listed separately because there can be spatial, temporal, auditory, kinesthetic, and visual dissociation. Individuals can experience themselves in trance both "here" and "there" or have the ability to see themselves sitting in one part of the room and also across the room or somewhere else at the same time. This phenomenon exemplifies trance logic where we can be "here" and "there" at the same time. We can be both six years old and sixty years old in trance and it will seem perfectly logical. Auditory dissociation can be experienced by hearing sounds inside or outside the self. Everyone has had the experience of "hearing" a tune inside their heads or can imagine an orchestra playing in a band shell in a park outside one's self. Kinesthetic dissociation occurs when electrical impulses fire off that would send feeling messages to a part of the body. However, the person is unaware of the feeling. Sexual sensations may occur in the body but be numbed. Individuals may experience a feeling and express in the body, or anesthetize a physical sensation and express in a feeling. Perls et al. (1951) describe this process of how one may somatize an emotion of crying. The person, instead of allowing the feeling, cuts it off.

> Instead, he now suffers headaches, shortness of breath, and even sinusitis. The eye muscles, the throat, the diaphragm, are immobilized to prevent the expression and awareness of the coming crying. But the self-twisting and self-choking in turn arouse excitations (of pain, irritation, or flight) that must in turn be blotted out, for a man has more important arts and sciences for his mind to busy with than the art of life and the Delphic self-knowledge. (p. 269)

Visual dissociation occurs when we "see" images inside with the mind's eye while at the same time looking at objects outside.

Analgesia/Anesthesia is a numbing of physical sensation. In other words, a person may suffer an injury or illness but be anesthetized, through various chemical changes that take place, to such an extent that there is little or no awareness of resultant pain or discomfort. In some relationships, acknowledgment of physical pain is unacceptable, and partners learn how to use their natural ability to pay little attention to some pain signal that requires attention.

This phenomenon can be used effectively for pain management. It is common for people naturally to use anesthesia to override the signals from the body and keep up with the demands of the world. Unfortunately, the results are sometimes harsh on the body and on the spirit.

Amnesia is a natural memory loss and can be experienced in the hypnotic dance. When one partner begins to recount a situation, the other may forget about it.

Hypermnesia is an ability to remember minute historical details. Often hypermnesia in one partner is followed by amnesia in the other.

The therapist must demonstrate how the unconscious can influence behavior and that the focal point for change is located in the unconscious. The next step in the model contributes to this goal.

Determine the Symbolic Meaning of the Problem

In this step of the model, the therapist will want to utilize systemic, developmental, and intrapsychic data to determine what the partners are attempting to learn or master, both as a couple and as individuals. Within the symptom is the symbol of potential resolution to the problem. From this perspective, the symptom can be viewed as an ally.

Retrieve Resources

According to Lankton and Lankton (1983) resources refer to "automated patterns of feeling, perceiving, and behaving. Sometimes the resources exist in fact and frequently they must be 'created' by bundling together associated bits and pieces of experience" (p. 121). Erickson believed any experiences, even painful ones, could serve as positive resources. As he told Monde (Erickson & Lustig, 1975), "Getting a spanking as a child hurt, but it really is nice to know that you can have feelings, isn't it?" Experiences can be accessed through memory, metaphor, story, analogy, or associations. Examples of important early learnings that act as resources most people have include the ability to move into and out of feelings, the ability to argue, the ability to agree, the ability to accomplish tasks, the ability to say yes and no, self-discipline, persistence, courage, endurance, and the ability to feel pain. Every symptom is a resource, and every problem has a potential learning. Every new situation, such as confusion, has the potential for expansion into clarity. Erickson kept turning problems and solutions around so that life could be fluid and adventuresome.

Some people feel blocked in their ability to move forward because of their pasts. A difficult past may remain as an unrecognized resource and become a reason for people maintaining a particular symptom. Therapies that overemphasize the review of past hurts may actually serve to keep the patient unhappy.

Utilize the Symptom in the Intervention

Utilization of the symptomatic attitude, emotion, or behavior in the intervention is an important step in this model. Symptoms are attempts to master life conflict. If a person continues to become involved with the same kind of dysfunctional people, this may represent that person's attempt to master something.

Symbolizing the Solution

The use of a symbolic communication for solution generation can be a powerful instrument of change. Being multi-leveled in meaning, the symbol can provide a sense of comfort and contain a generative solution in the present and future.

One couple who sought therapy were embroiled in a power struggle over who was to be in charge of the relationship rules. The content of the battle was focused on household cleanliness and orderliness. One spouse preferred everything put up where it belonged; the other was more flexible. At a deeper level, the theme of the struggle was about individuation and separation or how to be both a couple and individuals at the same time and how to be functional apart from their original families.

There were some important family-of-origin issues that significantly affected this relationship, but the struggle needed to be calmed before these marital partners could begin this work. I asked them to take a table and place it in the middle of the room for one week with objects that belonged to each. Shoes from one partner and rumpled papers from another were strewn over the table. They were instructed not to process anything regarding the table during the week but to consider what meaning I intended the table to have. When they returned for the next session, both reported that the arguments had ceased, and they began to laugh with each other every time they had to walk around the table. Each person developed wonderful interpretations for the meaning of the table and were then able to begin work on the relationship.

Another couple came to therapy presenting with their eight-year-old daughter, Suzie, who felt angry and frightened because the husband's father had committed suicide. Being precocious, Suzie had asked her parents if she could come to therapy since she knew they had been seeing me. She was distraught over her grandfather's death and told me her other grandfather was dying of cancer. She seemed agitated, sad, and said, "If my grandfather were alive, I would kill him. I am angry he didn't talk to anyone. I wish people didn't have to die. I wish people could just go to live in the middle of the earth and live forever." In the course of the therapy session, Suzie told me that some time ago when her parents had gone out of town, she had taken a picture of them, torn it up, and put it back together again. I suggested that she draw a picture of her grandfather during the session and do the same thing. She thought that was a good idea and proceeded to complete the task. She told me her grandfather loved roses and she was intending to plant a rosebush in her backyard. I suggested that she take the pieces of the picture she had drawn and plant them when she planted the rosebush. Then, the conversation continued:

CK: Do you know what happens to roses through the year?
SUZIE: They put out leaves and buds and roses.
CK: Then what happens?

SUZIE: (said sadly) Then they die and the leaves and flowers just lie on the ground.

CK: The leaves and flowers become part of the earth again and give nourishment to the rosebush when it blooms again, and the new rosebushes that grow from it.

SUZIE: They do? (said hopefully) And all the people become part of the earth again too? (She was able to make the connection quickly.)

Suzie struggled with her murderous anger and expressed it by tearing up the picture. Because she also loved her grandfather, she wanted to put the picture back together again, symbolic of wanting him to be alive. The symbol of the rosebush was utilized to represent birth, life, death, and transformation, which gave her hope and comfort.

Suzie came back for another session and began by talking about the planting of her roses.

SUZIE: My father said he would probably go down with me on Saturday and get me little plants and we would dig a little patch and we'd plant them.

CK: I'd like to hear about that.

SUZIE: I'll name one color of the roses—the red ones—Paul (her grandfather's name). That's my favorite. And pink ones are going to be—I'll call the pink one (thinks for some time)—I'm going to call it Crystal.

CK: That's very nice. Paul and Crystal together growing from the ground up to make your backyard very pretty.

SUZIE: Can we do that hypnosis thing again?

CK: You mean so your feet and hands can have that nice, warm, funny, tingling feeling? Are you having that feeling yet?

SUZIE: (She begins to laugh) They're tingling!

CK: That's right. I wonder when that tingling is going to move up into your ankles?

SUZIE: It's already right around there!

CK: Up to your knees? And there's a special part of you, Suzie, that can let that feeling change, a lighter tingling, or a heavier tingling, or a medium tingling feeling to stay right

there in your left leg while you might now notice how your
right hand . . . begins to feel like lifting?

Suzie continues to move into trance, and as most children,
begins to move around in the chair and then becomes very still.

SUZIE: My left arm's heavy. My right arm feels real light. (Her
arm begins to lift) No, wait a minute. Now my right arm
is getting heavy.
CK: Oh, that special part of you decided to trade one feeling
for another, so the feeling that was in the left arm is now
the feeling in the right arm and that is, of course, the right
feeling to have, is it not?
SUZIE: How could I trade?
CK: I don't know, and you don't know, but that special part of
yourself, in the back part of your mind, your unconscious,
knows how to trade one feeling for another by focusing
your thoughts on another idea.
SUZIE: Can my roses have feelings? I was going to put like a
little plaque and put his name on it and have it sticking out
of the ground.
CK: What were you going to say on the plaque?
SUZIE: In honor of my grandfather.

She told me she saw herself standing in front of the plaque
in her yard. Her grandfather appeared in her trance. He
thanked her and said the plaque was very nice.
Suzie came out of trance and talked of other things until the
session was over.
When the next session began, Suzie wanted to tell me what
she had done about her grandfather.

SUZIE: And I took those pictures and I went outside while he
was there and I dug a little hole and I stuck the papers in
it and then I buried them.
CK: And you did that all by yourself? How did you feel after-
wards?
SUZIE: I felt a little better. And I just pretended like there was
a crystal over it. (She refers to the crystal amethyst stone I

have in my office as well as a children's story she shared
with me on a previous occasion about a crystal mountain.)

CK: A crystal mountain?

SUZIE: Uh, hum. And I wish my grandfather was alive. And if
he was alive, I would probably kill him.

CK: You'd feel like killing him because you are angry with him
and you're sad too?

SUZIE: If he was alive, I'd wish that I would never see him again,
'cause he made me feel so bad. And I don't want my other
grandfather to do the same thing that he does. It feels so
bad.

Suzie's maternal grandfather had just been diagnosed with
terminal cancer, and the anticipation of this upcoming loss on
the heels of the suicide of her paternal grandfather was overwhelming.

Suzie then changed the subject to tell me about a story she
heard on the news of a little girl being abused by her parents.
This is a metaphorical description of how she feels "abused" by
these two events happening so close together. She then returned
to discussing her roses.

SUZIE: Every morning I water it. Or at least, I try to remember
to. My pink one still hasn't grown a rose. But my red one
started out with a rose but now the rose is dying. But I
think if I—next time my baby-sitter comes—since she
grows roses, she could show me how to cut them and I
could cut them off and they would grow! And then maybe
I could cut the pink one which doesn't have a rose yet and
maybe another one would grow. And if I cut that off,
maybe two more would grow and if I cut that off, maybe
another four would grow, and if I cut those off, maybe
eight would grow, and if I cut those off, sixteen will grow,
and if I cut those off, 32 will grow . . .

(Picks up amethyst stone in office) I like looking at that
and seeing in the future.

CK: Yes. Since you're looking in it as the future, what do you
see today?

SUZIE: Well, Peter my brother. Something about a D on one of his tests. And my mommy is going to get her Ph.D. . . . Know when you get it [diploma] framed? The glass is going to get popped open and it's going to get torn. And my father is going to retire someday. He's going to have so much money that he's going to get a mansion and he's going to have, he's going to be really rich. And he'll get better from his asthma. I don't think that's possible. But they're going to come up with medicine so he can. And me? I'm going to become a dancer and I'm going to break my leg.

CK: And when it heals?

SUZIE: Then I'll get better and I'll be an actress and a singer and then I'll lose my voice and then, I'll get it back and then everything will be great!

Suzie was learning how to incorporate managing normal losses in life and to look forward to a positive future.

CK: It's nice to know so many interesting things can happen in the future, and you can enjoy looking ahead to the future you most want. It is fun to build things and watch them grow, just like your feet.

Distraction and confusion were used to shift her attention back to an experience where she felt some mastery. She was being taught at an unconscious level how to change one feeling into another.

CK: See if the tingling starts in your foot right now. (referring to an earlier session where she learned to numb her feet.)

SUZIE: It tickles!

CK: That's right.

SUZIE: I did it to my foot and my foot fell asleep and I couldn't get it awake until a lot later on.

CK: Ohhhh. Well, you might want to tell your foot, if you're going to put it to sleep, when it's O.K. to wake up, too.

SUZIE: How am I going to tell my foot when to wake up?

CK: Just tell your foot, "You can wake up in a moment or two."

SUZIE: I flipped it like that and it didn't wake up.

CK: Oh, no, because it went too far asleep.

SUZIE: It's a very heavy sleeper.

CK: That's right.

SUZIE: Both of my feet and also my nose.

CK: Very deep sleepers, hum? You know how hard it is to wake up yourself.

SUZIE: This morning? The minute I woke up, I wanted to take a siesta. Do you know what that is?

CK: Right. A little nap.

SUZIE: Uh hum. A little nap! I wanted to sleep the whole day!

CK: And a nap always comes to an end when you wake up. (Suzie picked up the amethyst stone in the office.) Well you can look into that little stone and you might see a lot of things in your future. What do you see in the future?

SUZIE: Well, when I'm 101 this office will be an apartment in somebody's kitchen and the fountain, there'll still be a fountain, but it'll look different. It will have weird purple things around it . . . the people who live here will be artists and they make marble sculptures with purple stones going around it like that. And in the middle of the water fountain there'll be a long purple pool.

CK: You can look into that crystal and see time go by?

SUZIE: I can see a special period of time.

CK: And what do you see there?

SUZIE: Peace. There'll never be a war . . . there'll never be a World War III. Thank goodness. And the USA will only have one more war. With Russia, I think. It says in Russia. It says, "R-U-S-S-I-A." Do you want to look into the future? When I looked into it (stone) for the first time, I started looking this way, and I moved it and then I moved it again. You have to move it to see the future. And you can focus on people if you want to. You can see what their lives will be. I'm trying to focus on the flowers, to see what will happen to them.

CK: Well, look into the future and look at your rosebushes . . . ?

SUZIE: Some will be dead.

CK: You think so?

SUZIE: I think they'll be dead before I am. A long time before I am.

CK: I wonder why that would be?

SUZIE: Well, roses don't live forever! They don't live as long as people do either. I love the roses.

CK: But they have children who have other children.

SUZIE: Yes, and in the future I go to Florida and become an artist, and I make a sculpture of the grave of my grandfather, and put the dolls all around it. Miniatures of it. And then I take the real dolls and I give them to my children. Except I don't think that I'll become an artist . . . I want to be an actress.

Suzie speaks metaphorically of how this tragic event will affect her into adulthood, but also how she will integrate it and turn her vitality toward her children and her own life.

Suzie continued the next few months to see me occasionally and report on her roses and how much she missed her grandfather. She could speak openly with her parents about her angry and sad feelings. Her parents worked also individually and conjointly on the impact of the two parental deaths on their marriage.

The therapeutic approach with the wife involved mostly supportive work. She could easily express feelings, and her father-in-law's suicide encouraged her to push through her reticence to tell her own father all she wanted to say before he died.

Since the death of the husband's father had been so sudden, the husband felt unfinished and empty. A trance session was used to suggest that the husband see himself with his father across the room and speak to him.

HUSBAND: (Breathing deeply several times) My dear Dad, It's been over a month since you died and I am still trying to understand what happened. I knew you were having problems and I knew you had tried suicide before, but I really didn't believe you would do it. I'm sorry. And I wish I could have been of more help to you. I don't think I knew how. In the end, you were going to do what you wanted to do.

I feel very sad, knowing how difficult each day was for you. Life was a real struggle. I can remember times in my life when each day was a terrible struggle and I started each day looking for it to end. I know how difficult and how wearing it can be. In the end, your desire to go on had just worn away. There are times when I also feel an incredible amount of anger towards you. I am angry at how much of your life was wasted . . . how you chose not to be in charge of yourself . . . why you created this absolutely hostile world—it was not true—it was a big lie . . . you could have had a lot more of what you wanted.

My anger also takes on a very selfish side. I feel angry at how what you did to yourself affected me. I have spent many years of hard work, trying to rid myself of feelings of helplessness, inferiority, and incompetence. It is not real, and I am angry at you for not allowing me to taste the world and its possibilities when I was a kid. I know you had a hard time taking care of yourself, but I guess I expect that you would have gotten beyond your fears to help me get more. Every time I get extremely anxious or depressed, I feel cheated by it . . . when I feel those kinds of feelings, I am glad you are dead.

When I found out about your suicide, I can remember feeling many things at one time. When I was shocked, angry, sad, and relieved . . . relieved that you were gone, it was as if an anchor had been removed from my neck, that I no longer needed to protect you and I could be who and what I wanted. I can feel it in my bones, I am sure of it. I am going to do important things and I couldn't do them while you were still alive. In a way, you did me a great favor. I feel like a horse that no longer has anyone pulling in on the reins.

I am also sad, and I miss you. There were things about you that I value and treasure. I know you loved me. I could hear it in your voice and see it in your eyes when you looked and asked how I was doing. I know you were proud of the successes I have had in my life and I learned from you how to be gentle, how to be caring about family and generous to strangers. I got a curiosity about the world and a sense of obligation to others. You had those qualities and I will try to have them too.

I miss you. I wish I could talk to you one more time. (Husband comes out of trance.)

When I was with my mother in Florida at the funeral, I had a sense of relief and I think that it was almost, in a strange way, that his doing what he did gave me permission to not have to be like him anymore.

CK: That's right. You can live differently.

I had a client a couple of years ago who was Jewish and when his father died, they cremated the body. He was here when it happened, and he had to get the body back up North. The only way, because of his circumstances, was to mail the urn. This fellow told me it was the most bizarre experience. He was standing at the post office after having taken a number, waiting in line to mail his father back home. And nobody else in the post office knew what was in the box that he was mailing. It was one of the most incredibly absurd situations and yet, as he waited for his number to be called, he said good-bye to his father. He told him how much he appreciated the things he had received from him and the sadness about what he didn't get. His number was called. He gave the package to the clerk. And the very moment he let go, *you* have that feeling of relief and release. He walked out of the post office and realized that an incredible weight had been lifted from him. His father was going home.

When you have a weight lifted, you begin to feel much lighter: a lighter step, a lighter walk, and your breathing is easier. You never know exactly how long something will take to be completed, just like the time it will take for Suzie's roses to grow. And as the rosebush grows, you may find yourself hearing the sound of the beating of horses hooves—free to enjoy the space, the air, and no more reins.

Suzie's father continued to grieve and talk to me about the memories of his father. I suggested one other symbolic assignment. He was to visit the city's rose garden. As he completed the assignment, he spent several hours a week enjoying the kind of roses his father used to grow. He was saying good-bye, savoring some of the positive qualities his father expressed, and feeling comforted by the rose garden. The symbolic experience was useful as a generative healing intervention. The rose garden and the roses Suzie was growing would continue to stimulate the father's own healing in many ways. He told me later that the roses touched him deeply. He did not understand the process but he knew he was experiencing an inner healing.

Erickson constantly worked on a symbolic level and responded to the patient's own symbolic communication to facilitate healing and change. He asked one patient to write his father's name on a piece of paper and flush it down the toilet, symbolizing the break in his dependence on his dad. He believed that "we all take a symbolic attitude toward a lot of things," (Erickson & Rossi, 1980, p. 147–148). The attitude of which he spoke is reflected in our language. For example, Erickson noted that we say things like, "That is something I would like to sink my fangs into" (p. 148), a symbolic expression of wanting to be involved.

In the next chapter, we examine what trance induction is from an Ericksonian perspective, how it can be accomplished, and how to use the interpersonal dance to help stimulate trance in a couple. Indirect suggestion and linguistic forms are also discussed.

5

Trance Induction

To stay within a framework of operating belief systems, it is important to join the ritualistic and familiar dance of the couple before intervening. The therapist must join the system and utilize the symptom to help create change. Trance induction is one way of entering into the patient's reality, utilizing the "as-if" context (we will act as if this perceived reality is real), employing the symptom to expand the couple's strategies for achieving satisfaction, and engaging the unconscious mind to develop future-oriented solutions.

Trance, the dissociation of the conscious mind from the unconscious mind, may occur in a variety of ways. It can happen spontaneously as in a daydream or a trance that develops from driving down a highway. A person may become lost in thought or in a fantasy and be so absorbed that time is lost and "space/time" is transcended. The past and future may be viewed as if they are occurring in the present. Trance may be induced in the context of marriage as in the case of couple rituals, play, or conflict. Each person focuses more and more upon positive or negative feelings at the same time she or he helps to limit the partner's attention to a narrower focus. Trance may be induced by the intentional activities of the therapist in a more formal direct way or through conversation and indirection. In this chapter, we explore how the therapist can induce trance intentionally, by utilizing both spontaneous self-induced trance that the patient creates unwittingly and by using the negative partner-stimulated trance that the couple cocreates. Before proceeding, it is important to note the differences between an Ericksonian approach and a more traditional approach to hypnosis.

The traditional approach follows a particular linear procedure with a number of specific stages and according to Zeig (1984) includes: the pre-induction stage, the induction, deepening, therapy, and termination. Pre-induction includes the process of establishing rapport, diagnosing the problem, dispelling any myths the person may have, and using suggestibility tests. The induction stage focuses on the use of direct relaxation suggestions, such as in the case of progressive relaxation. Deepening by the traditional hypnotist might include direct suggestions about going deeper, or fractionation where the hypnotist might suggest a person go deeper and then come back a little, and then go even deeper, so there are a number of deepening and awakening experiences. A number might be suggested to be visualized that would indicate depth of trance. In this stage, the hypnotist may use a test suggestion to elicit various hypnotic phenomena. The therapy stage usually consists of giving positive and negative suggestions to remove the symptom or to strengthen the ego, or to address the particular problem directly. Termination, the final stage, consists of bringing the patient out of trance and putting him or her in charge again (Zeig, 1984).

In contrast, the induction of trance used by Erickson is the use of a naturalistic event, the alteration of consciousness, by the therapist for therapeutic purposes. Erickson blurred the lines between induction and trance work itself. He moved beyond the traditional approach and would often begin with naturalistic talk as opposed to formal, authoritarian commands. Hypnosis occurs whenever a person's attention or consciousness is focused more and more narrowly. The Ericksonian therapist provides a context, or creates an invitation through intense rapport, or an environment that, if tailored to that specific individual's needs, meets that individual's requirements at that particular moment for entering into trance. Erickson was adept at pacing a person's experience at the moment to enhance the trance.

As all hypnosis is self-induced, the patient merely responds to the therapist's invitation. Most people enter a trance state or experience an altered awareness when they come into the therapist's office. They immediately begin to focus when they sit down in the office and the therapist invites an internal focus on personal attitudes, feelings, and behaviors. Actually, all therapies provide the invitation for trance, and each therapy has its own induction process (Lankton, 1980). The Ericksonian approach utilizes the patient's unique self-induced trance for new learning.

Erickson evolved his style from the formal, linear model to a style that was more interpersonal and included focusing attention, building responsiveness to minimal cues, associating the patient to memory of resources, pacing present experience, using confusion to disrupt the conscious mind set, encouraging dissociation, eliciting motivation of the patient and connecting the change to what the patient values, ratifying the response, and naming the experience hypnosis (Zeig, 1984).

The Ericksonian therapist might begin with what is being observed: "You are sitting in that chair, focusing your attention on me, wondering about hypnosis."

The next statement might be: "You can notice how your breathing begins to be different." With this statement we begin to focus the attention of the patient and build responsiveness to the minute shifts that occur when a person goes into a trance, all the while leading and suggesting these behaviors. However, when done indirectly, it may almost seem to the patient that the therapist is reading his or her mind.

"Have you ever been in trance?" the therapist may inquire. "Everyone has read a good book and become so interested that their attention is absorbed."

The only possible answer to the question is yes. The association to a learning every person has had continues to develop the trance, and the change in pronoun from "everyone" to "your" deepens the experience and a change in voice tone signifies the meaningfulness of the word, "your."

We may want to pace the patient's experience next by saying: "And you can have a feeling of heaviness in your body or lightness or another kind of feeling. Whatever feeling you have is a perfectly respectable feeling because it is your feeling."

Confusion may be used next to disrupt the conscious mind from thinking in the usual way. An example might be: "And reading that good book, you can become so absorbed that the images form in your mind in such an interesting and vivid way that . . . you can really feel like you are watching a movie and sometime later, you notice that you lost the page you were on. You are not sure what page you left, whether it was page 56 or 65, or 55, or 66, or just what was the right page that you left; was the passage you just read on the right side or the left and was the passage you just read the right passage that you want to read, or the left one that was the one left that was right?"

Dissociation follows confusion to continue to deepen the trance and depotentiate the conscious mind set. An example might be: "Your right hand or your left hand might begin to feel a sense of lightness. I don't know which hand your unconscious mind might select to have that feeling of lightness while your conscious mind observes with curiosity. It might begin with a little twitch, as your unconscious makes it selection."

To elicit motivation and connect change to what the patient values, we might next say as feedback to the patient's response to the suggestions: "Your unconscious mind has selected your left arm and hand to have that lifting experience; becoming lighter and lifting, lifting, all the way, that's right, to your face."

As the patient responds, the therapist can ratify the response and define it as hypnosis. "And you can really appreciate the pleasure and comfort your trance can provide for you."

At this point, the therapist may expand on the initial trance and move into metaphorical work or work in eliciting more trance phenomena. However, various language forms can provide the therapist with powerful tools.

UTILIZING LINGUISTIC FORMS
FOR ELICITING CHANGE

Through Erickson's intensive study of the dictionary, he discovered that there are multiple meanings of the same words. It is the context that gives words meaning. We create contexts linguistically and at both the conscious and unconscious levels. Erickson was adept at creating a context that the patient must accept as true. He might pose a question and concurrently a suggestion, "Have you ever been in trance before?" He structures the context for the patient and asks if the patient has ever been in trance before, but leaves it ambiguous: Before this trance? Before the trance that is about to happen? The meaning of "before" is unclear (Zeig, 1984). The context that Erickson creates that utilizes implication in this example is that something important is about to happen that will create change. The patient will move toward a goal, and any response that occurs is the right response. In the video of Erickson with Lee (Zeig, 1982), he spends a long time suggesting a hand levitation and finally when she does not respond by lifting her hand, he says with authority, "See, her hands have become immobile." Her behavior is framed as following his direction whatever she chooses. She accepted his frame of reference and, thus, any way she responded was defined as having done what Erickson suggested and also as the best way for her to respond.

Thus, the task of psychotherapy and hypnosis is, as in the previous example, to disrupt the conscious mind set and to expand the patient's definition of what can and cannot be accomplished. The therapist must join the patient at the level of her experience, acknowledge the patient's reality, retrieve previous learnings, and expand the reality toward a new solution. All of the language forms that Erickson utilized accomplish two or three of these tasks at the same time. They will activate unconscious processes, create trance, and deliver suggestions.

Several authors have outlined the various kinds of linguistic forms for use in framing suggestions. Erickson and Rossi (1979, 1981), Lankton and Lankton (1983), Ritterman (1983) and O'Hanlon (1987) have identified a number of these different indirect language forms that incorporate suggestion and accomplish the above tasks of creating the context, that depotentiate the conscious mind set, and that lead the patient into trance. Several of these linguistic forms are presented here.

1. *Embedded suggestion.* A suggestion that is placed within a statement or question and that, with an appropriate shift in voice tone to slightly emphasize the suggestion, leads another toward a specific goal.

Example: I wonder if *you will want to go to the movies this evening.*

Example: I don't know if *you will go into trance now.*

The embedded suggestion may also occur in the form of a symbol or metaphorical story such as Erickson's famous tomato plant story, which he told to Joe, a florist who suffered terribly from the pain of cancer. Erickson interspersed suggestions about comfort, security, peace, and not feeling discomfort as he described the planting, care, and growth of a tomato plant. The florist was able to sleep and actually experienced some physical improvement (Erickson, 1966).

2. *Illusion of choice.* A statement or question that offers only two alternatives, both of which will lead to a particular outcome.

Example: Do you want to go now or in a few minutes? The a priori assumption is that "we will be going" and only two choices about now or a few minutes are offered.

Example: You may go into trance as I am speaking words to you or during the pauses. The a priori assumption is that "you will go into trance," and that trance will occur as you listen either to the words or to the pauses.

3. *Implication.* A statement or question that leads another to think of the unstated thought and to behave according to that unstated thought.

Example: In which of these chairs would you like to sit? The implication is that the individual wants to sit in a chair. Another example might be: I do not know how your behavior will change. The implication is that "your behavior will change."

Implication can also include the "if-then" statement.

Example: If you go into trance, then you can find out so much more about what you can do.

One of Erickson's daughters, Betty Alice Erickson Elliott, told an amusing story about an interaction she had with her father when she was much younger. He was sitting down reading the paper when she approached him and challenged, "If you're such a hot shot psychiatrist, can't you give me a diet to lose weight?" Erickson slowly lowered his newspaper and looked at Betty Alice sternly and replied in a gruff voice, "Do you really want me to give you a diet to lose weight?" Receiving the message loudly and clearly that she should not challenge him because he would make it difficult on her, Betty Alice said, "No, sir!" (Betty Alice Erickson Elliot, 1989, personal communication). Erickson used implication quite forcefully in this example with voice tone and facial expression.

One spouse may use implication and ask, "Have you picked up the clothes from the cleaners?" This question assumes that some previous agreement had been made for the other spouse to pick up the clothes, or that some previous conversation had taken place. If the second spouse accepts the assumptions as having validity, she may become defensive and make excuses, which may then lead to further conflict.

Implication may utilize presuppositions such as when, after, before, as, to direct the following suggestion. For example: "After you talk to me for a few moments, you may go into trance." These particular forms are discussed below.

Now if we ask, "In which of these two chairs would you like to go into trance?" all three of these language forms have been utilized. There is the *embedded suggestion*, "you would like to go into trance," the *illusion of choice*, "In which of these two chairs," and the *implication* that the person will sit down in one of two chairs and go into trance.

4. *Truisms*. Statements that express something that is generally agreed upon.

Example: The sun rises in the morning and sets in the evening.

Example: Everyone knows what it's like to relax; everyone knows what it feels like when you've worked hard and feel satisfied.

5. *Open-ended suggestions*. Offering patients many possibilities for response will allow them to select the one that suits them the best. Resistance is eliminated because any response the patient makes is considered to be the right response. These suggestions can be offered for the patient to achieve particular

learnings in the session such as feeling comfort, going into trance, retrieving a particular memory, and so forth.

Example: You can develop a feeling of comfort by just sitting there, and taking natural breaths.

Example: You can use your own personal past experiences for learning how to deal with the present.

6. *Suggestions covering all possible alternatives.* Statements that cover all possibilities of a class of behavior cannot be argued against. With this suggestion, any response by the patient is the right response and is defined as cooperating with the therapist.

Example: You might want to find a comfortable position, either with your hands on your knees, or resting in your lap, or on the arms of the chair, or you may want to find a different position for your hands.

Example: You can go into trance with your eyes open, or you can go into trance with your eyes closed, or you can go into trance with your eyes halfway open and closed.

7. *Apposition of opposites.* Statements that include "the more of one thing, the more of an opposite will occur," describe two behaviors that change in opposite directions.

Example: "The more you have pain, the greater your surprise will be when you feel comfort."

Example: "The more you move into trance, the more your left hand can remain awake."

Example: "The more tense you are now, the more relaxed you can be later."

8. *Conscious-unconscious bind.* A suggestion that separates the conscious from the unconscious mind and predicts that they will do two different things. The bind is created by describing the mind as separating into the conscious and unconscious polar categories and the suggestion that follows each.

Example: Your conscious mind may create a certain level of tension while your unconscious can use that tension to move into trance.

Example: The unconscious mind is a storehouse of vast resources that the conscious mind can utilize.

9. *Binds of comparable alternatives.* Statements that offer similar alternatives but that create only two options at a time.

Example: "Would you like to go into trance as you describe your situation or would you like me to listen first?"

Example: "You might be able to have a memory of when you were ten or perhaps nine. I don't know which will come to mind first."

10. *Non sequitur double binds.* Statements that present double binds in the form of illogical connection but similarity in the content.

Example: You can go into trance now or you can learn by watching your spouse have a conscious alteration.

Example: You will go into trance little by little or your unconscious will have a symbolic experience.

11. *Puns.* A humorous play on words that have a similar sound.

Example: Pirate error (pilot error)

Example: Trance action (transaction)

12. *Oxymoron.* A term or phrase that carries an inherent contradiction.

Example: Postal Service

Example: Weapons for Peace

13. *Confusion utilizing direction, time, and condition.* Statements that use confusing juxtaposition of these three aspects.

Direction Example: You are sitting there, and I am sitting here, but your there is my here and my here is your there so you're here and I'm there.

Direction Example: You can develop a feeling in your left arm or your right, and the feeling in the left is the right feeling to have left, isn't that right?

Time Example: Your unconscious mind can make that change; . . . perhaps, next Tuesday or Wednesday, or Thursday. I certainly wouldn't mind if it were Friday, Saturday, but not Sunday. Your unconscious may select the Tuesday after next or the Wednesday before the last Monday that came right after the following holiday that was on a Thursday, was it not?

Condition Example: Your husband is warmer so his cooler is colder to you, but when you're cold, he's warmer and his hot is your comfortable, but his comfortable is your colder, but now, you are comfortable, are you not? So when you're hot, he's not, but he is comfortable feeling cool and what is the difference between hot and cold? When your hand is cold, and you touch him to warm up, he can appreciate that nice refreshing change in temperature.

Condition Example: The kids today have many changes in language. Something that is hot is not; something that is cold is hot, and you like it if it's cold not hot; so you are cold, are you not? Something that is bad is good. So when they say, "He's bad," they mean he's good, so being bad is being good and being good is really bad, and is that bad or good?

14. *Triple negatives.* The use of three negatives in a statement has the intent of creating confusion for the conscious mind to disrupt a particular train of thought. Because the unconscious does not process negatives, that part of the mind hears these statements in the positive mode. The unconscious operates with primary process or images, symbols and metaphors, and the conscious mind uses secondary process or verbalized thoughts. Primary process has several characteristics that include no negatives, tense, or any linguistic mood such as ". . . no identification of indicative, subjunctive, optative, etc. . . . ." In primary process the emphasis is on relationships between persons or things represented in metaphor, while the secondary process (conscious mind) focuses on specific persons or things (Bateson, 1972).

Example: You don't know if now is not the right time for you not to go into trance.

Example: You don't need to do anything with your conscious mind not to discover what state is not useful for you to allow your unconscious mind to communicate something meaningful.

15. *Verb tense.* The use of past, present, and future tense in suggestions will direct the unconscious mind to a time dimension as well as deliver a suggestion.

Example: You can go into trance now. (present)

Example: You went into trance many times before. (past)

Example: You will go into trance. You might go into trance tomorrow. (future)

Example: You have to go into trance now. (present perfect)

Example: You have gone into trance many times before. (past perfect)

Example: You will have gone into trance the next time I see you. (future perfect)

TRANCE INDUCTION UTILIZING LANGUAGE FORM

The following script is taken from a demonstration to a general audience to illustrate how the various language forms may be used in an induction, to suggest dissociation, various trance phenomena, post-hypnotic suggestion, and reorientation. The punctuation, . . . , represents pauses in the delivery. The therapist should use these forms in the interaction with a patient and in response to the patient's behavior.

You can begin to develop trance in a variety of ways by focusing inwardly, . . . perhaps, to notice your breathing . . . as it comes in and goes out . . . or you may want to put your feet flat on the floor and find a position of comfort by . . . focusing outwardly on the feel of the chair as it supports you (open-ended suggestion), . . . It's so good to feel that support (embedded suggestion) . . . One of the nice things about going in to trance is that there really isn't anything for you to do or anything for you to think about . . . because you can just sit there . . . where . . . you are and experience your own unique trance. Your conscious mind may want to do one thing for now, whether it's listening to my words or to the sounds outside the room, . . . while your unconscious mind may listen to something else inside (conscious-unconscious bind). Now, I don't know whether you'll want to close your eyes or you'll allow your eyes to become heavy in a few moments, or close them a little bit later (all possible alternatives), . . . so you can really begin to focus in on your own experience. You can see with your mind's eye with your eyes closed just as well as you can with your eyes open, and the more you develop trance, the more your unconscious mind may have a learning for the waking state (apposition of opposites). Every child has experienced the wonder of discovering something new (truism). . . . And I wonder what alterations might begin to occur in your breathing or your unconscious mind will notice a change (non sequitur double bind).

Just which nostril, the left or the right, your breath is moving in and moving out. . . . And if it is the left, your right hemisphere is dominant . . . and if it is the right, your left hemisphere is dominant (conscious/ unconscious double bind) or if your nose is stuffy, just when it will open, indicating the opening of something else, some new openness to learning. Those alterations can be a change in your breathing, or a change in a feeling . . . from one side to another; perhaps a sense of heaviness on one side . . . or a feeling of lightness on the other (all possible alternatives). A sensation certainly can be something that you experience (truism) and you're entitled to become curious about just what those sensations will be. A sensation can begin to develop in your hands; a feeling of tingling?

When you go into trance, it is not unlike what you feel when reading a good book, when you stare at the pages and you can see those words and those words can form images and pictures in your mind. It might be interesting for you to allow that feeling of tingling in your hands and your fingers to begin to spread, . . . perhaps up your hand and your wrist.

And when you absorb your attention in interesting images, those images can seem very real, just like when you read that good book and you feel a sense of excitement and pleasure, a sense of comfort, . . . And just as you're watching a movie, sitting in the audience, observing characters on a screen, wouldn't it be curious for you to watch yourself sitting over there, having that particular feeling of tingling (embedded suggestions) . . . and you can be sitting in front of yourself sitting there, just observing yourself with your eyes closed watching that trance action (embedded suggestion, implication, and pun) between yourself sitting there and in front of your self sitting here (confusion).

Most people have had the experience of looking through a photograph album (truism), and as you turn the pages you can see pictures of yourself. As you start at the back and move forward back in time, you can see yourself in pictures as you were younger and you can look at yourself at a distance within a small frame (embedded suggestion of dissociation). And how that frame can change. It can be black and white. It can be color. The picture can be large. It can be small. It can have many pictures on the same page, or perhaps, just one . . . And you can look through the book from the right to the left or the left to the right; there's no particular right way . . . But whatever right way you choose to move, there's always a picture that is left, for you to see (confusion through double reversal of polarities).

You only need to look at those pictures that you really wish to. And you are entitled to look at as many as you wish. (embedded suggestions) . . . You can pick out one that looks interesting from a time in your life you had a happy experience. Isn't it interesting how you can take a photograph of a pleasant experience and years later . . . review it and remember that happy time (embedded suggestion of age regression to retrieve pleasant feelings).

And wouldn't it be curious if you got up from sitting in front of yourself, making those observations, and left yourself right there (left-right reversal) and decided to walk out the door and into another room where there was a mirror (further dissociation) with three sides, like the mirrors you look at when you try on a new garment (embedded suggestion to explore further trance phenomena) . . . and you have the experience of seeing yourself to the right and to the left, as well as in front of yourself (focusing attention). There you are, standing with the new garment on, . . . looking at yourself, surrounding yourself. . . . And you can stand side by side, standing beside yourself, looking into the mirror (focusing attention and building expectation) . . . and as you look into the mirror, and see the image being reflected back to you, looking at you . . . it's really hard to know exactly who's looking at whom. Whether it is you looking at the image looking back at you, or you in the mirror, really observing you, looking at the image, looking back at you . . . looking back at you . . . looking back at you . . . looking back at you . . . goin-to-trance (intentional mispronunciation for suggestion of trance).

And there are many sensations that you can have. You go to bed in the evening and you wake up in the morning with certain feelings (truism). You can have a tingling sensation when your arm goes to sleep . . . And that can be a pleasant sensation, a pleasant tingling (suggestions for analgesia), . . . a sign that your body has made an alteration (implication). And that tingling can spread. It can begin with a finger or the area on the palm and spread, . . . almost imperceptibly, inch by inch, . . . And it certainly is all right to let that feeling develop into numbness, . . . if it's cold outside. Your fingers sometimes don't notice the cold when your body is enjoying skiing or sledding. And isn't it fun to enjoy the snow? You don't really notice the coldness in your hands because you and the others are playing, laughing, as you slide down the hill having delightful fun . . . a feeling of numbness, and yet, it's a feeling that is not unpleasant (suggestions for anesthesia). And that feeling can spread over the hands, up to the wrists, and perhaps, half-way up the arms. That's right. And that particular feeling of numbness in the right arm . . . that has that feeling the most can continue that feeling until I snap my fingers . . . just a little while after you reorient from trance (post-hypnotic suggestion) and just then, the feelings can return.

And you can begin that reorientation . . . knowing that you can return any time as you wish. . . . Finding yourself in front of the mirror, moving back into yourself, walking back in here . . . knowing that you can connect and reconnect with parts of the body (not all of the body until the snap of the fingers). Sitting in front of yourself; feeling your toes, and you can take all the time that you want in a moment to come back into this room, . . . knowing that your unconscious mind can utilize this experience in any way that it wishes, but your conscious mind may not know exactly what your unconscious mind knows (conscious-unconscious bind and reorientation) that you can use in the future. You can certainly look forward to discovering that surprise, that learning, as you will have already been using it when you notice what it is (future orientation). And you can open your eyes and come back here.

ATTITUDE OF THERAPIST

As with any psychotherapeutic approach, the therapist's attitude should (1) convey respect, warmth, and empathy for the patient and the particular difficulty each person has brought, (2) express confidence in the patient's ability to change, and (3) establish rapport with each partner without taking sides. The therapist may want to strategically side with one partner or both later. Each patient couple has developed the pain they experience for good reasons. Their belief systems, family-of-origin trauma, and unique make-up has led to the development of a protective way of interacting with each other. What they have evolved may be dysfunctional but understandable. The therapist begins to build rapport with the first contact and continues to maintain a warm and caring attitude. This kind of accepting attitude communicates to the patients that their reality is understandable, albeit painful, and provides a safe atmosphere for the psychological work to be done.

The therapist will also want to express confidence in the hypnotic work and an expectant attitude that the couple can change a dysfunctional relationship. The message to be conveyed is that they have the resources to develop a different relationship, even though no one knows exactly what the structure will be. This kind of attitude on the part of the therapist fosters hopefulness in the patients.

Forming a relationship with each partner is important but tricky in conjoint work. Each partner's reality should be paced and affirmed as that which is experienced by that person. Usually, both partners are cautious. Each is frightened that the therapist will designate him or her as strange or ill, and, on some level, would like the therapist to designate the partner as the problem. Each will make a case that he or she is the most wounded party and, therefore, the spouse should change some behavior. Each will present arguments and evidence to enhance this position. The therapist wants to communicate in a supportive way that there is a "dance" occurring between the partners and that each person may have individual issues that are being confused with what the spouse is or is not doing. Each person, then, participates in creating the hypnotic dance through his or her response to the partner's behavior. In the exploration of the "steps" that are being taken by each, both partners will begin to recognize the sequence of behaviors or the cue from one partner to begin a particular dysfunctional response.

The therapist may use the following steps in the beginning trance work: (1) absorb attention of both partners by communicating meaningfully to each of them, (2) use appropriate voice tone, (3) utilize any resistance to trance, (4) use conscious/unconscious dissociations, (5) depotentiate conscious processes, and (6) begin to use interspersals for therapeutic suggestions. This process may be used when working with an individual as well.

Absorb Attention

Attention may be absorbed and focused in a number of ways. The therapist can begin by having the patient focus more internally on physical experiences such as breathing or on the particular problematic idea. Trance can be developed through either externally or internally oriented attention. Externally oriented trance may develop by having the patient focus on some object in the room, whereas internally oriented trance may develop by having the patient focus on some internal experience such as breathing or a pleasant inner image that is elicited through anecdotal work.

If a person is resistant to allowing the attention to become absorbed, the therapist may suggest that the patient continue to look into the therapist's eyes. As the therapist goes into trance, the eyes can begin to enlarge slightly and remain open without blinking so as to engage the eyes of the patient. The patient's eyes will eventually tire and begin to blink, and the therapist can then suggest eye closure indirectly.

Voice Tone

Voice tone is important in the facilitation of absorption. An inviting tone and rhythmic quality can help deepen the trance, as the conscious mind becomes more and more focused on an idea. Speaking in a meaningful tone to emphasize certain words and shifting the tone of voice to a lower volume to deliver a suggestion is important in offering embedded suggestions beyond the awareness of the conscious mind. Erickson often used two different voice tones: one to speak to the conscious mind and one to speak to the unconscious mind (CP I, p. 438).

Example: You might begin to notice your breathing (regular voice), . . . and just how when you *breathe in and out something happens* (shift voice) . . . maybe it is a shift in tension (regular voice) . . . or perhaps, a *change in the level of relaxation,* or a *feeling of heaviness in your body, or lightness* (shift voice). Sometimes you can *feel a kind of pleasant tingling in one part of the body or another* (shift voice). Has it reached your fingers yet? . . . (regular voice)

Example: That one particular difficult idea concerning your spouse about which you have been thinking is perhaps expressed in a picture in your mind's eye or a word, or phrase, repeated like a refrain in a song that you can't quite get out of your mind, . . . and it goes around and around until it is quite difficult to *really know how to recognize the beginning and the end of a tune,* (shift voice), what comes before and what comes after, and when (regular voice) *you have forgotten that melody* (shift voice) until someone suggests moving on to the next verse (regular voice).

The therapist may find it useful to practice shifting voice tones by reading aloud the following trance induction for conjoint sessions:

. . . Perhaps there begins to be a slight alteration in what your conscious mind is focused on, while your unconscious minds orient to a new learning experience about yourselves and each other. Perhaps, you are wondering if _____(partner) is having the same or a different experience, an experience of being here together, yet separate. Separate minds and separate bodies sharing this space in time together, separately. And your conscious mind can have one thought, an idea that seems old and familiar, while your unconscious mind can use a new perspective, a different angle can make a whole new idea, but you won't really know what it is until you discover that you see differently. Every little child knows the experience of looking at something familiar and seeing something he didn't see before, . . . like a homemade wooden horse that is transformed into a great stallion . . . riding into a wonderful adventure, or the corner of the dresser until she bangs a shin. Then you are likely to walk carefully around the edges or find a way to cushion them.

Utilize Resistance for Trance

Resistance to cooperating with the therapist and developing a trance represent protective defenses against the possibility of harm. The cautiousness is a reflection of the patient's watchful eye both to determine the trustworthiness of the therapist and whether the patient thinks he or she has a particular ability. To sidestep any resistance to the trance experience and to facilitate trust-building, the therapist can begin by associating the patient's previous experience with the trance experience. Then the therapist will need to give permission for the patient to have a unique, individual response to the suggestions.

Some couples are resistant to using hypnotic work. In this case, conversational trance can be used to build rapport, put them at ease, and develop a way to communicate that alters the hypnotic shared negative trance they cocreate.

To a reluctant husband who was reserved and cautious about allowing himself to enter trance and who was an artist, I suggested that he already knew how to enter trance. He previously experienced shifting into an altered state of consciousness to paint. In addition, he was an experimenter in his art. He put together various textures, colors, and shapes that were unique.

In fact, he used automatic drawing on his canvas by entering into a restful state, as he named it, and allowed his hand to move over the canvas and "touch where the hand decided." This man reported that he could use his own trance state whether alone or in a house full of people.

He already believed that his unconscious assisted him in creating the images that appeared on the canvas, with which I concurred. Some of the work he showed me evoked feelings of high energy, passion, and sensitivity. He had found a way to touch his soul, I suggested, and he might be interested to see what would happen "when you allow yourself to enter trance in a similar way, perhaps, this time by listening to my words, or to your own inner words, or images of color and texture. . . . Or," I continued, "perhaps you want to allow your conscious mind to stay out of trance while I talk to your wife (who had already entered a trance state), and then you could find yourself absorbed in your own images as you observe her go into trance. Perhaps, there may be images not yet seen." This reference to his own work intrigued him, and he began to shift his consciousness and moved into trance.

Use Conscious/Unconscious Dissociation

In his later years, Erickson wanted to leave the power with the patient. The suggestions that encompass the conscious mind doing one thing while the unconscious mind does another reinforce the notion that there are at least two operations going on at the same time. The conscious mind learns in a linear way while the unconscious learns in a symbolic way. Both operations are important. However, Erickson emphasized the unconscious as the part of the mind that is more intelligent. It is that part that contains so many resources, memories of minute learnings that are the building blocks for later learnings and successful outcomes. Later, it was discovered that the conscious mind only has the capacity to remember seven pieces of information at a time. The unconscious mind is capable of learning many more pieces of information in order to allow the psychobiophysical processes to be maintained and new learnings to be generated.

Depotentiate Conscious Processes

The conscious mind is usually able to develop a few solutions to a particular problem. These solutions are often reviewed again and again by couples in an effort to solve a conflict. The conscious mind will often become focused or locked on an idea for a solution, even though it may be unworkable for the other partner.

For one couple who had been working with me in therapy to develop more separate selves instead of an enmeshed relationship, a problem arose during a camping trip. Fran had gone hiking with a friend while Jim went rock climbing. On reaching the summit, Jim began to really notice how much he wanted his wife there so he could show off and have her take pictures of him. He began to feel somewhat resentful that she was, for the first time, doing something for herself. Jim believed that he had worked through these feelings by the time he climbed down the mountain. However, when the couple met at a later time, he mentioned that a young girl had asked him to take a picture of her. She then jumped into his lap and hugged his neck. Fran felt punished by this comment and quite confused, yet jealous and frightened. Jim had had an affair years ago, and his comment to Fran brought up old hurtful and angry feelings. During the next therapy session, Jim took responsibility for this behavior and said he realized that a younger part of him that wanted praise and acknowledgment immediately became hurt when he did not receive it. He let Fran experience his anger in an indirect and immature way, and he apologized to her. Still, she could not let go of feeling abused and frightened that she would be abandoned. Even when Jim reassured her how much the weekend had meant and how much he enjoyed her, even though he had been hurtful, Fran could just not stop obsessing about it. Trance work was employed at that time and confusion was utilized to depotentiate the conscious mind and help Fran move away from the repetitive spiral of negative feelings and images.

"Jim and Fran, you are sitting here trying to find a way out of these difficult feelings. Sometimes the presence of the past is upon us suddenly without warning, and you really don't know where the feelings come from. The past is back there, then. The future is ahead, a tomorrow to look back. The present is now, here. But, sometimes, it is difficult to see a future tomorrow when the past pays a visit to the present . . . and then you are in the past which is the present trying to find a future which is the past but you know it is the present; . . . and looking ahead just a little ways . . . to the future present, knowing that the past was another time and not yet knowing how the past can be a present for your future . . . and many changes have been made to create the presence of the future that you want with each other, . . . and how you can begin to focus on those changes just now, being able to talk in such a different way, feeling heard and acknowledged, which allows a feeling to shift from the way it was in the beginning . . . of the feeling . . . to the middle part of the feeling . . . to the end of this feeling . . . now . . . so you can talk further, . . . later . . . with more clarity and calmness."

At this point, further trance work was utilized to help Fran to rediscover a feeling of safety, a feeling she had lost in her own negative trance.

Using Interspersals

Erickson developed the technique of interspersing therapeutic suggestions within a conversation for a specific goal. He used the technique to absorb a patient's attention and to distract a patient from interfering with the therapy. The therapist may utilize this technique to elicit cooperation and various resources that are not fully used or are misused (Erickson, 1966). These embedded suggestions may also be inserted into an anecdotal or metaphorical story to elicit various trance phenomena or to help change attitudes, emotions, or behaviors. Chapter 7 addresses the construction of metaphorical stories.

To illustrate conjoint trance work, an example follows from a marital session.

One patient couple came to therapy embroiled in a particularly intense conflict. Each time the wife became depressed, she complained that her husband was not attentive enough, or accused him of having an affair. The husband would become incensed that she would even have those thoughts and begin vehemently defending himself. She would react with more disdain, assured that she was correct, and her depression would lift temporarily. This response would escalate the conflict, which would end with the wife hitting her husband and the husband leaving the house. In response to his leaving, her anxiety began to surface, as well as fears of abandonment. However, her depression did not return until the couple felt more peaceful with each other, and she began to attend to her own sadness. As the assessment proceeded, the husband revealed that sometimes he felt abandoned by his wife, and he would withdraw, offering her the signal to begin complaining. The ensuing conflict brought both partners out of dissociation from their own feelings and changed the psychobiological state to one that they could more easily handle.

The following is a partial transcript demonstrating how to pace and support each partner, formulate the working hypothesis, and ready the couple for the trance work. This is also an example of how to use a conversation to move a couple into trance through a counterinduction.

JOE: I just don't know if I can take this any more. Jane keeps attacking me and either accuses me of having an affair, or of not being attentive enough. I feel like I can't do anything right. She's got that certain look and then I know, "look out."

JANE: I don't attack you. You are distant most of the time when I need you to talk to. It makes me furious and I feel all alone in this relationship.

CK: Joe, you're really frustrated at trying please Jane, and what you're doing just doesn't seem to be enough for her. You haven't quite yet discovered just what is going on between you or why you're working so hard to make her happy.

What you may know is that there is a certain tone or look or group of words that sends you into a negative experience.

The affect is paced here to support Joe. An implication is used to suggest that Joe will discover something important about himself and his contribution to the problem, so that the frame of the problem is presented as being a shared difficulty. There is also an implication that Joe may want to please Jane too much. He is indirectly instructed to identify the cue trigger for the negative trance.

CK: And, Jane, when Joe withdraws his attention from you, you feel abandoned and frightened, and then angry, and the feelings are very intense. Maybe he does something very specific like avoiding your eyes, or not responding to your comments, or having a particular look. Perhaps, you're not quite yet certain just how his pulling back is a problem for you, but you might be curious to find out.

Jane's feelings are supported and the message is given that clearly there is something undetermined going on between them and inside each of them to have such intense reactions. The implication is used to suggest that we are about to experience a learning about what is happening, what cues a trigger response into a negative trance, and that she can be curious as well as expectant in finding an answer.

CK: Could each of you tell me more about what happened before this last conflict?
JANE: I was feeling depressed and lonely that Joe was so distant. I started feeling angry and resentful so I told him.
JOE: You criticized me!
CK: Jane, before you were aware of missing Joe, what were you depressed about?
JANE: I don't know. I guess I feel depressed a lot. And then I look at our marriage and it seems so like my mother's and dad's that I feel worse. They were miserable for 50 years. I don't want to live like that.

Here Jane reveals that there is a conflicted parental image she carries with her and she expresses almost a phobic intensity to anything that resembles her parents' marriage. The suggestion is offered that she may be depressed about other issues as well as about Joe.

JOE: Jane seems depressed all of the time. It can't be just me. She doesn't eat much and mopes around. I really feel like going away.

Joe here seizes upon an opportunity to designate Jane as "the problem." He threatens to leave, although this is expressed as a quasi-feeling. He also jumps in before Jane can identify what is happening inside her and before she complains about him. Joe protects both of them from the knowledge of what may really be going on inside Jane.

CK: Joe, there is a feeling you want to go away from, is that right? And, perhaps, you would like to be able to change one feeling into another.
JOE: Yeah, frustration, anger, you name it. If only she could stop complaining.

The desire to leave the relationship has now been framed as a desire to leave a difficult feeling, and the implication is that he will be able to learn how to change his feelings.

CK: How old do each of you feel when you are fighting?

The direction is changed slightly since Joe continues to suggest that Jane is the problem.

JOE: I don't know, maybe 14.
JANE: I always feel 8 years old when we fight, just like I felt when my parents were fighting a lot.
CK: So each of you feels younger and you attempt to find an adult solution when you are 8 and 14, except you can only have 8 and 14 solutions. Eight and 14 were important times

for you growing up. I don't know what you can remember about those important years or what you can tell me.

The suggestion is given here that age regression occurs, and the resolution of adult conflict is too difficult for a child. In addition, a suggestion is given that there can be many solutions to a situation.

JANE: They were always fighting. My father was alcoholic and went on rages. My mother was depressed all of the time. She would yell back at him, and my brother and I would stay in our rooms. I often just turned up the radio, but you could still hear them. I felt anxious and scared most of the time. My father would rage and then storm out of the house. We never knew if he was coming back. I hoped he wouldn't. Then, one time, he left and had a car accident. I really felt guilty then. He recovered and things calmed down for a while but then, right back to the way things were.

CK: That sounds like a difficult family to grow up in. Joe, what about you?

JOE: I guess my parents were happy, though Mother seemed sad a lot. They never did too much together. My dad played golf and my mother had her friends. They never fought in front of us. My mother used to confide in me that Dad never did enough. That made me feel angry with her. My brother and I were close but not too much to either one of them. I really want a closer relationship with Jane than they had. I just don't know how to get it.

CK: Your parents were more distant than you want with Jane. It seems as though both of you have some fear of recreating your parents' marriage. Those are scary images to carry around, and I can imagine that when each of you begins to see something similar to those images, you want to do something quickly to . . . keep those images in that past time where they belong. Joe, when you see Jane being depressed, you remember your mother, feel frightened, and want to keep Jane from doing the same thing. Jane, when you see Joe distancing, you try to engage him through complaining to keep from feeling abandoned. The more each of you tries to keep the other engaged in the relationship and feeling happy, the more escalated the conflict becomes.

Both Joe and Jane indicate nonverbally that they agree with these systemic and interpersonal hypotheses.

Now the fighting is reframed as helpful and protective of the relationship. A working hypothesis at the systemic and interpersonal level is presented to the couple to encapsulate and present as manageable a conflict that seemed hopeless, confused, and uncontrollable.

CK: Your conscious minds do not know how to stop having these fights because they believe that you have no more management of your own feelings of anxiety and fear because you haven't yet learned what that particular tension in your body really means. And isn't a feeling a certain kind of tension . . . And just what kind of tension is it? . . . Is it a heavy tension, . . . a medium heavy tension, . . . or a lighter heavy tension? One patient of mine described the feeling as a kind of electricity that gets turned on and moves through your body. And just where do you feel it in your body? And what is that tension or electricity telling you about yourself and what you are needing?

Here the conscious mind is fixated by offering a statement with which both must agree, and the unconscious mind is sent on a search by utilizing an embedded suggestion to "know how to stop having these fights . . ." and "no (know) more management of you feelings" by learning that the feeling is really only a tension in the body. The suggestion to be curious about the tension is made, and suggestions for trance are indirectly made with both words and voice tone. An implication is made that each person needs to focus inwardly rather than seeing the spouse as the problem.

CK: Your conscious minds may not know what you need but your unconscious knows clearly.

Now, a more extensive trance induction begins that is conversational and that includes making a distinction between
being together and apart, dissociation between unconscious and
conscious minds, confusion to depotentiate the conscious mind
sets, hand levitation, early learning set, and the beginning of a
metaphorical story.

> "Both of you are sitting here . . . together yet there
> apart, . . . sitting separately . . . together. I have an idea
> that your unconscious minds noticed something im-
> portant when you first saw each other. Your conscious
> mind was orienting to certain pleasant characteristics
> of each other. Your unconscious minds became fo-
> cused in a different way, . . . noticing that there was
> an opportunity to really have some kind of healing of
> old wounds take place, an opportunity you haven't had
> previously, . . . and expectation, . . . a hopefulness that
> your life would be different. There were other details
> you began to notice like—perhaps your eyes are feel-
> ing heavy and you can close your eyes—sensations,
> like a feeling of lifting your spirit . . . and your un-
> conscious can select a hand to begin to feel lighter,
> whether the right or the left; it doesn't really matter.
> Whatever right hand is selected to lift up is the right
> hand that is left for you to notice some difference in
> feeling, and that hand that is left is the right hand to
> be left for that right feeling. I don't know which hand
> your unconscious will select, but perhaps, your uncon-
> scious shared minds will decide. As you first met each
> other and made that very important decision, . . . a
> decision to be together . . . you began to develop a
> shared unconscious mind, a mind that acts for your
> benefit . . . that shares so many resources between you.
> Many important learnings are there from the past, to
> utilize in the present, and ready you for your future.
> Every little child who gets ready for the next devel-
> opmental stage and crawls around on all fours, one
> day stands up and looks at the world from a new per-
> spective. The most remarkable change begins to take

place. Objects in the room begin to shrink just a little. The child begins to move one foot in front of another and balance in just the right way to have a very intricate and complicated learning. And once it is learned, it goes into your unconscious mind . . . in a way that you don't have to think about consciously. This is one learning among thousands . . . that you begin to build upon. Learning how to tie a shoe . . . is a very difficult task at first. But once you finally learn how to hold a shoelace . . . how to loop the lace around the other and tie the knot just so . . . a learning you never forget and you really don't have to think about it. Learning how to button a shirt . . . takes intricate movements of certain muscle groups . . . and if you have ever put on a shirt that was made to button backwards, you know how difficult that is and that can help you appreciate the enormity of the task for a little child.

And maybe that feeling of lightness has intensified as your hand is now lifting up, lifting up toward your face, lifting up as an alteration is taking place. Shifts have already taken place as I have been talking to you. Your focus has become more inward, your breathing has shifted . . . slower, . . . your body temperature has changed. Being so focused, you can forget to notice that . . . you have a watch on, . . . but you don't feel it, and you can become so absorbed in an interesting movie that time goes by without your conscious awareness; the story is intriguing and time moves in a way that you forget to notice. You can forget your watch, knowing that your unconscious can keep you on track. The hands of a clock can move . . . without notice . . . and physicists tell us that time is a construction . . . something so arbitrary . . . really is nice to forget to notice how much time goes by . . .

At this point, trance work could now consider specific hypotheses for change.

Chapter 6 examines how to gather specific data and formulate working hypotheses to be addressed in hypnotic psychotherapy.

6

Assessing Couple Dynamics

To many couples, it seems as though a spell has been cast to keep them from the warm, loving, passionate feelings that they once experienced. In order to understand how the unconscious mind operates to protect each individual from perceived harm and how that protection may be expressed in the couple relationship, a thorough assessment of the relationship and individual dynamics is needed. This chapter examines the assessment of couple dynamics and how to build hypotheses on three levels: systemic, interpersonal, and intrapsychic.

Systemic refers to the entire family group, the patterns of communication that involve hypnotic loops that lead to amplification, deviation, or escalating symmetry or complementarity. The system also includes the larger ecological influence of other systems such as community or work environment. Boundaries that exist between the couple and outside environment, as well as between couple partners, are described at this level. The interpersonal level refers to the dynamics between the couple, such as the images of the partner and the marriage, as well as the style of managing anxiety stimulated between the couple.

The intrapsychic level refers to individual inner forces such as self-image, defense mechanisms, and level of ego strength. There will be obvious overlap between the levels. The therapist can begin to view the individuals in the marriage and the couple's behavior through a wide-angle lens and then change to an ever more narrowly focused one. The ability to shift the focus back and forth is important in the assessment process.

Adequate assessment is crucial to the process of therapy. To evaluate for intervention in the "couple's hypnotic dance," the unconscious interactional patterns between couples, the system they cocreate, the individual strengths and weaknesses they bring, and the developmental issues at stake are important variables to take into account. It is useful for the marital therapist to distinguish these categories and to construct therapeutic goals that are broken down into short-term steps.

Breaking down a process so that appropriate goals may be established is always dangerous to the process itself. Psychotherapy is built upon a relationship and becomes symbolic of the early relationship between a child and parents. It is in the symbolic relationship that growth occurs from new and more functional experiences rather than in technique or strategy. The therapeutic intervention should evolve from the relationship itself so that it emerges out of the identities of the patient and the therapist.

In order to develop a hypnotic strategy for intervention from the assessment and within the model presented in the previous chapter, the therapist may explore various intrapsychic, interpersonal, and systemic hypotheses regarding the relationship pattern, cyclical dynamic operations, reciprocal and individual behaviors, affects, attitudes, and needed resources. Effective therapy is build upon these hypotheses. Although Erickson inevitably began with the simplest explanation of a person's problem, his interventions always addressed a hypothesis. To break the process down further, there are three important steps in developing hypnotic strategies: (1) gather data to make an assessment regarding individual developmental and systemic aspects of the problem, (2) formulate working hypotheses, and (3) set therapeutic goals that address what resources are needed.

GATHER DATA

There are several questions that the marital therapist may ask to facilitate this process of gathering information.

1. *How does each partner define the problem?*

As the therapist collects data from the patient, special attention should be paid to how the person defines the problem. As each marital partner delineates a hypothesis, the language used in description should be noted. The particular perceptions that may be in conflict and to which each partner seems wedded can be useful in identifying developmental sources for the problem. The definitions are often related to early experiences or to world views that have evolved over time.

In this step, multiple descriptions of the problem will be gleaned. Each partner's (if both attend therapy) perception of the other and the conflict, family-of-origin material, and developmental and systemic conflicts will provide a variety of data from different viewpoints. Being able to shift perspectives is valuable for the therapist to understand the assessment data and then to treat the couple with more flexibility. As descriptions are gathered, the therapist should closely observe the patient's behavior to detect unconscious communication. A couple who came to therapy to manage the escalating conflict between them told me of the wife's sexual abuse by her stepfather from age eight to eighteen. This terrible history influenced her developmental evolution. At age thirty she had also found herself being pursued by both men and women in sexual ways and felt disgusted by their advances. As she recounted the story she looked coy, raised her skirt to uncover her knees, and winked at me several times. When I asked her about the behavior, she was unaware of it. Later, the referring therapist mentioned her seductive behavior. Unwittingly, she may have participated as an adult in the sexual advances by her unconscious behavior. (We should note here that the victim of sexual, physical, or emotional abuse does not participate in childhood abuse at any level. The adult is always the perpetrator.)

This patient exemplified what most patients miss in their perceptual experience: the cybernetic relationship between persons and the world. Gregory Bateson (1972, p. 146) suggests that we are unable to see entire circuits but only arcs of circuits, put off from their matrix by our selective attention. Thus it is only the arc of behavior coming from someone else that is usually perceived, not the entire circuit. Delozier and Grinder (1987) add, "If two people, whether it's business or marriage or brothers and sisters, have a close, continuous relationship over a long period of time there is an overspecialization that occurs—unless they are extraordinarily conscious and have a balance system . . . They begin to play arcs in each other's circuits. They represent circuits in one another. Circuits that are in each of them but may atrophy over the years to the point of becoming nonfunctional, just as muscle disuse will cause atrophication" (p. 45). Bateson believed that we respond to our own self-generated representations or images of the contextual world, and these representations make up our descriptions. Each description is limiting but useful and each adds to the mosaic that is formed when the descriptions are combined.

Being able to describe as much of the whole circuit as we can is important in achieving an entire picture. The only way to more accurately accomplish this goal is by creating multiple descriptions. Gregory Bateson asked, "What is the pattern which connects . . . ?" (Bateson, 1979, p. 8), which only multiple descriptions may highlight. The recurring themes and perceptual distortions between couples may be discerned by this process.

The content of the conflict may not be as important as the recurring theme that can be identified. A theme is an identifiable story line or "melody" in the symphony of couple dynamics that is played, sung, hummed, and drummed through a variety of topics. Frequent themes include:

> "He is supposed to be my father, or she should be my mother and meet my every need."
> "He or she will ultimately abandon me so I will leave first."
> "Do not hurt your mother (wife)," or "please your husband at all costs."
> "Intimacy means suffocation."
> Having many rules about what your partner should do will create the marital bliss of happily ever after.

These themes often evolve from family myths passed down through the generations that influence the development of the couple system.

The myths we learned in our families that told us who we are, what happens in life, and specifically what we should do, symbolize the values around which we structure our lives. The stories of the systems and participatory roles have entranced us so that we tend to repeat patterns of behavior from long ago, patterns that are out of awareness. For example, one patient struggled with ambivalence about pregnancy. She felt more comfortable with the idea of having a boy and became tearful and agitated when she thought of having a girl. She knew that her great-grandmother had lost a girl child at birth, her grandmother had given up her daughter to her sister to raise, and her mother had aborted a girl child. The patient did not realize consciously that the family imperative commanded that she would have to give up her daughter as well. She had developed severe pelvic disorders and her gynecologist told her that there would be difficulty in becoming pregnant. There may have been several reasons for the physical problem. At a symbolic level, the pelvic problems became a boundary against her acting out the family imperative.

Themes often coevolve between couples and fit in with the family imperative of each partner (see Fig. 6.1). The themes reflect a particular behavioral redundancy between a couple and includes the symptom that coevolves within patterns of the relationship. The patterns are mutually reinforcing but constantly change to maintain the "fit" with each partner.

The attitudes, affects, and behaviors that accompany recurring themes should be identified and used in formulating the target therapeutic goals. The therapist can decipher more appropriate attitudes, feelings, and behaviors.

2. *What are the problematic images of the relationship?*

The description each partner carries within is also a key to the problem image that is maintained regarding the other partner. Each person maintains a problematic description and an image of the partner and the relationship. These descriptions and images are often the result of early wounds. The inner movie that is produced by an individual's history may run cer-

Wife's definition of problem: _____

_____

Husband's definition of problem: _____

_____

COEVOLUTIONARY THEMES:

Wife: _____

_____

Husband: _____

_____

    Images: _____

_____

Negative induction sequence: _____

_____

BASED ON:

Problematic attitudes: W: 1) _____

                                  2) _____

                                  3) _____

                            H: 1) _____

                                  2) _____

                                  3) _____

Problematic emotions: W: 1) _____

                                  2) _____

                                  3) _____

                            H: 1) _____

                                  2) _____

                                  3) _____

Problematic behaviors: W: 1) _____

                                  2) _____

                                  3) _____

                            H: 1) _____

                                  2) _____

                                  3) _____

Figure 6.1. Problem complex

tain scenarios in response to particular expressions, gestures, or language that is reminiscent of something from the past. One partner may look at the other in a certain way that suddenly triggers an intense reaction, which, in turn, triggers the inner movie of the other partner. When the outer reality mismatches the inner image in positive or negative ways, the result may be painful feelings that include feelings of shame.

To identify the problematic images and scenarios is important in developing a hypothesis. Whether "he's a monster," or "She's a witch," or the image of a past figure is haunting the relationship, the therapist needs to identify the image. Many images are at play in most relationships. A woman who had an abusive, aggressive, seemingly powerful father will probably marry a gentler man who is kind, nurturing, and soft. Because her father was in the role of nurturer/aggressor, she may have a conflicted view of caring. She may both love and hate her husband until she works through the conflicted father image. She may love his nurturing nature because she feels safe temporarily. However, she may hate his gentleness because she is also likely to perceive it as weakness and inadequacy.

3. What are the shame-based negative inductions that occur?

Negative cocreated inductions are often shame-based. These inductions can be observed by the therapist and include nonverbal and verbal behaviors. Shame often is experienced in interpersonal interactions and may be internalized and easily induced by others in different contexts. Shame is that feeling of humiliation for having certain feelings, thoughts, or behaviors originally communicated from significant people to children. Fossum and Mason (1986) define shame as "an inner sense of being completely diminished or insufficient as a person" (p. 5). A person may feel so exposed and incompetent that he or she is stripped of any sense of self-worth.

These feelings may begin at an early age, even a preverbal age. Main and Weston (1982) videotaped infants who responded to their mothers returning after a separation. The infants showed ambivalence toward their mothers by both hugging the mother and pushing her away or maintaining a blank look. Other more insecure infants reacted with active avoidance behaviors. Helen Lewis (1987) suggests that these reactions may indicate the forerunners of the development of shame at being rejected. The child may move to anger and rage to avoid the feelings of shame.

In the analyses of adult conflict where the early development of shameful feelings can be recognized, shame may be the basis for negative interpersonal inductions and individual defenses. The push toward perfectionism, power, achievement (Kaufman, 1980), or other strivings that allow an individual to avoid the terrible experience of shame can become powerful trance inducers in couple communication. An example of a shame-based negative induction might be as follows:

WIFE: We need more money to operate the house (said accusingly).

This statement elicits shame and triggers an inner movie of the husband's father being discounted by his mother, or a movie of him being a terrible husband. The implication is: You are inadequate and I feel afraid.

HUSBAND: I don't understand why you can't manage the house account (said accusingly).

This statement elicits shame and triggers an inner movie of the wife's mother being discounted by her father, or a movie of her being an inadequate wife. The implication is: You are irresponsible and I feel afraid.

WIFE: I can't talk to you about this, and the bills keep piling up. Never mind, I'll just take care of it like I always do.

This statement elicits more shame and inner feelings of abandonment. The implication is: I will act more adequate, but I want you to take care of me.

HUSBAND: You bitch. Leave me alone.

This statement elicits anger and rejection and inner feelings of abandonment.

The implication is: I will push you away so you cannot be the first to leave emotionally.

The attention for each partner is internally focused, and each has probably experienced some form of dissociation at this point. A negative trance state has developed for each partner as a result of the shame-based induction.

4. *What are the problematic attitudes, emotions, and behaviors that are leading toward dysfunction and dissatisfaction?*

Distinguishing the limiting beliefs, or the patterned emotional responses that seem uncontrollable, and the concomitant behaviors is useful in analyzing the symptomatic pattern between couples. One couple with whom I worked described the beginning of their relationship as romantic and passionate, with both partners feeling that they had finally found the one person who would make them feel connected and nurtured. The wife reported that she had mistakenly believed that this second marriage could provide her daughter (and herself) with a new "dad" without any conflict over the old one. She had actually wanted to replace her first husband and believed that she could do that without any grief or pain. Although she realized that this belief was unrealistic, she continued to press her new husband to act in fatherly ways toward her and her daughter. She pressured him to be the perfect father but interfered with his parenting because she was afraid he would be too heavy-handed with her daughter. This woman's hope of having a rescuer from her unhappy previous marriage, a savior/father, was a problematic attitude that placed her husband in an impossible role. He, on the other hand, attempted to fill the role by being overbearing, demanding of her daughter, and harsh. He had expected to fulfill every nuance of the father role with the stepdaughter, but, instead, found himself pushed to the outside of the relationship between the mother and daughter. He desperately wanted to be loved and appreciated and believed that, if his wife would only listen to him, he had the solution to the problem of their acting-out child.

Distinguishing the defenses utilized by each partner that elicit complementary defenses is an important aspect of this part of data gathering. The various defenses employed indicate the kind of distortions that are occurring and in order for stability to be created, reciprocal defenses are elicited. For example, anger and hostility often elicit the same or passive withdrawal. Projective identification will elicit what is being projected. An individual who believes he is victimized by others and projects this idea onto his spouse will elicit victimizing behavior. The response elicited is called countertransference by object relationists. To play on words, there is a "counter-trance/ference" that occurs. The original "trance/ference" is a mutually created induction where the spouse becomes age regressed and the other partner sometimes age progresses and becomes a parental figure. The counter-trance/ference is played out through these roles or in the ensuing battle over who is allowed to remain the child and the parent.

If the conflict is complementary or symmetrical, the therapist can identify the patterned response of defenses. Escalating complementarity might include the husband who gives orders as the wife becomes more bumbling. Escalating symmetry might involve the husband who criticizes the wife and is criticized by the wife in return. Of course, these roles may be reversed. The therapist can identify the resulting process of mutual devaluation and ritualistic trance behavior by distinguishing the kind of conflict, the defenses utilized, and what behaviors trigger the negative trance. The therapist should also distinguish what behaviors trigger a positive ritualistic trance (J. W. Wade, 1989, personal communication). The trance is ritualistic because the same theme or communication occurs repetitively at certain times in the relationship and is triggered by the same cues (Figure 6.1).

5. *What are the developmental issues and uncompleted tasks involved with the problem?*

The early life of each partner in a couple relationship is often the basis for particular problems in the present. Whatever symptom emerges may be in some way rooted in the distant past in distorted perceptions, affect disturbances, and inadequate nurturing. Sheldon Cashdan (1988) suggests that "the nature of the patient's difficulties can be traced to arrests in the development of the self and anomalies in splitting" (p. 53). It is important for the therapist to have a good background in developmental theory. In identifying the developmental lacks in each person, it is useful to keep a schema in mind. Once developmental problems are identified, the marital therapist may then be able to assist each partner in providing these experiences through trance work and/or task assignment.

Disruptions in attachment early in life often result in difficulty in marital bonding as well as adult bonding in general. Adults who experience loneliness and emptiness and have a reticence to be close and withdraw from others usually have had difficulty in early bonding. In families where abuse occurred, children were often required to behave as adults. When a caretaker pressures a child to be an attachment figure or is ambivalent about nurturing a child, the child is likely to develop an anxious attachment to the caretaker. The caretaker will threaten to leave if the child refuses to act as an attachment figure. The child becomes overly responsible, angry, and guilt-ridden (DeLozier, 1982). To compensate as an adult, an ambivalent attachment to a partner can occur.

The separation-individuation experience is a universal experience that occurs throughout life, not just in an early phase of life as some of the developmental theorists suggest. This process is seen in the experience of every contact with other people. It begins in meeting another, developing a relationship, and moving toward and away from the other within the relationship. It is seen in every phase of development as we attempt to learn both how to be individuals and to be in relationship to others, a paradoxical situation that is a both/and process, not an either/or event. This dynamic culminates in death, the final separation from relationship as we know it.

Developmental Stages[1,2]

The following is a brief developmental schema to assist the therapist in making an assessment of deficits and strengths.

[1]Lifestyle impacts developmental stages. Those who lead healthy and balanced lives are likely to move through transitional phases easier to experience different stages of development. The methods people use to attain satisfaction may either lengthen or shorten the life span.
[2]Women experience developmental stages somewhat differently than do men. The therapist should take these differences into account.

0 to 6 months: The child should have developed an attachment to the mother or caretaker and can form a mental image of this individual. Early notions of splitting between the "good and bad parent" occur depending on the availability of the mother to meet the immediate demands of the infant. The mother or caretaker needs to feel warmth and caring toward the infant. The interactions between mother or caretaker and infant will have an impact on the individual as an adult.

The marital therapist may want to determine the quality of attachment each marital partner has made with the other. The quality of contact each person makes may reflect a disruption in development from this time period. The hypnotic work will then involve addressing the recreation of attachment experiences in symbolic or metaphoric work.

5 months to 9 months: A sense of separateness from the caretaker occurs during this time. There is a "psychological birth" as differentiation from the parent begins. The definition of "me" begins during this stage. The child begins to physically move away from the caretaker, although it continues to use her or him as a home base and moves back when needed. Crawling and walking begin at this time as the baby begins to experience the need to explore the environment. The caretaker needs to support this beginning separation and yet be available to the child who comes back to make certain he or she is still there.

1½ years: This period is termed by some object relationists as the period of rapprochement. Here there is anxiety over separation from the mother or caretaker. The child must learn how to be separate and maintain a sense of safety. During this time, the child begins to name himself or herself and identifies with the mother or caretaker. Object permanence is established. If the child's caretaker leaves the room, the child can carry an inner image to provide a sense of security until the caretaker returns. A failure to achieve object constancy and permanence can create a defective capacity for evocative memory, and stifle the ability to mourn (Masterson & Rinsley, 1975). Masterson (1981) suggests that the child who is reared by a borderline caretaker will have dependent and regressive behavior reinforced and separating-individuating behavior punished. The internalized image of self and caretaker will take on polar dimensions. Part of the inner caretaker image will be tinged with criticism, hostility, anger, and attack; part of the image will seem loving, supportive, and approving. On the one hand, the self-image will be devalued, with feelings of helplessness and guilt and an affect of chronic anger and rage. Beneath the surface is an abandonment depression. On the other hand is the polar opposite of the self-image, which includes being compliant, obedient, and good with an affect of warmth and confidence. Underneath this affect is the desire for reunion with the caretaker (Meissner, 1988).

The marital therapist will want to evaluate the couple's differentiation from their primary caretakers to determine how much of a separate self each partner has brought to the relationship. The period during adolescence where separation is an issue again may need to be distinguished from the present period. How often each partner feels a need to be in touch with a parent might be evidence of a lack of differentiation. If object constancy or permanence is a problem, the hypnotic work will then have to address how to be separate and safe and yet connected.

2 years to 3 years: The process of separation should be completed during this time. Inner images of the self and others are formed and splitting of the images of good bad self and good bad caretaker continues. Object constancy continues to be developed until three years of age so that mother or father can leave the room, and the child can maintain an image of her or him inside to feel safe.

The marital therapist may evaluate object constancy with both marital partners to determine if separation anxiety is related to an early problem. Some partners are not able to maintain either an image of the partner or a feeling of connection when separated for a period of time. Having them carry a picture of the spouse and look at it or having them carry an object that belongs to the partner is useful. This object can act as a "transitional object," a symbol for the individual, which will carry the feeling and image of connection when they are separated.

Otto Kernberg (1979, 1984) suggests that there are three stages of development that reflect the mother-child relationship comprised of "bipolar intrapsychic representations:" introjection, identification, and ego identity. These representations contain three elements: an image of the self, an image of the other, and an associated affect. Introjection is a swallowing whole of the images of self and object evolving from experiences with the primary caretaker, and these experiences are given positive and negative valences. The identification stage reflects the ability of the child to develop a sense of self as one who can have an impact on his or her world and manage feelings. Finally, the stage of ego identity reflects an integration of the self from all of the experiences with mother and father and can direct behavior.

The marital therapist should remember that the father plays an important role in the early development and the triadic relationship of mother, father, and child that begins as soon as the child is born. The representation of that relationship becomes internalized in the child as an image of the self, of the parents individually, and of the parents as a couple, and associated affects for experiences related to the dyadic or triadic dance.

3 years to 7 years: During this time, the child's world is magical. Events seem to occur because of some mysterious force. The ability to think logically is established. In addition, the child begins to think that others construct the world in the same way as she or he does. Defense mechanisms such as projection and repression are learned during this time.

The marital therapist might observe tendencies toward magical thinking in adults to indicate some learning difficulty from this period. Identifying particular defense mechanisms will be useful.

7 years to 11 years: The child during prepuberty will begin to be more interested in members of the same sex and learns how to be a companion. Any abusive experience at this age may lead to difficulties in sexual identity formation in the next stage.

11 years to 15 years: Adolescence is a critical period of growth. The ability to abstract is seen in this stage as concepts and constructs are discussed. Idealistic thinking is prominent as is a focus on physical appearance. The adolescent tends to have simplistic and definite views on certain issues and displays "I am right, you are wrong" thinking. Relationships with the opposite sex begin developing in this stage. If parents have difficulty facilitating the child's moving away and practicing with new relationships, they will unintentionally foster guilt and shame in the adolescent for having these natural desires.

Problems resulting from this period of growth may be exhibited in adulthood through serial affairs, sexual difficulties, serial marriages, or tendencies to change jobs frequently.

15 years to 20 years: This stage of early adulthood finds future goals being established. Choices begin to be made regarding interests, and directions are charted. Moving out on one's own usually occurs during this time. Difficulties experienced in getting ready to leave home and in the actual leave-taking may result in children staying home into adulthood and reluctance to establish a new family.

20 years to 30 years: This stage of adulthood usually is the time for the establishment of marriage, family, and career. Learning how to balance the stresses of relationship and the demands of career is often a problem for both sexes. The woman who becomes pregnant often turns her attention inward and away from her husband to manage the process of pregnancy and birth. If her husband has difficulty with managing grief over "losing" his wife to a little intruder, he may become resentful and pull back from her. If she feels abandoned by her husband, they could have problems reconnecting after the birth of their child.

30 years to 40 years: Around thirty years of age the old defense mechanisms that carried the individual through life often break down, and there is an upheaval and reevaluation of the self, marriage, and career. The beginning of the realization of mortality occurs in this stage. For women, there is often a push toward having a child.

40 years to 50 years: There is a push for career success in this stage of life. Anxiety over one's own mortality is often experienced. The natural changing of the family structure as children leave home emphasizes the passing of time. The "midlife" crisis may be experienced by either men or women. The crisis occurs in order to foster integration of different aspects of ourselves. We attempt to reconcile our polarities of loving/mean, unselfish/selfish, creative/destructive.

50 years to 60 years: This stage is characterized by preparation for older age. An interest in spiritual objectives and personal growth often occurs. Adults often find themselves becoming grandparents in this stage of life and need to reconcile certain disappointments they may have had with their own children. Issues of physical change and loss of physical power may arise.

60 years to 70 years: As many people continue to work well into their later years, this stage can be characterized as enjoyment of "elder statesperson." These people often become wise advisors and mentors to younger people. They give consultation on life issues to those who need guidance.

This stage of life may sometimes be the most productive time for integration of different aspects of the self. The most productive career work may be accomplished and enjoyed.

70 years to ??: This stage of life is characterized by preparation for generative living. Usually, there is a change in the work life either through retirement or slowing of production in some way. The focus of life becomes more directed toward living for oneself and doing those things that may have been put off at an earlier time. An ability to refocus is needed here as is an ability to be identified through something other than a vocation. Changes in health or the loss of a spouse may be major developmental crises in this period.

Developmental Stages in the Marital Relationship

Besides individual stages of development, the marital relationship is characterized by seven developmental stages and accompanying tasks: romance, disillusionment, conflict, reorganization, expansion, contraction, and stabilization of the relationship. In fact, it is often couples' experience that they move back and forth from stage to stage until they reach the stabilization stage. Once this stage has been achieved, there is less recycling through the other ones.

Romance: The beginning of a marriage is characterized by idealization and projection. The mutual positive state of consciousness experienced by both partners is a womb-like emotional tunnel that provides a wonderful state of security and belonging. There is a collapsing of the ego boundaries and a state of symbiotic union that feels nourishing and ecstatic. As life begins to return to normal, each person begins to redefine himself or herself as an individual and as a part of the couple. The developmental task here is attachment and bonding. There is a natural reestablishment of ego boundaries if the process works well. If there is difficulty in separation-individuation, there will be conflict.

One couple with whom I worked related the story of the beginning of their relationship. They had met at their place of employment, but company policy dictated that employees could not date each other. There was something highly charged, electric, and risque about being together. At work, they pretended not to know each other well, which only heightened the romance when they were together: wine, candlelight, and a wonderful secret. Finally, the intensity became excruciating and one of them took a new job. They married. Six months later they were in therapy complaining about the boredom. They felt confused and frustrated that the early feelings had shifted. When the secret that had united them in intensity disappeared, so did the excitement. When the context that gave birth to their connection changed, they discovered how the beginning of a relationship was allowed to define the marriage.

Disillusionment: This stage of the relationship marks the beginning of disappointment that one's partner may not be the idealized person one once thought. Coming to grips with a partner's humanness is difficult but it is part of the separation from the fusion. Disillusionment also stems from each partner's realization that he or she is not the ideal image of a person either. Intense fusion may be experienced during this stage, which can last years. The more intense the fusion the more ambivalence is experienced in terms of proceeding with the marriage or terminating it.

The tasks in this stage include developing a realistic image of the partner, negotiating movement between separation and togetherness, and developing an appreciation of who one's partner is, with both weaknesses and strengths.

Conflict: The next stage in the relationship is fraught with argument and struggle in an attempt for each person to define a self in the relationship. Who decides what will be the arena of growth in this stage. It is usually here that the hypnotic dance begins, and the early themes of struggle that may follow the couple throughout the relationship will be identified.

The task in this stage is the establishment of the rules of the relationship. Where each partner will set boundaries for the self and partner is negotiated with ensuing conflict.

Reorganization: This stage is characterized by an acceptance and reordering of idealizations to more realistic perceptions of this partner. If this stage has not occurred until after children are born, the reordering will entail accommodation of the role of parent in one's identity. There is a natural tendency for a pregnant woman to move her attention inward away from her husband. She becomes naturally absorbed with the life within and is in constant communication with another in the most intimate connection that can be experienced. After birth of the child, if the partners have difficulty connecting again (a move from an internally oriented trance state to an externally oriented one for the woman), there will be conflict and difficulty in the reorganization stage.

Expansion: This stage is characterized by the incorporation of new people into the relationship. The tasks of this stage include integrating a career and children into the hectic lifestyle. Each marital partner must make adjustments in time, energy, resources, and deal with the ensuing grief over losing the old relationship with just each other. The family of origin triangle of mother, father, and child that has been internalized is formed outside the person's mental image in actuality. There must be adjustments made to deal with the subsequent projections and triangular relationship dynamics that evolve over time.

Contraction: This stage is characterized by launching children, one by one, and the result is contraction of the system. As each child leaves home, the parents must contract and refocus more on their relationship. Their ability to pull back is dependent on their ability to deal with their own aging, dreams that may remain unfulfilled, and the desire to pursue other interests.

Stabilization: In many couples' lives there comes a time when whether they will stay together is no longer an issue. They have made a commitment to each other and the relationship. This stage finds the couple committed to resolving conflicts and working together toward a better future.

Generative Years: The generative years in a couple relationship can be some of the most fulfilling time together if the couple has been able to deal productively with their own issues and have come to some resolution of their own fears of mortality. There may be an emphasis on spiritual matters, an increase in the transference toward each other, and a deep appreciation of each other as individuals.

There are life-span developmental transitions that all couples pass through. They include marriage, birth of the first child, children going to school, adolescence, children leaving home, loss of parents, becoming grandparents, loss of spouse in some cases, remarriage, or living alone.

It should be noted that individual developmental stages often interact with the couple's developmental stage. These factors sometimes lead to conflict. Transitional times between individual growth stages and the family/couple developmental transitions can complicate the couple's ability to cooperate.

6. *What are the systemic issues involved in the problem that include functional boundaries, power, letting go of resentment, generational ghosts, context and distance regulation?*

Boundaries: Clear and flexible boundaries may exist between each individual in the couple system, between the couple and other subsystems (children, grandparents), and between the couple and other ecological systems such as friends, work, organizations, and so forth. Rigid or permeable, boundaries are those attitudes and behaviors that define the couple as an entity, and that separate them from the world. They also define the individuals in the couple relationship as separate from each other.

Difficulty arises when the boundary is confused between the couple and the outside world and other people are allowed to enter into the intimate experience of the relationship, an example of too permeable parameters. This problem may occur when one partner discusses his relationship with a parent to solicit intervention for the other spouse. Problems can occur when there is too much dependence or too little dependence on the outside for support. Couples may become overly involved with others and turn attention from the relationship or be underinvolved with others and look to the marriage to meet all needs. Rigid boundaries may be the cause when it seems difficult for a couple to maintain friendships.

One of the hardest problems for partners to overcome is lack of boundaries between one another in the relationship. Permeable boundaries imply a tendency to take too much responsibility for the other person to the extent of sacrificing one's own well-being, an inability to be alone or separate, or to hold separate opinions without feeling overwhelming anxiety. This tendency is often called the "urge to merge," or fusion of two people who feel inadequate. Sometimes two people come together in an attempt to make one whole person. One young woman patient became absolutely panicked if her lover failed to call her at least once a day. She began to feel abandoned and separated to such an extent that she experienced her own fear of nonexistence.

Power: Gregory Bateson has distinguished two important power relationships—symmetrical and complementary. Both aspects are important in functional relationships. When power is shared, there is reciprocity and balance. Relationships that are only symmetrical tend to be extremely competitive. There needs to be complementary exchanges, an ability to take the one-down position from time to time where one gives and the other receives. When there is struggle over power, conflict increases and communication becomes confused.

Letting Go and Holding Onto Resentment: The inability to let go of resentments is an important diagnostic criterion. The inability to let go may be a function of a lack of internal strength or may be rooted in a conflict from an earlier time. This dynamic often operates between couples when resentment plays an important role in the closeness-distance regulation. Each person in a couple relationship must experience enough of a separate self to disidentify with his or her own interpretation of a partner's behavior and accept another explanation or idea.

Generational Ghosts: Loyalties to previous generations and hierarchical boundary difficulty may interfere with the couple relationship. Donald Williamson (1984, personal communication) suggests that until the hierarchical boundary between parent and adult child is renegotiated, one can never fully differentiate and create a healthy marriage. These family-of-origin issues constantly interfere with the full functioning capability of the couple system. A family of origin may demand that adult children live in the same vicinity as the parents or they will be ostracized and perceived as disloyal. These pressures can stress a marriage to the point of divorce unless the couple is able to take the chance of disappointing their parents.

The marital therapist may want to discern if any other "entity" is living in the marriage besides the couple. A parent or a grandparent will often be present in the household; a ghostlike presence that complicates the couple's interactions and influences the pattern that is established between the partners.

Context: How the couple's context operates in influencing their relationship is an important consideration in the assessment of the problem. How well established they are within their own community or how isolated they are from it, both as individuals and as a couple, is reflective of how intimate they can be with each other. The more a couple can bring other support to the psyche of the marriage, the easier it will be for the psyche to weather marital storms. The strength of community connection is crucial to the ability of the relationship to withstand difficulties.

Distance Regulation: Kantor and Lehr (1975) have identified a cycle attachment and distancing. There is a constant movement back and forth between couples that is an expression of normal ambivalence. This movement regulates the need for closeness and distance. It may become a problem when one person wants closeness and the other wants distance.

7. What are the developmental processes for the therapist?

Where the therapist is developmentally in terms of the present stage of life, developmental tasks left undone from previous stages, and any unresolved family-of-origin issues will affect the process of psychotherapy and personal life. Where we are in our lives determines the kind of psychotherapy we do, the kind of spectacles we use to perceive our patients, and how we experience what Carl Whitaker calls the "dialectic process" (Whitaker, 1989, personal communication), the moving in and out of the family by detriangulating from one's family of origin and triangulating with the new family and spouse. Whitaker says that this process is like sex, "You can't stay in and you can't stay out; it's in the movement back and forth that gets it" (Whitaker, 1989).

8. *What hypnotic phenomena are utilized by the couple as resources, and which ones are over-used or under-used?*

Specific trance phenomena that are already used, as well as areas of strength such as the capacity for humor and play, and coping mechanisms during stress, can be built upon and broadened. Those resources that keep the couple from ultimate destruction in the midst of a difficult time can be utilized and accessed for change. Identifying the specific trance phenomena being employed is important (see Chapter 1). Most couples have the ability to stop a fight. They are not in conflict 24 hours a day. Often a couple will have hypermnesia for getting in but amnesia about getting out of the fight. The therapist will want to broaden the partners' focus on how they moved out of the conflict and teach them how to improve upon the solution. Both the trance phenomena the couples currently use and the phenomena that would benefit them should be carefully evaluated.

9. *What are the major defense used by each partner to defend against anxiety?*

We can consider all defense mechanisms to be forms of hypnotic dissociation; they provide shelter from a flood of overwhelming feelings. Defenses are developed in response to family attitudes that have evolved over generations. They may also be the result of parental criticisms or the family style of problem solving. People generally model attitudes and behavior after parents or in reaction work diligently to model the opposite. Assumptions regarding which family system attitudes were held and which repetitive behaviors were enacted after can be made based on the particular defenses people utilize. Children are taught either to use the same defenses as their parents or to use the opposite. For example, critical and derogatory or discounting behavior on the part of a family system may result in the development of a child with the same char-

	Husband Wife	Overused Underused
Amnesia		
Partner Amnesia		
Hypermnesia		
Age Regression		
Age Progression		
Positive Hallucination		
Negative Hallucination		
Dissociation		
Anesthesia		
Analgesia		
Time Distortion		

Figure 6.2. Trance phenomena

acteristics or who is passive, meek, and mousey. Determining which defenses are being used and checking assumptions about parental attitudes and behavior with the patient can help the therapist to hypothesize what resources an individual needs to resolve a present dilemma.

Some people have learned to engage in obsessive thought that may be accompanied by compulsive behavior such as overeating, having sex to reduce anxiety, compulsive raging, drinking, spending, or working. Often there is no awareness that a dissociated feeling may be the underlying motivation for the behavior. The affect of anxiety or fear is managed and kept out of awareness by repetitive thought, the affect itself, or behavior. This defense may seem to have an addictive quality to it.

Cognition may be dissociated from affect when a person feels stuck in the review of a repetitive feeling that seems to flood the conscious mind and appears to the patient to be uncontrollable. One patient believed that in order to "work through her feelings" she must spend hours going over and over them so that much of her energy was tied up in reviewing pain. She discovered that she could refocus her attention whenever she began the repetitive obsessional thinking (a post-hypnotic suggestion from previous trance work) rather than continue to review the feeling so she could find some resolution and relief. In trance, she learned how to distract herself from the feeling once she understood it to be an old solution to managing fear. She was able to view the feeling from a distance and examine it as having texture, color, and substance or form. To complete the picture of the feeling, she began to be able to differentiate degrees of anxiety associated with it and to experience where the feeling was in her body, as well as how heavy or light it seemed. As she employed her own resources in this interesting examination, she could then discover what was stimulating the fear and formulate a plan to diminish it.

All of the defense mechanisms involve a dissociation of affect from cognition or behavior. Defense mechanisms can include repression, suppression, denial, projection, intellectualization, reaction formation, conversion reaction, sublimation, and regression. Analytical and psychodynamic theorists have identified defense mechanisms as protective devices to deal with anxiety and unacceptable feelings.

Repression: Severe dissociation of affect and cognition from behavior so that there is no memory on which to base a present feeling, thought, or action. Example: A person may feel anxious whenever her spouse touches her in a particular way, but have no specific memory to relate to the reaction. However, she may later recall a relative from an incest memory as the difficult image begins to surface.

Suppression: Less severe dissociation of affect that may be expressed in a thought or behavior. Example: An individual who feels angry toward another for something may give herself permission to express the feeling indirectly through a biting joke.

Denial: Dissociation of affect or cognition from behavior and a defense against perceptions. Example: A person who drinks excessively may justify the behavior by reassuring himself and others that he can stop anytime.

Projection: Dissociation of affect or thought and perceiving another as having the unacceptable feeling or thought. Example: One partner may feel distant and experience the other partner as wanting distance. Often, the circular aspect of this defense can be recognized as it emerges in the following sequence: "I feel bad" becomes "He feels bad about me," which, in turn, changes into "I feel bad about him."

Intellectualization: Dissociation of affect with a move toward explanation rather than expression of a feeling. Example: One spouse may experience the death of a parent and be overcome with grief, whereas the partner offers an explanation that "it was time for him to die." The explanation is both an attempt to ward off feeling and protect the grieving spouse from "leaving" the first partner emotionally.

Conversion reaction: Dissociation of affect with a conversion often into a somatic ailment. Example: Anger in many people who experience migraine headaches can, in part, be expressed through the triggering of a headache.

Sublimation: Dissociation of affect from behavior. Example: An individual may replace a desire to act out murderous anger through safer means such as playing football.

Regression: Dissociation of cognition from affect. Example: A person who feels frightened may begin to dress, talk, and act much younger emotionally than his or her chronological age.

10. *What is the image of the family system, how is it being maintained, and is it part of the problem?*

Unresolved conflicts from the family of origin may be recreated in the present family system. Making the family that each person carries around inside explicit can be useful in understanding how certain conflicts are perpetuated. The couple can compare and contrast their own relationship with their parents' relationship. Unrecognized disappointments in a partner either being more like or unlike a parent sometimes contribute to dissatisfaction in the marriage.

11. *What is the temporal organization and the "futuring" ability of the couple?*

It is useful to identify how each person in the couple relationship handles time. If there is an overfocus on the past, present, or future, the therapist may need to help the couple make some adjustments. Some partners become too future oriented and see only romantic idealistic futures. Some partners remain too past oriented and see only negative limitations. In order to generate and evaluate future possibilities or goals, the couple must be able to perceive positive future goals and be synchronous in their time perception. When there is conflict that relates more to marital adjustment, "a person's future images often are mismatched with other people in his social network, conjoint plans of action with other people become desynchronized, and the emotion often is ambivalence about the expectations and intentions of other people as related to the self" (Melges, 1982, p. 288). There is a cybernetic spiral when anxiety interferes with a person's ability to perceive the future as positive. Melges comments, "The spiral mainly consists of excessive feedforward of fearful anticipations that feed into one another" (p. 288).

12. *What is the image of the therapeutic goal? What images does the patient stimulate in the therapist?*
The therapist may futurize the patient and project into the future where the patient may be and even how the patient will look (Gilligan, 1987, personal communication). These images may be valuable unconscious therapeutic resources for the therapist as long as the therapist keeps in mind that the patient may have different images.

13. *How able is the couple to facilitate the movement back and forth between separateness and togetherness?*
The tendency to fuse is present in all couple relationships. How easily the couple is able to move from a state of separateness to a state of togetherness is useful information. When the fusion is great, usually the ambivalence about staying in the relationship is great as well. Fusion can be viewed as a state of consciousness where marital partners experience the other as themselves. Once the level of fusion has been established during the course of beginning therapy, the next step will be to formulate several hypotheses for the direction of therapy.
The quality of the contact couples make with each other is important diagnostic information. Contact is the energy exchanged between people. It could be described as the connec-

tion of one's spirit with another. Genuine contact involves the meeting of mood or feeling where one is left with an experience of inspiration or being uplifted or transcending the mundane. Some people are quite cautious and careful about their part of the dance, whereas others are aggressive and desperate to be fed and often come across as wanting to "eat up" another. Richard Heckler (1984) suggests that "to contact the rhythm of someone's excitement is to connect with the deepest and most essential part of them, and this connection creates the conditions for further learning and communication to occur" (p. 120). The quality of contact is related to the experienced quality and satisfaction of the relationship system. Heckler suggests that contact may be related to the polarity of containment and releasing. Some individuals have difficulty containing their energy and it spills out over their own boundaries and the boundaries of their partner. Others may have problems in releasing and withhold their contact so that their partner is always pursuing. Usually, when one partner withholds feelings, the other releases them to an extreme. This process is an attempt to provide balance in the system.

When I was a young psychotherapist I worked in a setting that treated many rehabilitation patients. A young, mentally retarded man taught me about intimate contact. He had been born with a hole in his heart and, consequently, he visited the hospital often. One day I went to work and my staff told me Dennis was back in the hospital. When I went to see him that afternoon, he told me that he was going to see his grandmother who had died earlier that year. I felt panicked and thought I needed to protect and encourage him. When I attempted to reassure him that he would be back soon, he looked at me directly and intently, smiled, and said, "It really is all right to die." There was an incredible calmness that we shared in that moment, a feeling that we both had transcended his mental retardation and my emotional retardation and momentarily touched each other. The next day his heart stopped beating. Dennis entered into my consciousness in a profound way. I will always remember his boyish face and wise essence.

The manner in which a person uses contact will allow the therapist to discover the most appropriate way to approach him or her. Someone who is cautious and introverted will only withdraw more if the therapist is too effusive in the initial contacts. The therapist needs to follow the individual's cues in moving toward greater intimacy in the therapeutic relationship.

Each partner's repertoire of contact is important in identifying this element as a resource to draw upon. If the couple can utilize words, touch, gestures, or other ways to make contact, the range is broadened. When a partner has only one vehicle for contact such as words, there may be difficulty. One of T. S. Eliot's characters who is quite out of touch comes to mind when he says, "I gotta use words when I talk to you" (1986, p. 123). If couples attempt to force contact, the result is dissatisfaction.

There is reciprocity between people regarding their contact style. One partner who is aggressive in making contact may be met by the other's more passive style. Usually, partners attempt to balance the contact dynamic.

In *The Little Prince*, de Saint-Exupery (1943) illustrates the process for those who feel more cautious.

> Little Prince: "What does that mean—'tame'?" Fox: "It means to establish ties." "What must I do to tame you?" asked the little Prince. "You must be very patient," replied the Fox. "First you will sit down a little distance from me—like that—in the grass. I shall look at you from the corner of my eye, and you will say nothing. Words are the source of misunderstanding. But you will sit a little closer to me every day." (p. 84)

If partners have respect for each other's boundaries and the ability to contain and release in an appropriate fashion, intimacy is experienced. It is impossible and even undesirable to maintain constant contact with another person. There must be time to withdraw—to renew, rest, and assimilate the experience of the other person. If both partners can do this easily and with flexibility, there is a feeling of satisfaction. If there is overwhelming grief over separation, therapeutic work may be necessary to address this difficulty.

HYPOTHESIZING

Hypotheses may be created from systemic and developmental data and integrated in such a way that a therapeutic goal can be established and an appropriate intervention may be made. Observing the system between couples is important in creating a systemic hypothesis about the dysfunctional pattern that needs interruption. In fact, all that may be required is pattern interruption for the couple to move back on track.

Identifying the complex of problem behaviors, attitudes, and affects in the hypnotic dance is important in the context of asking what developmental task needs to be accomplished that was not completed during the early years. What is the couple attempting to accomplish by the symptom? Whatever experiences that were skipped because of a deprivation in childhood may be created in task assignment, in metaphor, or re-mothering or re-fathering during the intervention stage.

Hypotheses can be created on three levels (see Figure 6.3): First there is the the systemic hypothesis that addresses communication sequences, hypnotic loops, boundaries, ecological influence, or the amount of influence each of the other systems wield in a couple's life, and the "we-ness," or the feeling of bondedness and the sense that they are a couple. Forming a systemic hypothesis can reveal reciprocal sequences of behavior between partners. In addition, the family's influence on the marital relationship can be observed. To add to the investigation, the therapist can move to the next level of hypothesis building. The therapist may proceed to the interpersonal hypothesis where in various aspects of the caretakers that are projected onto partners to act out (through projective identification or splitting) may be identified. Also, the image of the marriage can be noted. The style of managing interpersonal anxiety, and the capacity to be alone and the capacity to make contact can be evaluated as well. The various developmental tasks that remain unfinished also can be identified at this level. The third level of hypothesis building may be on the intrapsychic level where individual conflicts are experienced. It is at this level that the conflict the individual has with the internalized image of the self, defense mechanisms that are used to manage anxiety, level of ego strength (the ability to deal with stress without breaking down), acceptable and unacceptable feelings, and perceptions of limitations are addressed. Once these hypotheses are formulated, the marital therapist may set the goals of therapy, identify needed resources, and focus on intervention. As therapy proceeds, working hypotheses can be changed as necessary.

The psychotherapist needs to remember three ideas:

1. Elements at each level affect elements at all levels so that a reciprocal influence is always present.
2. The psychotherapist needs to "dis-believe" her own hypotheses and to realize that she makes them up as a way to understand the information presented. Flexibility in hypothesizing is crucial to helping people change.
3. The unconscious mind of the therapist can be a valuable instrument for a trained clinician to create the jump from hypothesis to treatment goal to intervention. In other words, images or thoughts will develop in the therapist's mind out of the interaction with the client that will often stimulate intervention ideas.

THERAPEUTIC GOALS

Once hypotheses have been formed, therapeutic goals can be established. The goal of therapy may be conceptualized in terms of what developmental experiences the person needs, which behavioral sequences need to be interrupted within the couple context, and which attitudes, emotions, or behaviors need changing. Attitudes are usually changed by creating new perspectives through new information or new experiences that reshuffle old categories into more creative ones. The resolution of object relational conflicts that are played out in the marriage is important to the lasting satisfying functioning of the relationship. This resolution may occur through replacing conflictual images of caretakers with new images of functional and loving parental figures or directing and resolving intense feel-

Intrapsychic level

1. Image of self
2. Fears, defense mechanisms
3. Perceptions of limitations   Hypothesis: _____
4. Acceptable and
     unacceptable feelings
5. Overall level of ego   Needed
     strength: capacity for   resources: _____
     humor, for handling
     stress
6. Developmental age

Interpersonal level

1. Projective identification/
     splitting
2. Image of partner/marriage   Hypothesis: _____
3. Style of managing
     interpersonal anxiety
     a. withdrawal   Needed
     b. socializing   resources: _____
     c. aggressive/hostile
4. Capacity to make contact
5. Capacity to be alone
6. Couple developmental age

Systemic level

1. Communication sequences
2. Hypnotic loops   Hypothesis: _____
3. Boundaries
4. Ecological influence   Needed
5. "We-ness"   resources: _____

Figure 6.3. Hypothesis building

ings toward appropriate people rather than projecting these feelings onto the spouse.

Any or all of these goals may be set by the therapist depending on the developmental deficits, the level of motivation that the therapist can help the patient to develop, the ability of the therapist and patient to develop a caring relationship, and the ability of the therapist to enter into the other's reality. Setting long-term goals and breaking them down into smaller short-term goals will keep the therapist on track in the therapy process. In fact, there should be continual reassessment during the course of therapy of the short-term goals. When therapeutic goals have been created, a treatment plan can be formulated.

TREATMENT PLAN

The treatment plan needs to be individualized and specifically tailored to the couple in order for any intervention to be useful. Individual needs and concerns, resources, and potentials are the marital therapist's major focus. Because of the importance of customizing a plan to particular persons, the relationship between patient and therapist is much more significant than the use of any particular technique. Every intervention needs to evolve out of the caring concern of the therapist and any treatment plan must be held lightly. Erickson believed that the psychotherapist should guide the person back onto the path that the patient knew was the right one, rather than force someone into a particular "healthy" behavior.

It is usually best to begin at the systemic level in order to calm the crisis at hand. Couples often come into the therapist's office in a panic and in a rigidly looped communication sequence that they are unable to interrupt. This dysfunctional sequence of behaviors may be targeted for interruption and depotentiation. The marital crisis is an opportunity for personal and couple growth in the context of an intimate relationship. Once this crisis has been depotentiated, the developmental and intrapersonal levels may be addressed.

Conflict is usually the result of people trying to awaken themselves from a deadened state created by a system that may have maintained life only at its lowest possibile level. With appropriate interventions and a treatment plan, some new (pattern) story is about to emerge out of the upcoming change; a story that will enrich the spirit of the marriage. Alice Walker (1983) describes this search for new life and spirit as demonstrated by her mother in *In Search of Our Mothers' Gardens*:

> . . . I remember people coming to my mother's yard to be given cuttings from her flowers; I hear again the praise showered on her because whatever rocky soil she landed on, she turned into a garden. A garden so brilliant with colors, so original in its design, so magnificent with life and creativity, that to this day people drive by our house in Georgia—perfect strangers and imperfect strangers—and ask to stand or walk among my mother's art.
>
> I notice that it is only when my mother is working in her flowers that she is radiant, almost to the point of being invisible—except as Creator: hand and eye. She is involved in work her soul must have. Ordering the universe in the image of her personal conception of beauty.
>
> Her face, as she prepares the Art that is her gift, is a legacy of respect she leaves to me, for all that illuminates and cherishes life. She has handed down respect for the possibilities—and the will to grasp them. (p. 241)

It is these possibilities that emerge from a relationship to be discovered, cultivated, respected, and enhanced by the marital therapist. To nurture these possibilities, the therapist can develop strategies for interventions that will address each hypothesis. Some guidelines for developing these strategies are presented in the next chapter.

7

Utilizing the Language of the Unconscious

The vision quest or pilgrimage to find a treasure, a search for salvation, for the Holy Grail, or some hidden jewel that will bring enormous satisfaction to life is found in much literature. This metaphorical journey that humans take to find themselves and to find contentment and happiness in relationships is a universal journey. It is the journey through psychotherapy as well. The journey is facilitated with the language of the unconscious: myth, symbol, metaphor, ritual and images. Both patient and therapist create this language.

The rituals, symbols, metaphors, and myths of couples represent the essence of what holds a relationship together. They represent the "trans-cendent" quality of why people couple in the first place. This chapter describes the strategic use of ritual assignments, symbol, metaphor, myth, and images in the therapy of a couple relationship that fosters the "experience of being alive."

MYTH

"We tell ourselves stories in order to live," says Joan Didion in *The White Album* (1979, p. 1). It is these generational stories that maintain traditions, values, and life passages, and that act as the guideposts of every journey an individual and a couple makes. The stories or myths describe the universal themes of the unconscious: birth, the passage of life, death, and resurrection or rebirth. The cultural stories are myths that contain ritual, symbols, and metaphors. The myths reflect universal themes and serve and guide to the "inner thresholds of passage" (Campbell, 1987, p. 4).

Campbell describes myth as what ". . . helps you to put your mind in touch with this experience of being alive." It tells you what the experience is. For marriage, the myth reveals that it is "the reunion of the separated dyad. Originally you were one. You are now two in the world, but the recognition of the spiritual identity is what marriage is" (Campbell, 1988, p. 6). Campbell goes on to say that when people marry because of the hope that romance and passion will sustain the relationship, they usually divorce because all love affairs end in disappointment. Further, for marriage to survive, people must sacrifice false ego to the relationship. Campbell has identified two stages in marriage: the youthful marriage where the couple produces children, and the alchemical stage where the two partners experience the unity of the relationship.

Each marriage develops its own myth or story about how and why the partners married, stayed together, and continue in relationship. These stories often contain many resources from the partners' memories of how they overcame life struggles together. There are stories of how they worked out conflict, shared humorous experiences, and felt commitment to the relationship. The therapist can often use other partners' mythology to communicate meaning to their unconscious. The use of myth in literature can also be valuable in therapy.

SYMBOL

Erickson, late in his career, often used symbols to communicate to the unconscious and facilitate healing. Symbols are used in a variety of ways: (1) to "absorb feelings or deflect them" (Erickson & Zeig, 1984), (2) to speak to the unconscious about problem resolution, (3) to occupy the conscious mind while the unconscious goes about healing, and (4) to facilitate the process of poiesis, or calling something into existence that was not there before from the comparison of one thing with another (Cox & Theilgaard, 1986).

A symbol in a broad sense is the use of one object to represent another. In literature the symbol is a trope, a figure of speech that uses a change of meaning. It is the "use of a word in a sense other than its proper or literal one; in this sense figures of comparison" such as metaphor or symbol. An important distinction when defining symbol is that it is ". . . an image which evokes an objective, concrete reality and has that reality suggest another level of meaning" (Holman, 1978, p. 509).

We tend to live in two different worlds of experience simultaneously: the world of the left hemisphere and the world of the right hemisphere (Sperry, 1968). Although we know now that this dichotomy is not quite accurate because both hemispheres are operating all of the time, it is primarily in the right hemisphere that symbol, metaphor, ritual, and images influence an individual.

METAPHOR

Metaphors are a way of articulating experience in multi-dimensions. Metaphors contain perceptions of a whole event and sets of experiences by which we view and make contact with the world. They are descriptions of subjective events and, as such, may communicate to the conscious mind and the unconscious mind. Certain metaphors may assist us quite well in one stage of life and then need to be changed in another stage.

Mary Catherine Bateson stated that "there is nothing more toxic than a bad metaphor" (Moyers, 1989, p. 347). As psychotherapists, we attempt to give our patients new symbols or to change the meaning of their old ones. When our work with patients becomes stuck, we need to alter the old metaphors both for clients and for ourselves. Bateson said we are our own central metaphor and when the metaphor changes and has new associations, so then do we.

Metaphor is "an implied analogy which imaginatively identifies one object with another and ascribes to the first one or more of the qualities of the second or invests the first with emotional or imaginative qualities associated with the second" (Holman, 1978, p. 314). I. A. Richards has distinguished the difference between the "tenor" and the "vehicle" of the metaphor. The "tenor is the idea being expressed or the subject or the comparison; the vehicle is the image by which this idea is conveyed. . . . The tenor and vehicle taken together constitute the figure of speech, the trope, the 'turn' in meaning which the metaphor conveys" (Holman, 1978, p. 314). The metaphor's referential and emotive characteristics may extend beyond these meanings to communicate a truth.

Merlin the magician was able to harness the power of the dragon and, through casting a spell, create transformation. The shaman of the Western world is the psychotherapist. Resembling a "cure" that is evoked by some strange chant or ritual and involves a potion or the use of alchemy for a magical transformation, change is brought about through the "magic" of the therapist's language and the offering of self through a relationship. The alchemy dramatizes change through symbol, metaphor, ritual, and myth—in all of which Erickson was a master. These change agents allow the unconscious to create associations at a very deep level. The patient can then expand personal categories and definitions and move out of self-limiting beliefs. These vehicles become anchored in a person's unconscious to assist in the sailing journey through rough, calm, unknown, and familiar seas as growth continues.

Lenrow (1966) suggests that:

> Metaphors can also highlight a person's unspoken assumptions about his capacities for influencing his surroundings effectively in the future. In this way, metaphors can condense and make vivid the person's apparent view of his lot in life. Moreover, metaphors can highlight the client's active contribution to his situation and thereby imply choices open to him for modifying that situation. (p. 146)

The metaphor is an open-ended device for suggesting unlimited options for particular problems. In fact, there are many functions of metaphor as a therapeutic modality.

1. Metaphors provide a way for the therapist to speak to the patient without conscious interference. The patient cannot know for certain that the therapist is speaking about her and thus the patient is more open to the suggestion within the metaphor.
2. Metaphors may contain a humorous quality that can distract the conscious mind from experiencing intrusion. The patient may listen more carefully without any feeling of shame.
3. Metaphors, because of their symbolic nature, may stay in the back of a patient's mind for a long while and new meanings may be generated, depending on new contexts.
4. Metaphors suggest solutions to similar dilemmas that the patient has, and they offer hope that resolution is quite possible. New possibilities open up for the present problem as well as for future ones.
5. Metaphors provide poetic images that take on a life of their own and resonate within a person as the journey moves on.
6. Metaphors from different languages express certain emotions, actions, and ideas, and the particular cultural language of metaphors influences both the perception and cognition of the cultural language (Whorf, 1969).

Metaphor contains multiple levels of experience and meaning and communicates to the unconscious mind in a way that direct communication cannot. Turbayne (1962) suggests that there are other functions of metaphor that should be noted. Metaphors create perspective and shift attitudes because of a focus on one aspect and defocus on another. Several good examples of metaphor found in literature dramatize these points. The first is a poetic metaphor in the well-known poem by Robert Frost, "The Road Not Taken."

Two roads diverged in a wood, and I—
I took the one less traveled by,
And that has made all the difference,

Robert Frost (p. 131)

Robert Frost uses beautiful poetic imagery to suggest that life choices, symbolized in the two paths through the forest, mean that the cultural norm of how to live life may not be as fulfilling as risking something different. For Frost, the road not taken was the path few travel. He implies that for him, this road offers more creative opportunities and possibilities. He also tells the reader that he maintained an illusion that he might always return and take the other path, but he really knew he would not.

On the other hand, Dysart, the psychiatrist in *Equus*, like his patient, the boy who blinds horses so they will not see his sexual passion, blinds himself to his own latent passion for life. Since he can neither find his passion nor share it with his disinterested wife, he can only read about it. He describes himself as "the finicky, critical, husband looking through his art books on mythical Greece." He realizes his own tragedy when he describes himself: "I shrank my own life. No one can do it for you. I settled for being pallid and provincial, out of my own eternal timidity." In a powerful metaphor, Dysart pleas for a new perception, a new language, a way to create meaningfulness. He says, "the thing is, I'm desperate. You see, I'm wearing that horse's head myself. That's the feeling. All reined up in old language and old assumptions, straining to jump clean-hoofed on to a whole new track of being I only suspect is there. I can't see it, because my educated, average head is being held at the wrong angle. I can't jump because the bit forbids it, and my own basic force—my horse-power, if you like—is too little. The only thing I know for sure is this: a horse's head is finally unknowable to me." This metaphor challenges therapists' tendency to become wedded to a particular theory or belief system in psychotherapy.

A. R. Ammons (1972) creatively expresses the recursiveness of systems and the "mirroring" that other people provide for us in a lovely poetic metaphor.

Reflective

I found a
weed
that had a

mirror in it
and that
mirror

looked in at
a mirror
in

me that
had a
weed in it

A. R. Ammons (p. 170)

In literature, the magician or sorcerer has spent much time discovering forces in the universe that reveal more about one's self and provide ways of viewing the world that result in more satisfying relationships. The sorcerer is a healer. He or she is concerned not only about healing physical problems but about healing the psyche as well. The practice of sorcery helps people remove psychological scars and create new perceptions. The sorcerer learns that the best instruction is provided through opportunities to experience something in a different way, rather than by directly telling someone something. Although Erickson was by no means a sorcerer, he often used symbol, symbolic experience, and metaphor to teach by using one's resources that have been discounted or forgotten consciously.

The metaphorical story or analogy may be a vehicle for opening up new ways of thinking, perceiving, and behaving. It should always be couple-focused and be designed for their particular situation. One couple came for therapy and revealed that I was number six in a long line of skilled therapists with whom they had spent four sessions, but they believed that I had some "magic" that the others did not. I told them that I had been given a gift of a magic wand. The wand had come with an instruction booklet because if one were to cast a spell incorrectly, it would happen backwards and I certainly would not want to make their situation worse, particularly since we would only have four sessions. They assured me that they had heard of my reputation and wanted to stay longer than four sessions. I said I understood their well-conceived plan, but that their pattern indicated that there might be some cosmic systemic influence that would compel them to leave after four sessions. (They were both therapists who had been married for the third time for four years and understood the significance of a systems orientation. A cosmic system was a somewhat different twist, however.)

In order for them to receive the full benefit of this therapy, we would just plan on four sessions. Now, the instructions accompanying the magic wand stated that the practitioner must hold the wand in the right hand unless you are left-handed, which would of course mean that the right hand would be the left hand to hold the magic wand, unless you are standing in front of a mirror. In that case, the right hand would be the left hand reflected in the mirror image that was to hold the magic wand which was of course the right hand which was left. The magic words must be uttered as you wave the wand over the couple. "It has been a while since I have read the instructions, but I believe I can remember them," I told the couple. They began to laugh and to help me with various magic words they knew as children. And I added, "Abbra Caddabbrah, the magic words go, the story is told, the dream will unfold." I began to tell them the following story about a monk and a nun.

Benjamin had been a monk for four years. His close friend Marie, a nun for four years, often studied with Benjamin and had many close times and meaningful conversations. However, they both felt something was lacking; some emptiness crowded into their awareness. Both desperately desired to know the meaning of life. They had studied for short periods of time with many teachers, but there seemed to be a missing puzzle piece to life. So, Benjamin and Marie began a long, tedious, and harrowing journey to find the wise one who could enlighten them. The monk and the nun searched many countries. They travelled great distances to lands where the ways were foreign and unusual. They were so intent in finding the wise one that they paid little attention to the journey itself, the interesting sites, the fascinating people, and the strange customs. Finally, they discovered the Master in the highlands of a distant country. The Master allowed the monk and the nun to come into his abode to discuss their concerns. Excited and relieved to have found the one person who could tell them what they had so long searched for, the monk asked the Master, "What is the meaning of life?" and the nun pleaded, "Yes, oh please, what is the meaning of life?" The Master smiled lovingly at them both, took out an old piece of parchment and wrote several lines on it. He gave the parchment to the monk and the nun and instructed them to leave. Once outside, they opened the parchment and realized that the lines were written in a strange language. Somewhat discouraged, the monk and the nun searched for someone who could interpret the unusual writing. They found no one.

Again the monk and the nun returned to the Master and asked him, "Please, sir, what is the meaning of life?" The Master instructed the monk and the nun to take the parchment with them early in the morning and to observe the sunset. Thinking this a rather perplexing directive, Benjamin and Marie nevertheless did as the Master had instructed. The sunset was beautiful, and the couple sensed the presence of something so magnificent that they could not speak. Later, they returned to the Master and shared the experience. But again, they asked, "What is the meaning of life? We know you have the answer!" The Master told them to take the parchment and go into the garden and sit with a rose. The monk and the nun did so and watched a rose for such a long time that they began to feel as though they were a part of the flower. They sensed that they were merging and moving into the rose in such a way that they could see themselves travelling together on a molecule inside the inner galaxy of the rose. It was a magnificent trip where they saw a world like the Milky Way, only inside a flower. There were sparkling colors never seen before; shapes and angles, and other strange but friendly creatures.

They returned to the Master, told him of the experience and

once again asked, "What is the meaning of life?" Patiently, the old Master told the monk and the nun to go and spend time with those they loved and give freely of themselves. "Really take your time to slow down and understand the relationship. And always at the end of the day," the Master said, "Ask yourself, how is my spirit?" Many years passed.

One day, Benjamin and Marie returned, looking serene and peaceful. They had discarded their religious garb and wore casual looking clothes and matching gold bands on their left hands. They came to the Master and gave him the parchment. The Master opened the parchment and saw that the lines had been erased. The former monk said, "I finally understand the meaning of life." The former nun said, "The meaning lies in the space between the lines." And the two became Masters.

The couple who heard this story decided to remain in therapy for nine months and were able to work through many issues.

The vehicle in this metaphor was a journey the couple took to find themselves and each other. Much like Dorothy who looks to the wizard for answers, the couple in the story looks to someone outside themselves, the Master, for meaning. The symbols of the monk and the nun were used to suggest that the couple was committed to another, Mother Church, and could not fully be together. The unconscious can have many associations with this indirect association, such as being tied to one's own mother or some other caretaker, so there cannot be a commitment to a personal relationship.

The number four that is repeated is taken from their own story of the number of years together and the number of therapy sessions they would allow themselves with each therapist. I discovered in the process of therapy that both partners had a major abandonment experience at age four when they were growing up. The number took on some kind of magical unconscious quality in their lives until they had therapeutic intervention.

Words have multiple meanings and create unconscious associations. Erickson was able to utilize metaphor for indirect associative focusing and to speak at different levels at the same time. The first book that Erickson read was the unabridged dictionary, and that made him tremendously aware of the deep meaning of words. In the only known video of Erickson working with a couple, he uses a familiar induction of the early learning set about remembering the alphabet and numbers. He uses sexual connotations when he asks, "Is the 6 and upside down 9—a 9 an upside down 6? Which way do the legs of the number 3 go? Is the 3 a letter 'n' standing on one end?" (Zeig, 1988). He later repeats these numbers in a metaphorical story and seeds the notion that a mature man and woman can function together in a sexual way and know how to be a man and a woman. Erickson recounts that at age 16 he went with his father to work delivering milk to the surrounding farms. At one farm, a young girl asks her mother, "Who is this strange man?" Suddenly, Erickson experiences himself to be a man by the little girl naming him as such, and he goes on to describe the wonder of the realization.

He also directs part of the story to the woman by suggesting to her that she can recall her feelings of being a woman. Zeig comments that this "was a sensitive story about a girl empowering a boy, and it was a bridge to create some good feelings between the couple with whom he was working (Zeig, 1988, p. 34). Zeig goes on to say that Erickson "seeded concepts, built responsiveness, and discharged resistance" (p. 34) in the story.

In the video, the husband requests help from Erickson with the tension he experiences when he reads and writes. This request may symbolize the difficulty in "taking in" and expressing himself outwardly. Writing can be viewed with a sexual association by the husband using his writing "instrument" to have sex while reading could be viewed as taking in comfortably sexual stimuli from his wife. Erickson begins to use a sexual metaphor with both the husband and wife, who have recently married.

The wife is uncooperative when Erickson asks her several times for a hand levitation. After four attempts by Erickson, she will not do what he suggests. He decides to relate the story of himself at sixteen and how a young girl empowers a young man. The message to the wife is that she can empower her husband through acknowledgment and respect or she can disempower him by not cooperating.

RITUAL

Erickson often used ritual therapeutically with couples because of its powerful capacity for promoting change. O. Van der Hart (1983) explains that "rituals aim at instigating changes in the consciousness of those who perform them. Minimally, they must fixate the attention of those involved by which the messages of the ritual are also unconsciously digested" (p. 5). Erickson sent one couple who had been warring for some time and could not come together or pull apart on a therapeutic ritual exercise. He asked one partner to go climb Squaw Peak and the other to visit the botanical gardens. On comparing their experiences, they discovered that each person valued entirely different things, and they would be miserable if they stayed together. Erickson heard from them later that they were divorced and they both had begun to live more productive lives.

This ambiguous ritual became a way to act out in symbolic form the unreconcilable differences between them. They had been unable to come to terms with the difficulties in the relationship long enough to resolve them or to dissolve the marriage. Because of the ambiguity in the exercise that Erickson had so creatively designed, each partner projected his or her own meaning onto the assignment. Then, each person became clear about the direction to pursue.

IMAGES

All of the primarily right hemispheric stimuli, such as myth, symbol, metaphor, and ritual use images. Images are a window into the unconscious mind. When trance occurs, often spontaneous images arise that trigger certain emotions, and then behavior follows. Erickson's later work emphasized the use of images through symbol and metaphor. The images suggested various coping strategies and expansions of perspective.

In theorizing how images work toward helping us, Freud in his document, "Project for a Scientific Psychology" (1895), said that an experience of satisfaction produces an association between images: a wishful image, or an image of something hoped for in the future, and a perceptual image, an image or complex of images of actions required to achieve the wishful image. To Freud, wishful images were the memory traces of satisfactory experiences with caretakers when we were infants. Inhibition becomes a necessary learning or learning to delay gratification when "states of craving," having been through experience, alter into "states of wishing," and become further modified into "states of expecting"—states that allow reality testing (Pribram, 1971, pp. 82–83). These images more closely resemble unconscious processes than does thinking in words (Pribram, 1971, p. 183).

In 1971, Karl Pribram proposed that the brain operates like a special image, a hologram. A hologram is a photographic plate that, when a laser is beamed through it, creates a three-dimensional image. Any one part of the hologram can create the exact and entire image. Pribram (1971) believes that ". . . because of the way in which motor systems are organized only one step of an action can be performed at a time. Yet when you or I sit down to write, or type, or speak, or play the piano, we have stored in our brains a considerably detailed representation of how the entire action is to be achieved" (p. 217). He suggests that the representation operates like a hologram in that any part of a sequence or pattern can create an entire memory of an event or experience. He describes visual, kinesthetic, and behavioral processes as being transformed into action by an imaging process he calls the creation of the Image-of-Achievement "which contains all input and outcome information necessary to the next step of that achievement" (p. 243). Pribram says that the Image-of-Achievement "regulates behavior much as do the settings on a thermostat: the pattern of the turning on and off of the furnace is not encoded on the dial, only the set-points to be achieved are" (p. 243).

Perhaps images that are formed from the patient-therapist relationship/interaction in trance develop from the deep resonance and holographic patterns of experiencing that contain concurrently the past, present, and the future. As the patient has a new experience with a loving parental figure, the patterns of experiencing have associations of acceptance, understanding, and a belief that he or she can have a satisfying life. Not only does the patient then carry an Image-of-Achievement, but the therapist carries one of what the patient can achieve as well.

In contrast, Von Foerster suggests that the holographic theory of brain functioning is trivializing a most complex operation. The hologram "only gives you a single picture of what happens at the moment" (Segal, 1986, p. 106). Von Foerster says that humans are nontrivial and recursive in that we change our behavior in response to our internal states. We tend to function as holistic systems only in the present; there is no direct access to the past. He also contends that we trivialize things and people in order to create a sense of certainty. We end up taking our simple linear descriptions of reality for explanations. Hypotheses become confused with facts. He gives an "ethical imperative: act always so as to increase the number of choices" in the context of community (Segal, 1986, p. 147). This is good advice for the therapist.

What is clear is that no one knows for certain how the brain operates. All we can have at this point in our understanding is a description, a metaphor. Viewing the brain metaphorically as a hologram or as a more inclusive holistic system where images are inextricably woven into emotion, behavior, and attitude shift may be useful when thinking about symbol, myth, metaphor, and ritual as interventions. Creating change can be a matter of altering the sensory image, shifting an attitude, eliciting an emotion, and teaching a new behavior. The process is, of course, more complex than this list, but for our purposes, we will follow this paradigm.

The use of metaphor and indirect suggestion can stimulate unconscious thinking by "comparison contrast, memory association, congruity checking, identifying attributions to the memory you are having, and so on" (Lankton & Lankton, 1986, p. 51). The Lankton's have designed a useful structure to construct metaphors in the multiple embedded format (Lankton & Lankton, 1983, 1986, 1988) and have developed a variety of protocols to assist in this construction. The three basic protocols that all other protocols are built upon are the ones for attitude, affect, and behavior. They are briefly summarized here.

ATTITUDE RESTRUCTURING

In order to help a patient change a troublesome attitude, a metaphor can be constructed that involves the following steps.

1. The attitudes and behaviors to be changed are scrutinized from the protagonist's perspective.
2. The opposite behaviors and attitudes from the perspective of another protagonist are evaluated or the same behavior from the perceptions of some significant other is examined.
3. The consequences of the behavior should be related to the perceptions held by both the protagonist and/or others who are involved tangentially.

AFFECT RESTRUCTURING

In order to assist a patient in changing a feeling or learning management of an affect, a metaphor can be constructed that involves the following steps.

1. A relationship can be established between a protagonist and any person, place, or object that involves any affect.
2. Movement in the relationship can be described that can include moving away from, moving toward, moving against, or moving with.
3. The internal physiological changes can be described that accompany the strengthening feeling the protagonist experiences and that may reflect the patient's behavior.

BEHAVIOR RESTRUCTURING

Behaviors can be targeted for change by designing a metaphor to use the following steps.

1. The protagonist's behavior is described, which is similar to the desired behavior to be acquired by the patient.

2. The protagonist's internal experience is described, which is used to support the new behavior that may also be used by the patient. The internal events are reinterpreted.
3. The behavioral descriptions are repeated several times in different contexts in the story.

These three protocols can be used alone or together to build and link new attitudes, affects, and behaviors to future changes. All problems are based on faulty attitudes, emotions, and behaviors. In fact, it is likely that particular attitudes people carry lead directly to the level of pain they will experience in their lives. The emotions and behavior in which people persist and that seem automatic probably lead directly to the level of satisfaction they will experience (e.g., "I had a panic attack last week" indicates that some external force caused the patient to feel overwhelmed with anxiety rather than that the patient created the feeling).

We might carry this line of thinking further and suggest that there are complementary and symmetrical influences of all attitudes, emotions, and behaviors, that systems theory studies. However, we do not really treat systems. We treat individuals who influence each other. The basic unit of change resides in restructuring attitudes, emotions, and behaviors. Thus, breaking all hypotheses down into these component parts is crucial to successful intervention (Wade, 1990, personal communication).

Outlining in trance how to make changes in one or all of these aspects can assist an individual or couple in creating more satisfaction. For marital partners, a couple structure protocol for metaphor building can be used as a more elaborate structure to address all three elements at once or only one at a time.

Most couples evolve a chronic, recurring conflict, which is painful and frustrating. A partner usually becomes focused on a behavior that is irritating in the present, then reviews all of the incidents where this behavior was frustrating in the past, and then the present frustration escalates into deep disappointment, anger, and sometimes despair. The irritant becomes a block to one partner being able to move close and feel intimate.

Instead, the affect of feeling alone may be experienced, accompanied by a feeling of having to put up with another "child." The irritant acts in some way to keep the couple apart or it pushes them apart when they have exceeded their tolerance for closeness. In order to interrupt this cycle and to use resources that have been forgotten or have not been built upon, the metaphor can serve as a powerful instrument of change.

COUPLE STRUCTURE PROTOCOL

After the interactional sequence has been identified and the inner images of the marriage, parents, and self have been disclosed, the therapist can ask what changes in each of these images need to be made through shifts in thinking, feeling, and doing. What resources are needed to help partners demonstrate appropriate developmental intimacy and age skills that will be reflected in thinking, feeling, and doing? What major trance phenomena are already being utilized? These resources may be elicited or taught through metaphorical stories and the symbolic interaction between patient and therapist. Other intervention strategies will be discussed in Chapter 8.

The metaphor should address the systemic hypothesis and the image of the marriage first. If the structure of the couple's system is dysfunctional, say, when there is an imbalance in the symmetrical/complementary dynamics for example, a restructuring of the system can be suggested in metaphor. Second, the interpersonal hypothesis and the image of the family of origin may be the focus of metaphorical work to deal with distortions in perception. This level should be followed by the intrapersonal focus and the image of the self. All of these image patterns contain complexes of behaviors as outlined earlier.

Care should be given to utilizing the trance phenomena that are under- or overused for each level of hypothesis. A single metaphorical story may be created for each of the hypotheses or one inclusive metaphor may be used to address specific attitudes, emotions, and behaviors.

In order to construct metaphorical stories that address the couple's dynamics, several elements should be incorporated.

The story should include (1) protagonists who deal with a conflict involving some other character, (2) an antagonist, (3) a central motivation to achieve some goal, (4) an exaggerated reaction to the problem, and (5) a storyline or chain of causally related events that affect the protagonists (Meredith & Fitzgerald, 1972). The protagonists can be constructed to deal with a thematic conflict symbolic of the patients' problems. They will struggle with someone else or some situation from which an important life learning will occur.

The antagonist will symbolize what the patient needs to overcome, such as fear or the resolution of a conflict. Often this character provides a mirror for the protagonist to see the "darker" side, the side of the protagonist that needs to be balanced through the resolution of a conflict or coming to terms with something unfulfilled. An exaggerated example of these two sides of a person represented by the protagonist and antagonist is found the *The Wizard of Oz* where Dorothy searches for an answer from the wizard to the question of how to get back to Kansas. The wizard is only a normal man pretending to have magic powers. The wizard represents a split-off part of Dorothy which she seeks. Her search is really a vision quest of sorts to find herself and her own power. This theme is examined throughout literature, film, and theater. In the novel *Shoeless Joe*, by W. P. Kinsella (1982) and the film created from the novel, "Field of Dreams," the protagonist carries guilt and anger toward his father (the antagonist) over their unresolved relationship. His father had died before any resolution could take place. Because he follows a dream by listening to a voice that tells him to build a baseball field, the protagonist is finally able to meet his father, a former baseball player, face to face. The most incredible part of the experience is that his father is 25 years old. The conversation between the protagonist and the father is a powerful transforming experience for the son who begins to understand his father's humanity. Healing takes place through that experience. This encounter allows the protagonist to reclaim his own humanity, to get in touch with his feeling that his father should have been more (a universal wish), and to come to terms with his own disillusionment over his sense that he too should have been more.

Each of these metaphorical stories contain a central motivation to reach a goal of self-discovery and resolution of some conflict. The motivation of the protagonist to build a baseball field on his farm is a driving internal force, at a conscious level, to do something extraordinary, and, at an unconscious level, to resolve an inner longing to love and respect his father. In addition, the metaphorical stories contain an exaggerated reaction to the problem, and a storyline or plot.

The storyline is designed to achieve two objectives. First, it can retrieve a memory experience or build through association an experience that will act as a resource for the patient toward resolving whatever problem is being addressed. The retrieval and building up of these resources can lead to generative learning of new present and future experiences. Second, the therapist can embed suggestions within the story line, while at the same time, building responsiveness by pacing and leading. The therapist will observe the responsiveness and build feedback from the patient into the metaphor and trance (see Figure 7.1).

Within the metaphor the attitude shift that needs to occur, the emotion that needs to change, and the behavior best suited to a positive outcome are addressed. The particular trance phenomena that couples utilize may be incorporated into the metaphor and used to create the desired outcome. In the *Field of Dreams* the primary trance phenomenon used is dissociation. The healing experience with the protagonist's father incorporates a unique kind of age progression and dissociation and surprise as the son speaks to his father who is younger than he is. Once the protagonist understands the factors that shaped his father, coming to a sense of forgiveness is easier.

The movement of action in the metaphorical story should follow a certain direction. The "first moment" sets the stage for the beginning of the metaphor, which is followed by the introduction of characters. The action in the story begins to rise. Then a complication is introduced for dramatic effect and interest, which culminates in a "crisis." As the story progresses, there is a reversal in the crisis, which leads to some solution, and the story's conclusion may be open-ended, with a moment of final suspense that leaves the patient wondering what the

Hypothesis to be addressed: Systemic, Interpersonal,
Intrapersonal

Change of attitude, emotion, behavior that needs to occur:

Trance phenomena utilized:

Protagonist:

Antagonist/other:

Conflict or Problem:

Motivation and Goal to be achieved by protagonist:

Reaction to problem/Protagonist:

Reaction to problem/Antagonist/other:

Storyline:

Ending:

Figure 7.1. Metaphor construction worksheet

resolution must be. The story may also end with a suggestion
that there is another metaphor to follow in another session.

Depending on the developmental stage of the couple, several
protocols may be used. For couples who are in the early years
of their relationship, who may be in the conflict stage, and may
have many family-of-origin issues, the first protocol is used. At
this stage, the couple may not have fully entered the marriage.

Never Coming Together or Pulling Apart

The metaphor can be constructed around the following steps:
    1. The couple falls in love.

2. The families disapprove so an evil spell is cast that keeps the partners together and yet apart in endless loops.
3. The couple asks for help from a healer who has been through a similar struggle.
4. The healer helps the couple create a counter spell or helps undo the spell so that they can fully be together.

This protocol can be used for the romance stage as well as the conflict stage.

Resolving the Mid-Life Crisis

The metaphor can be constructed around the following steps:

1. Each person becomes aware of a sense of boredom and projects it onto the partner.
2. Each person comes up with an outlandish scheme or experience that he or she engages in secretively.
3. To achieve the goal of the scheme the partners need each other. They cannot do it alone.
4. The scheme involves some risk, something out of the ordinary and beyond a conservative course of action.
5. A transformation takes place. Some newly acquired motivation results, a new direction. This could come in the form of accepting some new challenge, such as a new job position in a different part of the country.

This protocol may be used for the disillusionment or contraction stage.

The Generative Stage

The metaphor for this stage can be constructed by the following steps:

1. A person is at the end of a long, tedious, and important task. He or she feels sadness upon the completion of a

project and experiences boredom because there is no
new challenge. Internal conflict ensues.
2. Each spouse creates a new project independently of the
other.
3. Some new venture is attempted that involves letting go
of something old and performing a new action.
4. Renewed energy in an outside task provides more interest for the relationship.

Conjoint or individual work can be done utilizing either the
simple attitude, affect, or behavior protocols or the more complex couple structure protocols. The next chapter details various strategies that can be used alone or in conjunction with the
previous metaphorical constructions.

Understanding the patient's own metaphor plays an important role in the effectiveness of psychotherapy. The patient's
metaphorical descriptions can reveal both the problem and the
path toward its solution once the therapist begins to recognize
the particular language of the metaphor. The language that we
use and the resulting associations we derive from the language,
whether in the form of visual pictures or feelings they elicit,
create a sense of joy or pain.

The patient's metaphor can be understood in a variety of
ways. The context in which it is communicated will lead toward
an understanding of the meaning. An individual's or couple's
life circumstances will influence the meaning of the metaphor.
One young man came for therapy and complained of little zest
for life and an overwhelming feeling of depression. He lacked
the learning to connect well with others and felt quite alone in
his community. He related that he had even allowed a huge
plant to almost die from neglect. The plant had been with him
for years. I asked him if there were any life left in the plant
and he replied, "Maybe a little." Then I suggested that he bring
the plant indoors in order to nurture it, to water and fertilize
it properly. He agreed and began to describe what was happening to his plant. Metaphorically, he was describing himself.
"He didn't know he was going to come back but he's taking root
and the leaves are growing new shoots. I feel so ashamed for
letting him down." As the plant began to grow and develop,

this patient began to take better care of himself. There was never a direct verbal connection made between the plant and the patient. At an unconscious level, this young man was aware of how he was avoiding taking care of himself. A depression that he carried from his family of origin prevented him from nurturing himself. Once the plant responded, he began to tolerate more intensive therapy.

The patient's metaphor is usually ripe with affective and cognitive connotations, as shown in the preceding example. Because it is primarily a symbolic creation, the therapist cannot create meaning from a logical point of view. The therapist can allow the patient's metaphor to wash over her, to be absorbed, and to attend to her own metaphorical associations, and to allow the unconscious mind to dance with the unconscious of the patient. There is a resonance that occurs in an empathic relationship between the unconscious of the patient and the unconscious of the therapist. This unconscious process is symbolic of the early mother-child relationship (Chessick, 1965; Whitaker, 1982, personal communication).

Every communication between therapist and patient happens at several levels. Erickson was adept in communicating at the content level and the symbolic level, and he knew that the symbolic level addressed psychodynamic issues as well as the relationship between patient and therapist. In fact, every communication between patient and therapist addresses these levels simultaneously.

Elaborating on this concept, Ahsen (1978) suggests that every important developmental event a person experiences is encoded in eidetic recall. An eidetic image is an image that contains the picture, the somatic response, and the meaning or emotional response. A change in the image can produce a change in the somatic and emotional response. These images may be encoded in a pattern of symbols that stimulates affective and somatic responses. Trance work stimulates and utilizes a patient's symbols.

Theodore X. Barber (1961) believes that hypnosis is effective because of the imagery it creates within an individual through suggestion. When trance occurs, often spontaneous images or feelings arise.

Case Example

Susan complained bitterly that her husband would not complete caretaking tasks around the house. Her reaction was so severe that she became depressed, moody, and sullen. She expressed vehement anger toward him. The reaction seemed to be stronger than was called for by the situation. She recalled experiencing similar feelings in her family of origin when her mother was unable to be with her in the way she wanted. Her parents were from Germany and had escaped the country after it was occupied by Hitler. They maintained the Old World values and had difficulty amalgamating them into American culture. They continued to pressure her to take care of them in their old age. The eldest child was expected to look after the elderly parents. They would not accept any boundaries set by Susan, and she remained furious and enraged and demanding that they love her and do what she expected. After one poignant hypnosis session with her, Susan came back saying that she kept having an image of a golden snake covered by glittering scales, and with sparkling eyes and ruby red lips that kept smiling at her, tempting her to let out all her fury and passion.

SUSAN: The serpent looks evil to me. He is tempting me to do something I don't want to do. I could easily interpret this snake. My psychoanalysis did a number on me. He probably has something to do with sex.

CK: It is certainly very hard for you to really *see the serpent as an ally*? Do you think the serpent in the Garden of Eden was Evil?

SUSAN: Yes, I see him as a tempter.

CK: He certainly tempted Eve with consciousness and, therefore, pride; he tempted her with the tree of knowledge and bade her to go against God's wishes.

This image frightened her because she felt the image was evil. The serpent was beguiling her, inviting her to both release feelings and guard her feelings. She related that the symbol of the serpent had great meaning.

The serpent often was the guardian of treasure and served

to keep out any who would attempt to steal the treasure. The translators and interpreters of the *Septuagint* defined the Hebrew "tanniym" in the Old Testament as referring to the great dragon, or serpent, Satan. One of the best examples of a description using this term is Job:40–41, where the dragon is characterized as having an "impenetrable hide, gleaming eyes, fiery breath, and smoking nostrils." In the translation from Hebrew to Greek, the translation of dragon is pride, vanity, or idleness. He is referred to as "leviathan" in Psalms 74:13, Isaiah 27:1, and 51:9. The dragon is "an allegorical symbol for the sin of pride, personified . . . in Satan" (Evans, 1987, pp. 40–41). The Old Testament dragons are related to the Oriental myths whose theme is that a god slays the primordial dragon in an effort to bring order to the world (Evans, 1987, p. 40). The great dragon, Satan, was cast from heaven and took the serpent form of the dragon in the Garden of Eden. The Archangel Michael battles the dragon, a battle that ends when the deceiver is cast down to earth where he tempts Eve to be disobedient. The Fall was a fall from innocence to knowledge, and with knowledge people develop pride in their own abilities. Adam and Eve eat the forbidden fruit and develop consciousness. This is the beginning of initiating their own life, and "life really began with the act of disobedience" (Campbell, 1988, p. 51).

The "pride" this patient had developed was found in her ability to suffer. She had spent many years feeling rejected, used, and unacknowledged by her Jewish parents who came from a culture that was different from her own background and who maintained the old family traditions. In their belief system, the daughters were to take care of the parents when they were in need. They were expected to sacrifice their own needs for those of their parents. This patient painfully struggled with wanting and demanding her parents to adopt more up-to-date values and to accept her for not following the family dictates. The more she demanded they be different, the more her parents attempted to manipulate her by forming coalitions among other family members, and sending messages through the patient's relatives and children to her. All of the messages indicated that the patient never did enough. She ended up feeling guilty, depressed, and so full of rage that she was afraid to allow herself to express the feelings. However, she also operated with the notion that she had to keep reviewing her bad feelings, hours on end, to be purged. The serpent in her dream was a powerful image that represented the invitation to continue in the same way, or to use him as an ally to discover how to stop the painful, intense, feelings of rejection, rage, shame, and guilt.

After the conversational hypnotic session reviewed previously, this patient decided to expand upon a ritual I suggested to help her let go of her demand that her human and imperfect parents be idealized parents, to help her accept them, to learn better ways of protecting herself around them, and perhaps, even to enjoy some aspects of them. She visited the family graveyard, and in the plots designated for her parents, this patient buried a baby spoon and several other artifacts that represented herself as a child. Everyone in the family except Susan planned to be buried in the family plot. Susan used the family plot to "bury" the demanding infant part of herself. She symbolically moved into adulthood through this difficult and emotional hypnotic ritual assignment. When she returned and visited her parents, she experienced herself as being able to maintain enough distance to protect herself and to be nurturing to them. As her work in psychotherapy continued, she began to focus on nurturing herself appropriately instead of expecting her parents to continue in that role.

As this patient began to resolve some of these developmental issues, her tolerance for her husband's lack of caretaking of the house, a metaphor for caretaking of herself, increased. As she backed away from complaining and pressuring her husband, he was freer to offer more caretaking duties around the house.

The next chapter examines strategies that may be utilized based on a couple's primary use of trance phenomena. The therapist is encouraged to develop couple strategies based on each couple's particular needs and developmental deficits.

8

The Strategic Use of Trance

The marital therapist has at his or her disposal a treasure of pearls in the unconscious that can be used for change. Believing that every individual contains within all that is needed for life, the pearls can be elicited and utilized through a variety of techniques. Each couple should have an individualized and flexible treatment plan; no couple should be forced to fit a prescribed model or be pressed into the therapist's definition of health. The techniques presented in this chapter may serve as stimuli for the creation of effective interventions.

It should be noted that Erickson utilized both direct and indirect work. He emphasized a permissive and simple approach noting that ". . . hypnotic techniques must be tailored to fit the individual needs of the specific situation. Therefore, users of hypnosis should be fully cognizant with all types of hypnotic techniques and fully appreciative of his subject as a personality" (Erickson, 1964, p. 162). He emphasized that the hypnotherapist should be able to change from one technique to another as necessary. (Erickson, 1964). When he used metaphorical stories, Erickson would directly answer an individual's questions about the relationship of the story to the problem (1990, Betty Alice Elliott, personal communication). In response to whether Erickson preferred a more indirect approach late in life, his daughter commented that her father believed, "Either a direct or indirect approach may be used in working with patients. It is a matter of therapeutic judgment and experience, to determine which will be more appropriate for that specific patient in that specific situation" (Klein, 1989, personal communication).

When a patient is caught in a conscious limitation and has difficulty cooperating with the therapist, an indirect method seems more useful. The indirect approach tends to bypass conscious resistance and often gives the patient a generative symbol for health, balance, and well-being.

Before discussing strategies, it is important to examine one other aspect of hypnotherapy. Hypnosis, as all psychotherapy, operates within paradoxical communication. In asking a patient to develop a hand levitation, for example, the patient experiences a paradox: "I'm doing this, I'm not doing this." It seems as though the hypnotist is causing the patient to perform in this way, although the patient "knows" he or she is actually levitating the hand. Because dissociation occurs, it is as though the levitation is happening apart from the person. It is the paradox that creates dissociation (Hoorwitz, 1989).

Symptomatic behavior parallels trance behavior and also operates within paradoxical relationships. Problematic behavior often occurs when a person feels caught in a paradox of "I'm creating this symptom; I'm not creating this symptom. It is happening to me." If one spouse is struggling with some symptom such as compulsive behavior, anger, boredom, or depression, and communicates to the other about this symptom, the message is, "This is happening to me. Rescue me." When the spouse responds to the one-down message of "help me," the other goes one up to be of assistance either through advice or performing some behavior for the other. Then the first partner often moves to the one-up position again and says that this advice is not good enough; it is not working. There is a movement back to the one-down position as the spouse communicates that "this symptom is overpowering me; please help me." The spouse may try one or two more suggestions or even take over, going one up again. Of course, this response is perceived by the other spouse as "not enough," and the first spouse goes one up by taking this position and then goes one down again. Often, the couple will visit the psychotherapist when the rescuing partner has failed. The trance state that has developed during this process, which is a shared dynamic state, is often experienced as negative and frustrating. The hypnotic dance is in need of alteration. The therapist may then take over the position the rescuing partner had maintained, and the same process may occur again, this time with the therapist who fails to solve the dilemma, just as the rescuing spouse had failed. The therapist is induced into the negative hypnotic dance and may end up carrying the frustration and anxiety for the couple home to his or her spouse and then draw the partner in to cocreate a negative hypnotic dance of their own. This cycle can expand to children, the children's friends, and cycle back the other way.

However, if the therapist can create a therapeutic double bind, the patient may be able to give up the symptom. The patient might say, "I am producing this symptom, but I am not producing this symptom." The therapist agrees and suggests that it is useless to eliminate the symptom, but perhaps the patient can experience more or less of it. Alcoholics Anonymous operates on this principle by encouraging problem drinkers to admit they are alcoholics. Only by surrendering to the problem can one control it. By moving from a symmetrical position of self-control to a complementary position of surrendering to a power greater than the self, the alcoholic believes that the only way to be in control is to give up control (Bateson, 1972).

The double bind is the stimulus for trance. An altered state results when an individual feels caught in a paradox. As a way to make meaning out of some experience that maintains "both/and" logic, the logic of trance (i.e., something is both one way and the opposite way at the same time), a person develops an altered state of consciousness to protect from the anxiety of tremendous confusion. In the logical world, something can be only one way at a time, not "both/and." In the world of trance, it is easy to experience being here and there, being in the future and in the past, and being different ages at the same time. Adults who take up a sport they may have played as youngsters often report having this experience of being both fourteen and forty-three. They can play baseball as adults and have new experiences but keep feeling those old childhood feelings of standing at the plate, facing the pitcher, and desperately wanting to be a hero, or at least not a failure. The challenge is to avoid the humiliation that may have been felt as a child.

There are several methods of using trance in couple therapy: one person trance work, conjoint trance work, and conversational trance work with one or both. Trance and other hypnotic interventions are designed to block interpersonal or intrapersonal signals that have altered partners to begin symptomatic behavior. These interventions are used to create a counter-induction so that the signal for symptomatic behavior is no longer activated or holds a different meaning. Depending on the assessment of the couple relationship and the various trance phenomena that are already employed and those that may be taught by the therapist, one or more methods may be selected. When there are individual issues that are affecting the relationship, one person trance work may be used where one spouse is hypnotized while the other observes the process. Frequently, if one spouse becomes entranced, the other also drops into trance. The therapist may also see the partners individually but still address the couple system. None of these techniques should be employed before the "teachable moment."

The "teachable moment" is that moment when individuals or partners pause in the confusion from the interaction and drop into a light state of trance. This strategic time to begin trance work occurs in each therapy session. It is the moment that can be used therapeutically to disrupt the usual context in order to change a way of perceiving or a redundant behavioral sequence, or to change the meaning of an emotion. Often, this moment occurs in a state of confusion or when the therapist has said something that rings true for the patient.

When couples require individual work, working with them apart in more formal trance and conversational trance may be indicated. Separating couples may be more beneficial than conjoint work when the partners continue to be uncooperative with each other in the sessions, and every attempt by the therapist to support one partner is perceived as abandonment by the other. The therapist can follow the same model and assessment procedure as with a couple seen conjointly.

Conversational trance work or more formal trance work can be useful when doing therapy conjointly. The therapist may want to work with one spouse at a time while the other observes and then gives feedback, or the therapist may want to work with both at the same time. Conjoint work can be valuable in increasing bonding and feelings of connectedness.

The following trance phenomena and associated structured and indirect interventions may be used with either conjoint therapy or individual work around couple issues. The therapist can decide to select one of these interventions based on the trance phenomena already practiced by the couple, which may be found in the symptomatic process between them. These phenomena will already be utilized by the couple and can be expanded in a more positive direction. The intervention should be designed to address one of the systemic, interpersonal, or intrapersonal hypotheses the therapist has developed from the questionnaire data.

DISSOCIATION

Dissociation is the ability to separate affect from cognition. When we view ourselves separately from our problems, or do not feel pain, or see ourselves in a mirror in the next room while we are sitting in this room, or view a scene from our past in a movie, we are employing dissociation. Being able to perceive ourselves without the bounds of the body can be a resource to be used in intervention. One aspect of an experience is often split off from the others in dissociation. For example, arm levitation in hypnosis can be experienced as happening apart from an individual. The subjective experience says the arm is really not there.

Dissociation exists on a continuum. It can occur in mild form during ordinary life experiences and it can be more intense, occurring during trauma when certain parts of the personality are completely split off from conscious awareness so that there is an amnesiac barrier. Multiple personality disorder is an example of extreme dissociation. We can experience dissociation from feelings as a result of shock or trauma. Over time, a patient who maintains the dissociation of affect from cognition will be unable to recognize core feelings such as anger, shame, pain, fear, joy, guilt, and loneliness. In this case, feelings need to be stimulated and released.

We can also experience a dissociation of cognition from affect. The intensity of the affect may need modulation and management if a person is so aware of feelings that the feelings cannot be tolerated or experienced in a balanced way—neither so much that the patient becomes dysfunctional, nor so little that the patient has flat affect. People may obsess with thought, dissociate from affect, obsess about feelings and dissociate from cognition, or maintain compulsive behavior and dissociate from affect and cognition. Several interventions that utilize dissociation follow.

Mental Rehearsal

Mental rehearsal is a technique that can be used with individuals to practice a response different from the patterned one that may be dissatisfying. There are several steps through which the marital therapist may want to take each partner.

1. Have each partner review the problematic behavior of the other partner. Then have each review his or her dissatisfying response at all levels in a waking state: attitude, behavior, physiological response.
2. Have each partner select which trance resource would help change the response.
3. Suggest that both partners avoid psychological interpretations of what is wrong with themselves or with their partners.
4. Have each construct a scenario with the trance resource and follow the scenario with the desired response.

One young wife who had been reared in an alcoholic family where there was loud conflict in the form of yelling, screaming, and hitting would begin to have an anxiety reaction with sweating palms, heart palpitations, dizziness, and feelings of rage whenever her husband would raise his voice or yell about something even when it was unrelated to her. She reported that she became foggy but extremely frightened, and that she would keep thinking that her husband should never raise his voice if he loved her. Because she was frightened that her husband would hit her as her father had done, she would usually scream back at him as a way to stop his behavior. He would become confused and feel controlled over something that had nothing to do with his wife. Because she could dissociate fairly well, I suggested that she construct a scenario in which her husband would raise his voice over something unrelated to her and she could dissociate more readily. She practiced going deep into a forest to a special secret place where no noise could be heard at its full volume. The husband realized that he was being self-indulgent and acting immaturely when he yelled loudly in reaction to frustration. He began to review a scenario in which he would first yell for a shorter period of time than usual and, if need be, go for a walk. During the process of therapy, each was able to learn to identify and manage feelings that had previously felt beyond control.

States of Consciousness Dialogue

A powerful intervention that utilizes dissociation is to have the patient dialogue with different parts of the self that are in conflict. Beahrs (1982) and Watkins and Watkins (1979) suggest that we are all conglomerates of different "selves" or states of consciousness that are "co-consciousness." People in painful conflict often wish that a part of themselves would dissolve or disappear. Because they have difficulty appreciating what each state of consciousness does for them, they are likely to want to eliminate the state. Separating the different ego states involved in a conflict and framing the "negative" part as an important, useful, or protective part are often helpful in the integration of these aspects of the self.

A mistake therapists often make is to ask patients to move from one intense state of consciousness to another by focusing on a conscious selection of alternative forms of action. Patients then end up being "resistant," and they struggle with the therapist. As a result, everyone feels like a failure, which is not good for the therapist's reputation, state of mind, or for the patient's potential to master the problem. Rather than attempt to move from a negative state into a positive state, it may be more useful to transform the negative state by first dividing it into parts and then encouraging some dialogue among the parts.

The therapist may ask the patient to identify those aspects of the self that are in conflict and name them. These parts may take on male, female, or animal identities and will represent different qualities of the individual. In working on a marital issue directly, the therapist may want to ask the patient to name the part of the self involved in the conflict that is represented by his or her spouse and to develop a dialogue among the states of consciousness.

The states of consciousness may be divided into emotions rather than personalities, and a similar working through to integration may occur. One adult woman of about 34 years old, who was married and was hospitalized for cocaine abuse, talked of an incredibly abusive family background. Her mother would beat her, numb herself through alcohol regularly, and withdraw into the bedroom. Her father, attempting to be both mother and father, moved too close to this woman and made her his confidant, companion, and wife on a symbolic level. She spoke of this background as though it had been normal. It was a shock to her to discover that functional families are not abusive. Her family background created difficulty for her in divorcing from her father and establishing her own family. This woman identified a pattern in relationships with men of enraged outbursts and pushing them away, followed by depression and confusion about what had happened. She could only label feelings that she had when she was unhappy about a potential partner's behavior. As I explored with her the complex of feelings that she called anger, she identified first a feeling of disappointment in her partner. The disappointment washed over her like an enormous wave when her partner failed to match the inner image she maintained about a man in relationship. She described the men to whom she found herself attracted as kind but quite distant and withdrawing in the face of conflict. When a man would act in a gentle manner toward her, she would feel needy and desperate to have his attention and would sacrifice all of her desires in order to please him. This patient said she was searching for mothering in distant, emotionally unavailable partners, a recreation of the relationship she had with her mother.

The next stage in the complex of feelings was depression. She said, "The next feeling I have, if I think about it, is rejection. Then, instead of staying with that feeling, I push the man away and reject him in anger." She attempted to master or manage the feeling of rejection by flipping it into rejection of the other. Rather than being the one left, this patient could feel more powerful if she left the relationship first.

In initial trance work, this woman could dissociate easily. Once in trance, I asked her to anthropomorphize each of these feelings, and speak to each one as if it were a person (see discussion of my work in the chapter on "Diabetes Mellitus: Learning to Think for an Organ" [Achterberg & Lawlis, 1980]) In each of three chairs, she placed Loneliness, Depression, and Rejection. In dialoguing back and forth she discovered how each of these feeling "entities" were allies. Loneliness comforted her, Depression was a protector, and, when she sat in the chair for Rejection, something curious happened. She crouched into a little ball, her voice became quite young sounding, and she began to weep. I asked, "How old are you?" and she replied, "I'm four." She began to recount a situation where she wanted desperately to be with her mother, but her mother was drinking and completely unavailable for any contact. She felt rejected and alone, and she told me, "I can't get out of this feeling. This is the feeling I have all of the time." I suggested that she sit in the first chair and be herself.

ck: "Perhaps you could nurture this little four-year-old child."
pt: "I don't know how. I just feel so bad." (This woman had two children of her own, and had described earlier with warmth and pleasure how she took care of them.)
ck: "What would you do if your little one came to you crying and feeling rejected and alone?"
pt: "Well, I would hold her. (She closed her arms naturally around herself.) And I would tell her that she will be O.K., that I will keep her safe, and that I love her." (She kept repeating these statements to herself and sobbed. Finally, her voice changed and sounded steadier and calmer. She

stopped crying and began to feel more peaceful and comfortable.)

CK: "Your unconscious mind can remind you to talk to this little one from time to time."

PT: "I don't know what happened, but I feel better."

CK: "Your unconscious mind can continue to provide you with a sense of comfort and security and can continue to do the inner work you need for balance and satisfaction."

This patient began to interact differently with her current partner. She could no longer maintain the old ritualized pattern because she now had different associations and meanings for the feelings. She realized that the feelings belonged to a much younger person who was frightened and feeling abandoned and alone. At this point in therapy, we began to explore other resources from which she might draw to nurture herself. With the help of the hypnotherapy and hospital program, this woman went from being a brusque, intimidating, potentially explosive person to a kinder, more understanding, tolerant individual. Three months after her short hospital stay, she called to tell me she had broken off her relationship. She discovered that she was less needy and had found a man who was much more available.

This patient learned a great deal about being able to differentiate feelings, understand them, manage them, and change one feeling into another. She was amazed to find that she could exert mastery over emotions and behaviors that had seemed completely out of control. She discovered a power she did not know she possessed.

Learning how to change one feeling into another is useful for people who feel controlled by spiraling emotions. Dissociation can be a valuable instrument for change and management of strong feelings.

Dream Within a Dream

Dream within a dream is a device that utilizes dissociation, confusion, and deepening for trance work with individuals or couples. The therapist may want to have the protagonist—former client or a made up person—have a dream in which the dreamer dreams another dream related to the problem at hand.

One dream may carry a story line or just be a description of the protagonist's conflict, and the dream within can carry a well-developed metaphor and the "fundamental image," that is, an organizing image around which a story is built and which will enhance aspects of the person. Ego strengthening techniques may be incorporated into the dream within, such as, "You can really feel a sense of confidence growing every day as your unconscious continues to utilize your own inner resources to provide you with a greater sense of personal safety. You can have the ability to meet your own needs."

At times, one spouse will have a dream associated with the couple work. It is valuable to use the dream in the session as unconscious material, which the couple may have communicated about in their sleep. The therapist may also have the couple have a dream about the dream in the session. The therapist may use variations, such as suggesting each person have a dream about the other.

Dissociated Review of Past Event

If an individual or couple is blocked from experiencing feelings or cannot contain them, a significant event from the near past may be reviewed as if the person were watching it occur on a video cassette recorder and monitor. All of the controls can be used—start, stop, pause, fast forward, and rewind. By slowing the event, the therapist can assist the individual in discovering the point at which he or she used anesthesia to numb feelings and dissociate from them. In cases where the patient is unable to contain emotions, the therapist can pinpoint where the dissociation from cognition takes place and work with the various "controls" on the VCR so that containment of the affect seems possible.

Entering the Skin

When the couple is locked into a conflict but nonetheless wants to resolve problems, the therapist may have each partner "enter the skin" of the other, taking on the feelings, perspective, and central life dilemma. The couple can review from the perspective of the other partner a scenario that involves the conflict in which they feel stuck. Being able to experience the emotions, beliefs, attitudes, and the "insides" of another can lead to a deeper understanding and willingness to cooperate. There is an electrical resonance between marital partners that is unique. Exchanging "skin" can enhance the connection and make the resonance more pronounced.

Catching the Holes in the Sound

Often partners become mired in a struggle over something, and, rather than being able to hear the one another's feelings, they become reactive and blaming. The therapist may want to suggest two activities in trance: First, that each partner listen for the "hole in the sound" or what is really being experienced by the other by focusing in the sound of his or her speech and the space in and around the sound. The space in the sound reveals what one's partner is really feeling and struggling with, which has little to do with the other spouse. The problem is separate from the partners, and a focus on the problem can be beneficial. However, when the partners are too stuck to objectively separate the issue from each other, catching the hole in the sound may be useful. Second, the patient may be taught to listen for the pause between when the partner stops talking and one's own response. This pause is the space in which the decision to respond in a certain way is made after having reviewed several responses on the inner movie screen. Often people will complain that their responses are not within their control. Once they begin to listen for the hole in the sound, they may be more inclined to select the response that will have a better outcome.

Siding Descriptions

Couples often come into the therapist's office with entrenched interpretations of their partner's behavior. The interpretation usually involves some malicious or pathological intent where none actually exists. The patients usually want the therapist both to believe their interpretation and to help them let go of it. An example might be a wife and husband who are fighting over the husband's temper tantrums. The more she demands that he act like an adult rather than a child, the more he may defend his behavior. The therapist can respond with: "Does your husband have a temper tantrum when things do not go his way (the wife's description) or is he overcome with fear and panic and having difficulty knowing how to manage these feelings that therapy can help him master?" (Hill, 1986, personal communication). The negative frame for the husband's behavior is placed side by side with the more positive, workable frame, so that both partners may focus differently and move out of their looped, hurtful communication. As the wife begins to alter her perception of her husband, viewing him as having some difficulty over which he can gain control rather than as hopelessly immature, the husband can begin to work more competently to manage feelings.

Being Inaccessible

When one person always feels the need to be accessible to the other and consequently centers his or her life around the partner, the relationship eventually becomes enmeshed. Often, the passion dies. However, taking the time to take care of personal needs protects the individual against exhaustion and burn-out. Burn-out occurs when an individual sacrifices his or her own needs to take care of those of another. In addition, the other person will feel overly indebted and begin to experience exhaustion.

Fusion results when dissociation is over-operating so that neither person has a strong sense of himself or herself as separate. Couples can utilize dissociation to become appropriately inaccessible and to foster the movement back and forth from a psychological sense of being together and to one of being separate. The therapist in conjoint or individual sessions may use suggestions that facilitate this movement.

AGE REGRESSION

Age regression is the ability to experience oneself as younger —physically, emotionally, and cognitively. During stress in relationships, people usually regress to their most vulnerable age when they felt small, helpless, unprotected, and alone. However, it is also possible to regress to pleasant times. One patient was regressed to retrieve a feeling of worth and importance from a favorite birthday party, from the first time a boy recognized her in front of her friends, and from earning her first paycheck. There are several techniques that utilize age regression as a trance phenomenon.

Stopping the Internal Dialogue

Because people usually employ the same resource over and over, they often become stuck in a state of consciousness that may not be useful for a particular problem. In relationships, we have a tendency to activate familiar resources. We tend to create a familiar world by reviewing and overlaying the past onto the present in order to reassure ourselves that the world continues to *be*. Our usual reactions to stress—whether frustration, fear, depression, or disappointment—are learned. They reduce anxiety. Soon they become well-developed skills. All of these skills become important functions in a person's life, ones that may not be growth-enhancing in themselves, but that may, in an altered form, serve as accessible resources.

There are several ways to stop an internal dialogue that helps maintain an unproductive state of consciousness. If one partner develops an internal dialogue of anger, criticism, and sarcasm related to his or her partner's behavior, changing this state of consciousness may be difficult. The therapist may want to suggest that being irritable or angry is a reminder that the patient might be avoiding taking responsibility for the acts that brought him to the state that elicited anger. An alternative interpretation might be that the feeling exists to alert the patient to the fact that she or he had been avoiding something that needed attention, that is, the feeling was actually a resource to restore a sense of inner balance.

In order to interrupt the internal dialogue, the therapist can work with the patient to disarrange the usual context by helping the patient to alter his or her perspective. The therapist might suggest that the patient take all of the defenses revealed through the internal dialogue and visualize them in the form of shields. These different shields serve to protect the individual and couple from the difficulties of everyday living. The shields represent all of the the activities in which a person engages that have some protective quality. Each shield may have a different form, color, and decoration. The therapist can work with the patient to change the look, structure, color, or protective location of a given shield, and the attitudes, emotions, and behaviors connected with it.

If a patient is stuck in obsessive thinking about what he or she cannot do, the therapist can suggest that the individual lie to change the inner dialogue. For example, knowing that a patient constantly rebukes himself and obsesses about how incompetent he is, the therapist might suggest that for a period of eight days, the patient should lie to himself. Rather than telling himself that he is incompetent, the patient is to lie and say that he is extremely competent. The purpose of this exercise is to teach the patient that both are lies. This paradoxical strategy is similar to those designed by Erickson to create therapeutic double binds.

Another method to help a patient interrupt the inner dialogue and to change his or her state of consciousness is to make a visit back in time. Erickson believed that one's perceptual history could be altered through age regression techniques such as those described in *The February Man* (Erickson & Rossi, 1989), where an adult person may go back in time to a past event when the patient was younger and more vulnerable. The adult can act nurturing or protective of the child or give some advice. Adding to this technique, the therapist may wish to create in trance the "holding environment" of an individual by suggesting a warm, nurturing female figure and a nurturing male figure to go back in time with the patient to a younger, more difficult age and to protect the patient as a review of a traumatic incident is completed. The two figures may help change the outcome of the trauma or they may be there to protect the patient from danger and harm.

Developmental Task Completion

A nurturing figure may be used with a patient who is age regressed to relearn those developmental tasks that have been either incorrectly learned or completely unlearned. The therapist may want to take the patient in metaphor back through the phase of maternal infant bonding, where, especially during nursing, the infant suckles and licks the area around the nipple, gazing; where infant and mother look into each other's eyes with delight, touching; where infant and caretaker feel each other's skin with sensual pleasure, smelling; where infant and mother or father enjoy each other's scent, hearing each other's voices, and moving in synchronized rhythm. The therapist may suggest in trance that each parent hold the infant and move through these early attachment behaviors to complete the crucial task of attaching (Erickson, 1988, & J. William Wade, 1989, personal communication). The developmental tasks that were incomplete may be recreated through age regression. Object constancy, for example, can be learned by the patient as one nurturing caretaker suggests how to take a "picture" of the other caretaker and look at it on the inner movie screen while that caretaker is out of the room.

Affect Bridge

The affect bridge, first described by Watkins (1971), allowed a patient to retrieve an original feeling or event and to place it in the appropriate context. The therapist may ask the patient to focus on the recurring feeling or body symptom and use that feeling as a bridge back in time to the first time the patient experienced the emotion or symptom. Using this technique, the therapist may discover what developmental task was left undone. The original conflict, which may be operating hidden from view, can be brought to light. A link to the present problem may be made clear to the patient, thus allowing the therapist to proceed with the resolution of the problem.

Retrieval of Resources

The couple may be asked to go back to a more positive time, to remember the warm feelings and the strengths they experienced in each other. Revivifying thoughts, feelings, and behaviors and then linking those resources to the present can be accomplished by asking the unconscious minds of the partners to develop a solution to the present problem while holding on to those positive feelings (Protinsky, 1988).

Alternate Past Selves

The couple may be asked to go back in time to meet themselves the way they were when they were first together before they married and to give their younger selves advice to help them avoid certain obstacles. Additionally, the couple may go back to a time when they were courting. The couple then may be asked to see themselves paired up with different partners and to converse with them. They may be regressed to children and meet to talk about their fears or joys. Each partner's adult self may accompany the child self and dialogue with the other partner's child and adult self.

AGE PROGRESSION

Age progression or pseudo-orientation in time is a trance phenomenon whereby individuals or couples are progressed into the future to a time when a particular goal has been accomplished. They can review the goal in terms of attitude, affect, and behavior. A patient may select the future time or the therapist may select a general future time indirectly accompanied by amnesia for the suggestion. Richard Bach (1977) commented on the importance of an imagined possible future: "You are led through your lifetime by the inner learning creature, the playful spiritual being that is your real self. Don't turn away from possible futures before you're certain you don't have anything to learn from them. You're always free to change your mind and choose a different future, or a different past" (p. 51). Several age progression strategies can be beneficial to couples in conflict.

Crystal Ball Technique

Erickson used this technique by having the patient hallucinate several crystal balls. In each crystal ball the patient was induced to see various emotionally significant experiences at different times. The scenes were locked in the ball in order for the patient to review each scene, which included behaviors and emotional reactions. Then, the patient was projected to a time after the therapy had ended and the goals were achieved. The patient reviewed the crystal balls of the past from this safe distance. In another series of crystal balls, the patient was asked to review his or her accomplishments, which were resolutions to the problems reviewed in the first set of balls (CP IV, pp. 397–407).

Unconscious Insight with Pseudo-Orientation in Time

When there is a need for understanding a current problem that is so emotionally charged for the partners that they cannot discuss it objectively, couples can be hypnotized conjointly and projected into the future. From this perspective the present problem can be viewed as evolving from some time in the past, a current difficulty, or an anticipated difficulty in the future. A more objective viewing of the therapy problem by the couple can lead to moving out of an escalating looped communication (CP IV, p. 424–426). Erickson suggests that the procedure begin with inducing at least a medium trance state and with having the couple dissociate from the surroundings. Suggestions for the unimportance of the day of the week or the particular month are given. Each partner can then move into the future to look back at the past—which is actually the present—from a new perspective. The fresh understanding of the problem will also contain the solution because the new perspective is from the future when the problem no longer exists. Suggestions for noting how the problem was resolved are given. These suggestions are followed by amnesia for time and place, but with an awareness of one's identity. The couple can often gain unconscious insight over the present difficulty with this strategy.

Alternate Selves of the Future

Partners can be age progressed to meet their future selves if they proceed along the same path they are presently traversing and if each partner makes particular desired changes. Three different futures may be constructed where dialogues take place with each future couple. The first two futures were described previously. The third future includes the partner being absent as in divorce.

It is typical to consciously imagine several different futures with one's partner. In trance, the unconscious may be tapped for ideas unknown to the conscious mind concerning the future.

Time Projection Through the Next Developmental Stage

When couples are floundering around a transition from one developmental stage to another, time projection that addresses task-specific behaviors, attitudes, and emotions can be useful. Suggestions concerning the accomplishments of previous stages through metaphor may be given to elicit feelings of self-confidence and an attitude that this task can be successful. Age regression may be used in conjunction with this strategy in order to resolve any past difficulty that may be keeping a couple from proceeding through the next developmental stage.

TIME DISTORTION

Time distortion is the ability to experience time as expanded or contracted in duration. The physicist Stephen Hawking (1988), uses the phrase "psychological arrow of time" to describe time moving from the past to the present to the future and our memory of the past as something stable and ordered. The second law of thermodynamics states that with the passage of time, disorder increases. Thus, the increased disorder differentiates the past from the future. The present and future are often perceived as unstable or disordered because of constant change. The past is perceived as fixed until some experience in the present stimulates a new perspective on the past, at which point, we could say that the past changes.

The subjective perception of time often is quite different from the actual duration of time. Cooper and Erickson (1959) suggest that "when there is a 'marked' difference between the seeming duration and the clock reading of a given interval, we say that 'time distortion' is present" (p. 2). The "seeming duration" is that perception of how much time has elapsed. Sometimes, the more we enjoy an event, the more we shorten the time to enjoy it. The more painful we find an event, the more we expand the time to suffer.

Couples often experience time expansion when they feel loving toward each other. The process of sexual relating and orgasm for couples who are satisfied with each other is often an experience in slow, intense pleasure. For those who are angry with one another, sexual contact can seem to last about thirty seconds. In the midst of a conflict, time becomes contracted, slowed to an agonizing pace, and painful feelings seem to go on forever. In the flash of a few seconds, couples may review all of the other painful events in their histories that have been perceived as unfair and the result of the partner's "mean and inconsiderate" behavior. Two basic strategies may be used to help resolve conflicts, condensation of time and expansion of time.

Condensation of Time

Time can be subjectively shortened in trance so that partners can move beyond a particular conflict to its resolution when they feel warm and connected. The therapist may ask the partners to have a five-minute therapy dream about the problem in which there is some kind of resolution represented.

Eliciting this phenomenon can be accomplished by suggestions of pleasurable experiences—for example, vacations that seem to rush by or activities such as painting or singing where one's focus is highly concentrated. This resource can be linked to reducing the subjective upset of a marital partner's behavior.

Expansion of Time

Perceived time can seem as though it is passing much more slowly than the clock actual shows. However, positive feelings between partners can be suggested to expand in duration, with negative feelings contracting in duration. For many people the distinction among past, present, and future is only an illusion, even if a stubborn one.

ANALGESIA/ANESTHESIA

A naturally occurring trance phenomenon is anesthesia or analgesia, where physical feelings are forgotten or changed by focusing on something that absorbs attention (CP IV, p. 224). Everyone has had the experience of developing an anesthesia for the sensation of certain clothing, shoes, or underwear, for example. A splitting headache can move so far into the background when a person's attention is absorbed by an interesting story or an exciting sports event that the headache is hardly felt. We can fail to notice all kinds of physical sensation.

Often when there is sexual unresponsiveness with one partner, analgesia/anesthesia is being utilized for protection. There may be a natural numbing response because of early trauma or restrictive teaching where loyalty to the family system prevails over physical pleasure.

Anesthesia can be used by women who want to experience childbirth without medication or patients who have chronic pain. Any kind of chronic discomfort eventually affects a couple's relationship by becoming a focal point around which the couple system may organize. The therapist may begin indirectly inducing anesthesia by asking about the pain and then diverting attention to some other more pleasant topic. Suggestions about the numbing effects of snow, ice or Novocaine can be made to enhance the anesthesia.

AMNESIA/HYPERMNESIA

Amnesia is the natural forgetting of events, whereas hypermnesia is the ability to remember minute details of events. Amnesia can be viewed on a continuum from temporary forgetting of the recent past to a deeper forgetting wherein traumatic memories and feelings are buried. It is often the case that a person who is adept at amnesia will marry someone who is expert at hypermnesia. Conflict arising from "archeological" expeditions that dredge up buried artifacts from historical experience can lead marital partners into painful pursuits and withdrawals. In the midst of a painful conflict, amnesia for loving feelings is utilized as is hypermnesia for hurtful behaviors, so that the downward negative trance spiral is difficult to stop.

The therapist should foster hypermnesia by suggesting to the couple indirectly that they may want to review their courtship and particularly their satisfying times together. The partner who is able remember minute details can be asked to stimulate the memory of the other spouse by recounting places they went, people they were with, and objects they may have purchased to represent those good times. A review of how the two overlooked certain irritations then (negative hallucination) and actually forgot them because their focus was on the pleasant feelings and resonance between them can be suggested by incorporating negative hallucination and the ability to use amnesia. Hypermnesia can be employed to have a partner really notice something important about the other spouse that may have been overlooked and that contributes to the well-being of the relationship.

POSITIVE AND NEGATIVE HALLUCINATION

Positive hallucination is the ability to perceive something that is not there. Everyday examples include seeing a particular book on the shelf only to discover that, once it is removed, it is not that book at all. Many people have had the experience of regularly driving into a parking lot that has a protective automatic arm that raises and lowers as each automobile pulls in to park and seeing the arm as actually there even though it has been broken off. These hallucinations can also take the form of auditory hallucinations. Positive hallucination may be used by the therapist to suggest that each partner view in a crystal ball or on a theater screen the particular response he or she wants to make in a stressful situation.

A second kind of hallucination that is naturally occurring is negative hallucination. Negative hallucination is the ability not to see something that is actually there, for example, when someone cannot find house keys that are in full view. That individual may look at the keys directly but not be able to see them. Not noticing sounds, or physical sensations, or certain visual cues might be used as a resource in marital therapy. Most marital partners develop certain ideosyncratic irritations with their partners. Paying attention to "that tone of voice" or that "look" can cue the beginning of an escalating conflict. The therapist may interrupt the pattern by suggesting that spouses fail to notice certain cues and attend to some element that is more enjoyable (Lankton & Lankton, 1983, 1988). It may also be important to discover the person's association with the annoyance so that it can be completely resolved.

Depending on the goal of therapy and the trance phenomena that are presently utilized by the couple, one or more of these strategies can be used. In order to interrupt an interaction that begins with an intense fear and leads to negative feelings, the following strategy may be used. (This strategy should not be used if abuse is present.)

Fear is often unintentionally elicited by one spouse from the other, which marks the beginning of the dysfunctional looped interaction. The feeling triggers an age regression and negative trance state. When the feeling of fear can be identified by one or both marital partners to be a trigger for the hypnotic dance, the therapist may teach management of the feeling through the following protocol. The patient can practice and use the skills to interrupt a usual response, and the dysfunctional pattern will be interrupted. The following steps may be taken after trance has been induced. The quotations following each step are from the video tape of Erickson working with Monde (Erickson & Lustig, 1975), and are illustrative of the steps that teach a patient how to carry a feeling of safety and security with the hypnotic protocol.

1. *Suggest indirectly that the past events may be viewed from a distance.* "Now, while you go deeper and deeper into the trance, it is as if you're traveling a highway, passing this scene, that scene, in your life. And perhaps something very nice that you could recall that you haven't thought about for years."

2. *Retrieve a positive memory from childhood of safety and security that can be utilized in adulthood.* "And I think it would be most interesting if you would find some childhood, infantile memory that you haven't thought of for years—such as the time when you discovered you could stand up and the entire world looked different."

3. *Introduce further dissociation through using a trance phenomenon such as hand levitation and continue to suggest a positive childhood memory.* "And your unconscious is showing that jerky movement (referring to the patient hand levitation) because your unconscious has allowed your conscious mind to use fluid movement. And sooner or later, I don't know just when, you will be wondering about something that you would like to see."

4. *Have the patient visualize a happy scene and open his or her eyes to see the therapist as this scene is viewed.* "Now somewhere out of the past you'll come upon a happy scene. And I want you to visualize it. A happy scene . . . you don't have to have everything, just the happiness. . . . Let's see if you can open your eyes a little bit, and be alone with me. . . . And I want your attention just on me, while you sense and see that scene from the past."

5. *Have the patient memorize the positive feelings.* Monde remembers being two years old and splashing in a lake. Erickson emphasizes the good feelings. "And memorize all those good feelings, because there's a lot of them. It's a learning. . . . Just as learning an alphabet and learning to recognize letters and numbers is the basis for an entire future of reading, writing, enumerating, so are the good feelings of splashing with total abandonment in water. Something that you learn and will stay with you in later life to be used in a directed fashion."

6. *Elicit a second positive memory and review the good feel-*

ings. Monde has another positive memory of herself chasing ducks and being carefree. "And she needs to learn that enjoyment. 'Cause along life's highway are various things and you had to learn the things. And discover later how you can use those learnings."

7. *Have the patient close his or her eyes and have a negative memory from childhood.* Erickson asks Monde to have a bad memory with her eyes closed. She remembers kicking in a window at school and feeling shocked that it broke. Erickson reframes the event by saying. "It's nice to learn what a shock is, isn't it?"

Erickson paces, retrieves a memory and feeling, and reframes it into a new learning that he says an adult can have and understand, more so than a child. He follows this with retrieving a feeling of security and safety.

8. *Recall the positive feelings and suggest the patient can change the feeling by opening his or her eyes.* Erickson suggests to Monde that as soon as she shuts her eyes she will begin to feel uncomfortable and then comfortable when she opens them under his direction. He repeats this process and says: "And you can afford to suffer and feel miserable because you know that when you have really felt it thoroughly, you can open your eyes and banish it."

Erickson has Monde examine the uncomfortable feeling and suggests that she is getting through it. Then he has her open her eyes and see what she is doing across the room as a two-year-old child. She can maintain the positive feeling as an adult.

9. *Review the negative feelings again.* Open the eyes to eliminate the feeling. Review the positive feelings that were memorized while attempting to hold the negative feeling concurrently.

Erickson has Monde remember a spanking she received. He tells her she thought she was not going to live through it but she did, just like most troubles. She did live through it, and she can live through other troubles. He then has her experience a worse spanking and he says: "And there's gonna be some hate in you, for that spanking—hate and anger and pain. . . . And feel it all. And you're going to feel some 'never again.' And now you're going to feel 'I can live through this, and never again will I have that spanking and that hate and that anger.' " Erickson has Monde thoroughly review the feeling of pain so she will know that she can tolerate it. However, he suggests that she will never have that painful experience again as an adult. Neither does she need to maintain the hate and anger over this event that can remain in the past, but at the same time, be thoroughly integrated.

10. *Review a negative situation in the present in relation to the person's spouse using the retrieved safety resource, and then review the worst possible situation with the spouse and have the patient open his or her eyes to eliminate the bad feeling.* Follow this by reviewing the positive feelings of security and safety. Have the person review the negative situation with the positive resource.

Erickson suggests to Monde that the adult Monde will meet him, the one with feelings of security and comfort. He says: "Knowing that when discomfort strikes you, you can close your eyes and then open them." He then has her practice how to banish negative feelings by closing her eyes and opening them again. He gives her an important future-oriented suggestion when he says, "You can pretend anything and master it."

The statement, "You can pretend anything and master it," contains a powerful strategy for overcoming learned limitations and practicing a desired skill. Trauma can be resolved that may be keeping a couple from enjoying their relationship. In the next chapter, the effect that early trauma can have on a relationship is discussed in terms of marital conflict or psychosomatic illness, and specific strategies for resolution of these conflicts.

9

The Role of Trauma in Marital Conflict

Psychological trauma occurs when an individual suffers intolerable fear in the wake of an overwhelming life event. A child who experiences repeated family trauma may escape from the pain and fear through a dissociative process. During the trauma, the child may see with blurred vision or actually have out-of-body experiences to protect the self from danger. While the abuse is occurring, the child dissociates through the experience of being somewhere else, or watching from a distance, or actually *being* someone else. A series of traumas, shocks, and repression of feelings and memories can lead to emotional shutdown and overwhelming fear, which can become easily triggered by any symbol of that memory. A look, gesture, sound, touch, picture, facial expression, or tone all can act as deep trauma activators and stimuli for negative trance. When this state of psychophysiological alert is triggered as an adult, it may manifest itself in marital conflict, psychosomatic illness, depression, or "fading out," which is a period during which a person may dissociate and entertain himself or herself with another world or fantasy and be unaware of what is happening in the immediate environment. Once the person returns to a conscious world, there may be deep feelings of shame. This chapter examines the dissociative process utilized in reaction to trauma and its treatment through the use of Ericksonian psychotherapy.

When trauma occurs, several levels are affected: emotional, physiological, and behavioral. The affective experience may include a feeling of numbness, helplessness, feeling out of control, overwhelming fear, and depression. There is often an amnesia for the event and repression of memory and feelings. Later, an individual may demonstrate a startle response, extreme sensitivity to noise, emotional anesthesia, inability to feel, alexithymia, inability to recognize feelings, and conversion to somatic symptoms. Behaviors may include hyperalertness, withdrawal, moodiness, distancing from people, and difficulty in continuing friendships. Other behaviors may include overworking to maintain distance from others.

At a physiological level, certain dramatic changes occur. Inescapable stress depletes norepinephrine, dopamine, and serotonin—important neurotransmitters that are used by the brain to maintain the motivation for performing a task. Following inescapable shock, catecholamine is also depleted and results in reduced eye blink, coarse tremor, and reduced job functioning. The depletion of neurotransmitters results in startle responses, explosive outbursts, nightmares, and intrusive recollections (van der Kolk, 1987).

ADDICTION TO TRAUMA

Researchers (Bowlby, 1973, 1984) have suggested that an unresponsive or abusive early environment can stimulate the emergence of a hyperanxious state that can have long-term effects on a child's ability to manage anxiety and aggression (Green, 1978; Lynch & Roberts, 1982). The constant and inescapable stress of abuse elevates beta endorphins, which have been reported following surgery, gambling, and marathon running (van der Kolk et al., 1985, p. 72). The reason traumatized individuals reexpose themselves to stress such as abused children who often engage in self-destructive behaviors, or adults who recreate abusive relationships from the past, may be linked

to the endogenous opioid release that produces a state of relaxation. Some people are aware of the constant crises in their
lives.

One patient avoided paying government taxes for years. He
boasted about not having been prosecuted but knew it was just
a matter of time. He involved himself in one crisis after another
from an affair with the woman he eventually married, which
cost him his job, to financial deals that brought him perilously
close to disaster. His wife, because of strong religious mores
against divorce, stayed in the marriage. She recognized a pattern of selecting men who needed rescuing and then becoming
enraged and disappointed that the idealization of romance was
not realized. Her husband grew up in an alcoholic, abusive
family where beatings were common. His ability to trust was
minimal and emotionally he demonstrated a much younger age
than his chronological years. Each time he danced on the edge
of destruction, he experienced a feeling of euphoria. This behavior elicited both caretaking behavior and resentment from
his wife. The euphoria or pleasure release that follows an abusive act reinforces the behavior as a way to feel pleasure and
discharge tension.

Often, the psychological treatment of the trauma has emphasized revivification in hypnotic trance work, reliving the
trauma as a way to integrate it. However, if reliving is followed
by a conditioned endorphin release and subsequent hyper-
reactivity, bringing back memories of the trauma and reliving
them may actually make the symptoms worse and retraumatize
the patient. The therapist needs to ensure that the patient can
view a younger self from a safe distance where safety and security can be experienced.

Mary Jo Peebles (1987, 1989) has created an artistic example
of the "working through" process for post-traumatic stress disorder (PTSD) through analytic hypnotherapy. However, after
asking the patient to relive the terrible memory of awakening
during surgery, which resulted in PTSD, at the next session the
patient tells Peebles that she almost did not return because the
reliving caused more severe headaches and exacerbated her
other symptoms. Peebles then uses visualizing the scene on a
television monitor. Although Peebles is skillfully able to help

the patient resolve the trauma, it might have been easier on both the patient and therapist if indirect means had been employed much sooner. Therapy needs to be conducted with certain biological factors in mind. Erickson cautioned against the direct approach and suggested that the patient could review an event from a distance. He said, "You can . . . have the patient hallucinate a protective shield or an opaque cloth, and you can have that shield or cloth get thinner and thinner and more and more transparent in order to view the area of anxiety" (CP IV, p. 396). Erickson believed that the therapist would have more freedom to help the patient solve problems when the patient acts as an observer through dissociative review, the reviewing of a trauma from a distance either through metaphor or viewing the self from a distance, rather than actually reliving the historical traumatic event. To have patients relive trauma over and over essentially hypnotizes them in that traumatic pattern.

POST-TRAUMATIC STRESS DISORDER

Historically, the symptoms described above have been attributed to post-traumatic stress disorder, which is classified in the DSM-III-R as a psychological disorder. Post-traumatic stress disorder has been associated with war trauma (Kardiner, 1941). Later, the syndrome was described in relation to accidents (Lindemann, 1944), multiple personality (Braun, 1984; Bliss, 1980), rape (Burgess, 1974), incest (Courtois, 1988), abuse (van der Kolk, 1987), and borderline personality disorder (van der Kolk, 1987). Recently, the term "chronic shock" was coined by Carl Kirsch, M.D. (1987), personal communication) to describe the complex of symptoms experienced by adult children of alcoholics or any adult survivor of family trauma.

Anybody who has been through severe disruptions in family-of-origin life such as frequent moving, loss of employment by a parent, spanking and screaming as discipline, violence between parents, withdrawal of affection by a parent, death of a parent that is not grieved, or any event in a family that is perceived as overwhelming can become a victim of PTSD. If the event is not "named" to loosen the crystallized effect, integrated and understood, it may affect a person's behavior far into the future.

Many patients who present as depressed, anxious, or diso- riented and who have somatic complaints may suffer from chronic shock but they are often not diagnosed properly. They are sometimes diagnosed as having panic attacks, agoraphobia, depression, or anxiety. They may be viewed as experiencing marital conflict or somatic ailments. Correct diagnosis is cer- tainly integral to effective treatment. Patients who are assessed incorrectly often experience a diminishing of symptoms tem- porarily with psychotherapy, but eventually, the symptoms usu- ally return and the patient feels worse.

For no reason apparent to the patient, an individual may begin to experience nightmares, a flooding of feelings, uncon- trollable anger, or anxiety unrelated to the present. Usually, there is no conscious awareness of an event to which the feelings may be related. This "breaking through" of memories or feel- ings into the conscious awareness occurs because after so many years the defensive structure of the individual that kept certain events unknown usually breaks down.

The sequence in the process of developing "chronic shock" seems to follow these steps: (1) overwhelming life event or con- tinuous trauma, (2) emotional shock and numbing of feelings, (3) withdrawal, and (4) dissociation. The dissociation response is a survival mechanism used by an individual to withstand the trauma and maintain the self. This is followed by the devel- opment of a startle response, depression, irritability, sleep dis- turbance, and highly conflictual relationships in which reenactments of the trauma may occur. Within the marital re- lationship, various elements may act as reminders of the trauma, and the ensuing conflict may have little or nothing to do with the relationship itself.

STATE-DEPENDENT LEARNING

Erickson demonstrated that amnesias caused by trauma are psychophysiological in nature; the entire person is affected. There is often a "body" memory as well as an emotional state memory of the event. The dissociation that occurs and the con-comitant change in physiology can be treated through an "inner resynthesis" (Rossi, 1986) in hypnotherapy. Adult survivors of family trauma often present with an amnesia for the traumatic event but experience many feelings for which they have no conscious understanding. The reverse may also be true. The patient may present with an amnesia for the feelings and a memory for the event. The memory of one or the other is in the unconscious, but the individual has dissociated from the trauma in order to survive.

Cheek (1960) indicated that "hypnosis occurs spontaneously at times of stress, suggesting that this phenomenon is a state-dependent condition mobilizing information previously con-ditioned by earlier similar stress" (p. 108). He hypothesized that trauma leads to hypnotic dissociation in order to protect the self. This process occurs in a similar way to some animals who, in the face of danger, "freeze" and become cataleptic.

State-dependent learning (SDL) is not a new concept but it is an important one. In 1971, Fischer defined stateboundness: "Meaningful experience arises from the binding or coupling of (1) a particular state or level of arousal with (2) a particular symbolic interpretation of the arousal, experience is state-bound and can thus be evoked either by inducing—naturally, hypnotically or with the aid of drugs—the particular level of arousal or by presenting some symbol of its interpretation such as an image, melody or taste" (p. 373).

In some experiments with SDL, a group of subjects was taught nonsense syllables after having been given alcohol to the point of inebriation. After sobering up, members of the group were unable to remember the nonsense syllables. After becoming drunk again, they could remember them quite well. In addition to a drug effect, SDL has been shown to occur in certain mem-ory strategies, stress, and states of emotion (Henry, Weingart-ner, & Murphy, 1973). Sleep and circadian rhythm have also been shown to have SDL effects (Holloway, 1978). Bower (1981) reviewed the literature on mood-contingent SDL. It can be con-cluded that there is mood-dependent recall. The data suggest that mood that is natural, hypnotically induced, or drug-in-duced can be linked with the encoding and recall of memories.

There is a special neuropsychophysiological (NPP) state where each learning takes place. When the same NPP state occurs, whatever was encoded or learned in that state returns. From the literature on multiple personality disorder, we have discovered that what seem like strange phenomena are really extremes of a response pattern available to everyone. Multiple personality disorder occurs (often from severe child abuse) on the extreme end of a continuum of normal dissociation from daydreaming or natural everyday trance states through "repression, ego-states, extreme dissociation, and multiple personality" (Braun, 1984, p. 173). Different personalities often carry differences in immune response and disease states—one alter personality may have diabetes and another not, one might have excellent vision whereas the other needs glasses, personalities might have different heart rates, pain thresholds, and allergic responses. Current work is being done to determine if healthy states can be contacted and utilized in people who dissociate within a more normal range. Understanding that internal states are always interpreted by the individual can be useful to the therapist.

Patients who describe the startle response to loud noises or hallucinate some traumatic event from childhood and inappropriately overlay it onto the present have a certain level of high arousal and interpret it as "I will be killed." It can be useful for the therapist to help the patient re-interpret the kinesthetic experience in a more appropriate way than as a matter of life and death.

THE EFFECTS OF TRAUMA ON MARRIAGE

Adults who have traumatic family histories will tend to form enmeshed relationships with their spouses. The fusion is a defense against memories of being abandoned as a child. The worse the perceived trauma, the more an adult may fuse with another. There may be an "anxious attachment" between partners where they may trade overfunctioning behaviors and overresponsibility or counter-dependency. Any act of autonomy by one partner may raise abandonment fears in the other. To protect against the early memories of feeling so alone and helpless, one spouse may rage against the other. If one partner has little attachment to his or her family of origin, that spouse will likely pressure the other to provide all of the emotional support so that nurturance from the outside can be kept to a minimum. There may be a tendency to isolate from the community and draw the boundaries around the marital dyad very tightly (Krugman, 1987).

This suffocating fusion may cause each partner to feel trapped and alone. One couple told a story about such severe enmeshment that the wife obsessed about leaving the marriage, something upon which her religion frowned. The husband grew up in a home where rage was expected and conformity was demanded. He carried strong feelings of insecurity and fear, and to defend against them, he would follow his wife everywhere she went. He convinced her to work in his office so they could be together during the day. Anytime she wanted to meet friends or play tennis, her husband would drive her and either wait for her to finish or demand that she call him three times during the time away. If she "forgot," he would rage at her until she was remorseful. The wife grew up in a home in which her mother was victimized by her father's rage and belittling attitude and behavior. She never saw her mother stand up to her father and, as a result she grew up believing that women were weak and needed to be taken care of by a man, even if he were harsh in his manner. This wife had tried to bend to her husband's demands but she became increasingly depressed and angry, and she began to exhibit passive-aggressive behavior. Finally, she started to develop an interest in her tennis partner who treated her more kindly than her husband. Eventually, they found themselves having more than a game of tennis, and this wife's husband discovered their affair. At this point they entered therapy.

Another potential effect of trauma on adult marriage is that people who were abused as children often develop high susceptibility to being hypnotized (Hilgard, 1972). Rossi (1986) explores how trance becomes triggered through state-bound mechanisms. This same mechanism can operate between the marital partners. When a stimulus, which may be a spouse's behavior, triggers a certain state, a memory bubbles up and a psychophysiological process occurs suddenly. A state of alert and alarm penetrates the mind-body and the person will age regress and may have the same feelings he or she did as a child during the abusive event. Positive memories can be elicited in the same way. However, the individual who has had an abusive background will notice more of the startling and sudden alarm reactions than positive feelings. Thus, one or both spouses may be susceptible to a negative trance in the context of marriage. There may be a "flashback" to an earlier experience and a person can hallucinate a completely different experience of the partner than the partner has of herself or himself. Calof says that "to the survivor (who lives outside of time), the level of perceived reality of a 'flashback' to an earlier event is equal to the original experience of the event itself, or to ongoing present-day experience" (1989, p. 11). This experience may occur to someone who has had to endure other abusive experiences in being reared. The rather dramatic response of one spouse often elicits further reaction from the other spouse, which elicits further reaction from the first spouse. Circularity, reciprocity, and shared problems in identifying the feelings or dynamics result. As the dual reaction becomes escalated, neither partner may be able to described what is happening to him or her. In fact, they may only be able to express anguish, pain, anger, and fear through blaming and attacking maneuvers.

If early trauma is not resolved and integrated, it will interfere with facilitating a functional marital relationship in terms of appropriate perception of one's partner, the ability to manage affect such as pain and joy, and increased clinging or distancing behavior. A neglected or abused child has increased physiological arousal. The caretaker can reduce that arousal through nurturing behavior such as touch or verbal soothing. If the child is treated brusquely time after time, the level of arousal will be easily triggered and there will be ensuing panic and a chronic move toward quickly calming oneself through whatever means are immediately available—food, sex, alcohol, drugs, or compulsive behavior. As an adult, consolation may take the form of a dependent process in relationships where an individual will sacrifice his or her own needs in order to stay connected to some other person.

TREATMENT

Ericksonian hypnosis can be useful in the treatment of chronic shock that manifests in couple conflict or psychosomatic illness. Once this problem is assessed, it can be suggested that individual issues be given some separate treatment time where hypnosis is used with psychotherapy to retrieve amnesiac memories that are present in disturbing fragments, to integrate them, and to help change the inner images and feelings. At the same time, the therapist will want to help the patient make distinctions between the spouse and the conflictual internalized parent. Where the spouse may have similarities with a parent, the therapist will want to focus the patient on more functional responses than were used when the patient was a child. These responses can be taught directly through dialogue or indirectly through metaphor. The reworking of a recovered memory through age regression, the February man (or woman) technique, distant viewing, or conversational time trance that reviews the trauma in trance and from a distance can lead toward the integration of the memory by capturing a view from a different perspective, the perspective of an adult who has many more resources at her disposal.

One way to begin this process is to have the person set specific goals. These objectives may require the uncovering of memories and the resolution of trauma, which may either be known to the patient or not. The therapist will need to determine from the assessment if the patient goals are reasonable. If the goals are reasonable, an important therapeutic objective will be to help the patient learn how to modulate affect by slowly stimulating feelings and memories through dissociative reviewing of safety and security experiences. Trance phenomena such as positive and negative hallucination and amnesia can be elicited to prepare the patient for later reconstruction of a memory if needed. We should note that some patients believe that they need to remember every terrible experience. Reconstruction of memories is useful when there are upsetting fragments that intrude on daily living. However, a review of negative memories for the sake of review is not often therapeutic.

The therapist can begin to help the patient identify gaps in memory through the use of conversational hypnosis by asking the patient to identify his or her date of birth and then by moving forward in time by marking each year with the particular school year. Because this is a universal experience, a memory of a school year can trigger significant memories. Remembering the teachers, specific experiences, places, and other details will often stimulate a memory. When the gap in memory has been identified to represent a potential problem time when the possibility of trauma occurred, the therapist may use conversational age regression to move back before the problem time and then continue to work backward. Because of the possibility of triggering a flood of uncontrollable feelings, work should include preparing the patient through practice with eliciting safety and security resources.

The following protocol provides steps that will help the therapist to facilitate the patient's recovery and altering of a painful or traumatic memory.

1. Induce trance.
2. Give an indirect suggestion for memories from the past to be reviewed from a distance, scene by scene.
3. Begin with a neutral memory such as the first time we stand up and discover that the perspective changes.
4. Interrupt with the elicitation of a trance phenomenon, such as dissociation through hand levitation.
5. Intersperse suggestions of a pleasant childhood memory with the elicitation of trance pheomenon and deepen the trance.
6. Elicit feelings of safety and security by describing, in metaphor, a universal happy scene such as caressing a pet and feeling completely loved and accepted. Suggest that these will stay with the patient to be used later in life. To review another positive resource, a second happy memory may be elicited and the suggestion given again that this resource can be used in later life. Emphasize feelings of safety and security.
7. Give a suggestion for viewing through dissociation the child some time before the potential difficult time. Begin to alter the experience by introducing a figure of

comfort to whom the child may tell what is happening. This person may be the therapist or a trustworthy teacher.

8. Utilize dissociation by suggesting that the adult part of the person may watch the child part experience something painful. The therapist should continue to dialogue about what is happening with the patient.

9. Elicit a feeling of safety and security again and suggest that this feeling can occur immediately when the eyes are opened. Continue to retrieve comfort and security and dissociation through distant viewing. It is important to pace the patient carefully.

10. Continue to work carefully toward the most traumatic memory and continue to alter the memory with a figure (or figures) of comfort. The therapist should slowly help the patient build coping resources by gently encouraging him or her to see the child having a painful experience and reminding the adult part to give to the child resources that were needed in past. The therapist should avoid moving too quickly. If necessary, the patient can be instructed to slow down the observed memory. The patient may be able gradually to allow the painful feelings to surface in the child so that the learning that takes place is that the feeling can be survived, integrated, and changed. The patient can then open his or her eyes and experience the feeling gone. The therapist can then suggest that the patient leave these feelings and this event in the past forever.

The trance phenomena of amnesia can be used for hypnotherapeutic work after the memory is reviewed in trance. The therapist can suggest that as the conscious mind is ready, the inner picture can be completed. These steps provide the therapist with only one of many ways to resolve trauma that may be affecting a person in the present with lowered self-esteem, depression, or difficulty in relationships.

Another method of memory reconstruction might be using experiential assignments such as having the individual walk through his or her childhood neighborhood to see up ahead the younger child who is aware of feelings about certain events. This kind of experience activates the trance state and many of the senses connected to the memory, which usually involve a kinesthetic experience of skin feeling, sound memory, smell familiarity, and visual recognition. This method can be a powerful facilitator of recall. However, it should not be suggested until a positive relationship has been established between therapist and patient and preliminary work has been done in eliciting and building resources for this more difficult work. The patient needs to have much ego strength and ability to manage feelings before activating more difficult and sensory memories. The therapist should suggest that the patient has the ability to leave the scene or to slow down the memories as a protection before the actual visit.

One woman who was involved in a relationship conflict revealed a severe history of physical and emotional abuse. She came for therapy to deal with traumatic memories that had begun to surface after an automobile accident. The memories flooded her conscious mind and interrupted her daily life. Her self-esteem was extremely low and feelings of shame pervaded her contact with others. One trance session was designed to help her slow down the memories and view them from a distance and to help her differentiate feelings and accept them without shaming herself. She experienced some neurological difficulties as a result of the accident such as balance and visual problems. She had a poor relationship with both parents and was in need of much reparenting and healing of early wounds.

The sixth session began with exploring her memory to discover a figure of comfort.

CK: Were there any adults to whom you felt close as a child?
PT: I'm sure I must—I can't remember.
CK: I remember asking one woman, "If you could go back and select the parents you always wanted, who would they be?" She replied, "Well, I always loved to watch Roy Rogers and Dale Evans. (My client laughs.) And they had all of those children they adopted to love and raise." She said that she wrote a letter one time to Roy Rogers when she was a child.

He wrote back and sent her a picture. She treasured that picture for years. Every time she looked at that picture she really knew in her heart that he loved her.

PT: (Moves into trance and smiles and nods.) I spent time at another family's house when I was in kindergarten, and I always felt comfortable at the house.

CK: Did you enjoy being there?

PT: Yes.

CK: Did you like both the mom and the dad?

PT: Yes, they were both nice to me.

CK: So, you have a variety of good experiences you can remember now, and perhaps others you have not thought of yet, from interacting in that other more normal household.

PT: Yes, that's right. (She begins to recount other memories.) I had a teacher who was very nurturing, but I wasn't appreciative at the time.

CK: It's always difficult to know how experiences in the present moment can be used later. You can't even imagine sometimes until you have that future perspective—looking back. (I orient the client toward trance.) You can perhaps now make any adjustments to follow those nice feelings of being nurtured and allow yourself to become comfortable.

PT: (Adjusts herself in chair.)

CK: Now you have been in trance before, and you can begin your own unique process of going into trance—either by focusing on your breathing or some other way of turning your attention—inward. It is certainly nice to sit here and go into trance—taking a few moments for yourself. We go into trance every few moments naturally, but it is nice to do that now. Your conscious mind can have one thought and your unconscious another. Your conscious mind may want to know you can be safe in this setting. You have a variety of experiences being here and being safe. Trance is merely a personal experience you create for yourself. And your unconscious has the ability to protect the conscious from anything it doesn't want to think about. Just like you have a bicycle right now with a third wheel to maintain balance, the unconscious mind is like having even another wheel to have that sense of balance occur.

When a person stands up from sitting down, there is a natural balancing of weight on your two feet that you learned long ago—a learning that went into your unconscious mind so you don't have to think about it now. When you stand up, your hands grasp the arms of the chair so there are four feet balancing—then two as you let go. Your conscious mind can entertain one train of thought, and your unconscious mind another, because in trance a person can do two things at the same time.

You have been able to create certain sensations in your body before—perhaps a tingling feeling or part of your body going to sleep or a changing sensation just for the delight of it. [Further development of trance phenomena continues for a while.]

Those treasures that are sometimes undiscovered reside in a variety of learnings. [Induction.] Every child who begins to learn to walk—learns that sense of balancing on the feet. All the muscles coordinate in a particular way, and we really don't think about how that happens consciously. Once a little child has discovered that she can stand up on her own two feet—though it may be unsteady—until her legs learn how to walk, one foot in front of another, that learning goes into your unconscious mind and after a while that child doesn't even think about walking or running or skipping.

[Beginning the metaphor to address the attitude that she can manage negative memories and can retrieve positive memories.] A friend of mine told me about a trip she took on a train. And as a part of you continues to develop the level of trance that you would like to experience today, another part might be curious about what a train ride has to do with a new learning.

My friend had no idea what she would learn when she took that train ride that day. But she boarded the train with a friend. They were quite excited because they hadn't been on a train since childhood. They were going to travel cross-country for the experience.

When they found their seats and the porter came by and clipped their tickets, they settled into what was going to be an interesting adventure. The train started—clappity, clappity sound that seemed so familiar—a sound that she recognized. This train was quite different from the ones she knew. It had a very special compartment—with television sets, a place to relax where you can barely hear the wheels as they carry the locomotive. They could barely feel the bouncing of the train— a pleasant sensation—kind of like a rocking in the back of your mind.

My friend decided to turn on one of the sets and sat there with her friend. She had picked up a brochure that described the workings of the set—different from the usual television set. The reception of the television wasn't very clear because of all the signals the train was passing through, as they passed through town after town. This particular television set, the brochure said, could be oriented in quite a unique way to the person who had the controls. It said, "If you follow the directions carefully, you can create your own film. You have the ability to select characters, a storyline, and how interesting this is—just like participating in a live book that you write yourself—having the ability and control to change any aspect of it."

There were various themes a person could select, but the one my friend particularly found entertaining was about visiting a family where normal kinds of activities went on. She had studied a lot about families but this one could be interesting—to really observe a family in a normal everyday interaction.

She pressed one button and a question flashed up on the screen. "What character will you select and what names will you give to the mother, father, and children? What ages will they be?" She made her choices and typed them in on the computer board attached to the television screen. There was a pause— and you could tell the computer was operating to incorporate new information while retrieving other information—putting it all together.

The instructions appeared on the screen: "YOU MAY BE-GIN BY PUSHING THE 'START' BUTTON."

She began to watch a movie about a family. [Retrieval of positive nurturing from parental figures.] The mother in this family was very kind. She could certainly be firm with the children if needed. As my friend was watching this mother on the television screen, one of the things she noticed was how that mother really gazed at her children—communicating love and affection by the twinkle in her eyes—and how the children received and took it in, felt filled up. And how the mother played with the children. When the dad came home from work, he would take time to relax. Then, he would play with them— either throwing balls or joking. They would laugh and giggle and have a wonderful time. Soon Dad said, "In a couple of minutes, we need to stop the game so you can do your homework." The children said O.K.—reluctantly. And they went upstairs to study.

My friend noticed that there was much love in this family. People could talk to each other and act respectfully and caringly.

There was one small girl in the family, who seemed to need more nurturing that the others. Her mother sensed the needs of that little child. From time to time, the mother would ask her how her homework was going with a sincere, concerned expression. Mother turned to the dad and said, "She is such a good child. We're lucky to have her."

Then the screen changed and another instruction appeared: "TO MOVE THE SCENARIO YEARS INTO THE FUTURE, PRESS THE GREEN BUTTON." [Future self for more resource creation.] My friend said she was so curious about what kind of future this little girl would have that she pressed the green button. The screen changed and another question appeared: "HOW MANY YEARS INTO THE FUTURE?" My friend pressed TEN and the computer hummed and oriented to a new time.

A scenario began about the little girl who was now a young woman, and she was in a classroom. She had become an excellent student. Others would ask her for help. The young woman noticed how the others respected her abilities and knowledge. If they had a question, she would be the first one asked. She watched as the others received help from her and appreciated and enjoyed her company.

In a moment, the screen changed again and another question appeared: "HOW MANY YEARS INTO THE FUTURE?" She pressed the number TEN again. The computer oriented to ten more years into the future.

On the screen appeared the little girl, the older girl, and an older woman who all had similar features. They began a conversation.

The older person interacted with the other two and told them: "You may have many experiences now that you do not yet know how to utilize in your future. You may not know how your past can be a future present, a gift." [Suggestion that the learnings now will assist her in the future just like her previous learnings.] "No one ever can look ahead and predict just how you will use those learnings," she said. "But I am here from your future, having accomplished many things in my years." She continued, "I am successful. I have that feeling of self-confidence that you can have when you hold your shoulders back, head up, chin down. And I never knew all of the steps to take in order to get here, but from this perspective, I can look back and review them, one by one. All experiences look different from this future perspective, standing in the future looking at you, my past selves." She said, "I want to encourage you every step of the way. Every step you take, every day, you have a learning that your unconscious mind can utilize for your own growth—and sometimes those experiences are playful. Sometimes they are work, touching experiences—sometimes humorous—but every single experience, even the painful ones, can be important learnings—useful to your future." She said, "I never really knew that until I read a novel by one of my most favorite authors. In that story, he described a strange experience where he was flying in a bi-plane—one of those old planes with no ceiling. He had a number of questions about the way his life was going. As he was lost deep in thought, feeling a sense of freedom you can have when you fly the skies, suddenly he had the sense that someone was sitting next to him. He turned to look and saw someone familiar. Indeed, it was a man who smiled at him and said, 'I am from your future. I'm your future self.' The pilot thought he had flown too high and was lacking oxygen and was hallucinating. The man continued, 'There are a variety of experiences that are important for you, and I have come back to tell you. Some decisions you avoid making, when these new experiences will make your life richer and more pleasurable. Actually, I've come to tell you that you will make the right decision because I wouldn't be who I am if you didn't. So, cheerio.' The pilot said, 'Wait! Who are you?', but he faded away. The pilot was left with a funny feeling.

Having a visit from your future self can certainly be something to think about."

As my friend watched that scenario end on the television screen, she had that sense of the train again. The rhythm of the wheels going down the track—the right track toward her destination. She could even hear the whistle blowing. The train pulled up to the station. She and her friend walked off of the train. The first thing she eyed as she stepped off the train was a beautiful dark brown horse tied up to a rail. The stationmaster walked up and asked her for identification and told her someone had left this horse for her enjoyment. She was astonished but went over to the horse and felt an immediate rapport.

Upon her return and visit with me, she said one idea stayed with her. "Your unconscious mind—always helps provide you with experiences of learning—and how you can look forward to all of the many experiences that you have so you can look back and review all of the steps you have taken—all of the learnings you have had—too many to enumerate—too many to keep in your conscious mind—but your unconscious can keep them. Too many treasures for your conscious mind to explore, but your unconscious can and it teach your conscious mind something new.

Before she left the station, the stationmaster said, "Oh, by the way, that person gave me something else to give you." It was a little present wrapped in colorful paper and ribbon. She looked surprised. He said, "Go ahead and open it." She took off the ribbon, the paper, and opened the box, only to find another box wrapped up, smaller of course. She took the wrapping off the second box and opened it, only to find a third box. She laughed and thought this must be a joke. She opened the third box, took the wrapping off, and folded in a piece of tissue paper was some object. She unfolded the paper, and the object came into view. It was a gold coin, dated 1896. She turned it over in her hand and examined it carefully. "What a treasure," she thought. "I wonder how many people have held this coin, this relic from the past." She decided to keep that coin in a special place, thinking that "you never know exactly how a present can be used in your future."

This patient continued to work hypnotically until she felt a sense of mastery over her world. Because her balance was so precarious when she stood, I suggested that when she stood up, she look slightly to her right instead of straight ahead. This technique helped her learn to stand, walk, and eventually return to riding horses by compensating for the brain lesion she had received in the accident.

Several strategies for intervention in the hypnotic dance have been suggested in this chapter that are based on the trance phenomena partners already employ. The next chapter examines how illness can play a role in partner conflict.

10

The Role of Chronic Illness in Marital Conflict

The context in which we operate, in which we interact, some-times evolves more quickly than we are prepared to experience. Additionally, the context influences our response to what happens to us. As the context evolves, so do our reactions. Bateson emphasized this notion in *Steps to an Ecology of Mind* (1972): ". . . the evolution of the horse from *Eohippus* was not a one-sided adjustment to life on grassy plains. Surely the grassy plains themselves were pari passu with the evolution of the teeth and hooves of the horses and other ungulates. Turf was the evolving response to the vegetation of the evolution of the horse. It is the *context* which evolves" (p. 155). As we are part of the context, we evolve along with both our inner and outer environment. Therapists sometimes ask their patients to move too quickly, to move at a pace that is beyond their own ego capacity, and then protections from the unconscious over-compensate for what is needed. At times this creates more of a problem than the original problem.

Changes can occur within at the level of physiology in response to the context, which will affect our perceptions, relationships, and experience of well-being. External changes at the social or community level may affect our physiology as well.

Evidence is accumulating to suggest that perceived stress from outside leads to experienced stress within in the form of lowered immunity and concomitant disease. Unconscious processes affect the immune system and operate as part of a suspected dance, though the exact steps are unknown. In fact, these processes sometimes affect physiology by targeting organs with dysfunction.

In ancient times people believed that illness was visited upon individuals because of their sins. Today there are some who are proponents of the notion that people "need" their illness; that is, people cause themselves to become ill because of their runaway emotions, poisonous lifestyles, or negative thoughts. Certainly, these factors play some part in the development of illness. However, the etiology for many illnesses in our culture that have some relationship to stress, such as migraine or asthma, is multicausative.

The marital therapist who treats a couple where one or both partners have an illness should be cognizant of his or her own beliefs about the development of illness and the maintenance of health. Erickson believed that psychosomatic symptoms could be unconscious communication about a developmental conflict. Genetic vulnerabilities, defenses against stress, lifestyle, and the systemic context in which couples operate may lead to the development of health or illness. A simple explanation of physical problems may suggest a subtle blaming of a person for becoming ill. The unconscious can also be an instrument to influence health in a positive way.

Psychologist David McClelland (1984) conducted an experiment to measure the presence of immunoglobulin-A content in saliva. This substance kills viruses that can cause upper respiratory infection. McClelland had a group of students watch a movie about Mother Theresa of Calcutta who ministers to the sick. Half of the group decided that she was a fraud and too religious. However, the movie stimulated a sharp increase in the immunoglobulin-A. The researchers also used projective tests to conclude that the students unconsciously benefitted from the movie.

McClelland also conducted experiments with a healer who used humor with people who were developing colds. The healer significantly stimulated their immunoglobulin-A levels. Thirteen of the fifteen who received the intervention kept from developing a cold, and three of the thirteen who received a placebo avoided developing a cold. The therapist and the marital partner may be able to stimulate patients' immune systems through the interactions. However, marital partners may also stimulate the immune system in negative ways.

Physical symptoms may develop within the context of marriage. The symptom may be an expression of an organ vulnerability breaking down after years of negative and unresolved stress that results in maintaining negative images. The marriage may be one of those stresses where constant conflict and pain become internalized and the outward manifestation may be a mind/body difficulty. As the symptom is exacerbated, the marital relationship may change to accommodate the change. We can look at an example of how migraine plays a part in marital conflict and consider some treatment considerations.

When physical dysfunction occurs, the marital dance changes to incorporate a new dance step. As the problem develops it can take on a life of its own, and the illness almost becomes an entirely different entity in the relationship. One patient, who had developed migraine headaches several years after she married, always succumbed to excruciating headaches when her husband acted more distant and feelings of abandonment would bubble up. She had grown up in an alcoholic family and could describe many events of abuse such as having to sit at the dinner table with a broom handle through her arms to make her sit up straight. This woman had little affect in her descriptions. In fact, she was alexithymic except when it came to headaches. She was aware of feeling depressed about the headaches. The headache became a signal to her husband to offer more attention and nurturing so that the pain acted as a distance regulator and intimacy barometer. Of course, he would experience guilt over his distancing behavior and feel responsible for her well-being. This overdeveloped sense of responsibility led him to feeling trapped and alone.

The husband had been adopted by his stepfather when he was eight years old and he felt that he was constantly criticized by him. He was sent away to boarding school. As a boy, this man had felt abandoned; first by his biological father and then by his stepfather. He became angry and bitter. He developed a sense of entitlement but also struggled with a tremendous sense of failure and shame, feeling that no accomplishment was ever good enough. Perfection became his goal in every endeavor. He learned quite well how to focus on the negative aspect of an achievement so the feelings of confidence that usually accompany a success could not be elicited to support risk-taking behavior in the present. He would think about what he failed to do, even in a successful venture, so that each positive experience was flipped into a negative one.

It became crucial to treat the fusion and accompanying age regression and partner amnesia in the marriage, the developmental deficits in each partner, as well as the emotional components of the migraine reaction and management of early signs of the migraine. The symptom that developed in this case served as a boundary and a protection from experiencing anger. The husband kept "seeing" his mother when he looked at his wife. He had given his wife his mother's wedding ring, and when his mother died, he could hardly bear to see his wife wearing the ring. His mother had died at a young age from breast cancer. In fact, she had overcome the disease when she was much younger. When new but familiar symptoms returned, she chose to avoid having treatment until nine months later (a suicidal act), when her own mother died. Unfortunately, by then the cancer had metasticized, and she died quickly. This patient felt unable to say goodbye to his mother and seemed to be mired in grief some five years after her death. This husband would withdraw from his wife when she reminded him of his mother.

At the beginning of therapy, the wife described herself in a vivid metaphor of living inside a bubble from which she could not escape. From inside this bubble, she watched time go by and herself being alone, an image that represented her worst fear. As she looked forward into the future, she saw herself alone, a bystander to life. She noticed in therapy that each time she felt angry with her husband, the migraine occurred. In individual sessions she worked with placing the headache outside of herself in a colored shape and moving it out of the office, across the parking lot, and into the bayou that carried it far away. She was able to succeed many times in eliminating the beginning symptoms of a headache and found that by practicing this technique at home, most headaches could be interrupted. Toward the end of therapy, this patient became more socially involved, had fewer somatic complaints, and felt hopeful about her marital future.

Her physician was contacted early in the treatment, and he worked to find a medication that would be helpful to her as part of the treatment. Whenever medical problems such as this one are treated with hypnosis, it is important to work in conjunction with a physician.

As with most physiological disorders, migraine has a multietiology. Migraines can be triggered by a variety of things—certain types of food, birth control pills, premenstrual onset, and so forth. Usually, psychological conflict precedes an attack. There is little evidence for a particular personality type being prone to these vascular headaches, but those who tend to suppress anger may be more inclined to them. In this particular marriage, the recurring headache became another entity in the couple relationship. As the couple began to work out their marital conflict, resolve their individual issues, and develop a new sense of intimacy, the wife's headaches occurred less frequently.

The husband resolved his grief feelings for his mother and was able to recognize that his overwhelming fear of saying the words "I love you" to his wife was rooted in the fear that somehow he would disappear completely. In trance, he described viewing himself descend into a cavern. As he became visibly uncomfortable, I suggested that he see himself with a climber's rope attached for safety. He had recently taken up mountain climbing after a therapeutic task assignment of climbing Enchanted Rock, a hilly area not far from the city. He knew the feel and security of the safety rope. At the bottom of the cavern was his wife and warm feelings of love and acceptance. As he came closer to her, the anxiety increased. He began to cry and said that he wanted to accept her love, but that he was afraid he was not worthy of it. His lips involuntarily started a sucking movement, and I suggested he could see himself move back to regain a feeling of safety. He described the sides of the cavern as having a soft, slippery, warm feeling. A metaphorical story was introduced that concerned the successful birth of a baby and the bonding that should occur through sucking the breast, gazing into mother's eyes, and naturally separating from mother with warm feelings of being comforted in a much different way than when in the womb. The story took the patient through several developmental stages and ended with the mother and father feeling pleased by their son becoming a man and establishing his own separate life. This story was designed not to attempt to change his historical experience, but to suggest appropriate stages through which a person should evolve. Safety feelings were elicited and associated to both being separate and together, and self-image building through the metaphor was incorporated. The patient recognized important growth when he could finally feel close to his wife without anxiety and tell her he loved her.

A final case is presented to illustrate Ericksonian psychotherapy in the treatment of illness. The patient requested assistance with two problems: allergies and her marriage. The patient was a 67-year-old woman physician who wrote poetry and came for therapy to deal with "contact" allergies, a medical condition that results in inflammation of the skin in various areas when different common materials touch the body. Additionally, she indicated that her marriage was highly conflicted. Her husband had been diagnosed manic-depressive many years ago and suffered with extreme lability of mood. He was abusive when in a manic swing and quite critical when depressed. She had no skin disorder before moving to a large city where she knew few people. The patient also told me several sessions later that she had difficulty taking anything at face value and could be quite contrary with others. Her first inclination was to disagree with anyone with whom she had a conversation. A preliminary hypothesis was formed that she indeed suffered from "contact" allergies or fear of not being able to control situations and other people. The symptom limited her involvement with others.

The patient was delightful, intelligent, well read, and had wonderful poetic analogies that were stimulated by the hypnotic work. The transcript begins in the second session with an association of trance with her writing and some resistance begins after a different idea is introduced, which raises her anxiety. Steps in the model used in this book are presented as the transcript proceeds.

CK: Sarah, you know that when you write, you alter your consciousness in a particular way to go into trance and really focus on ideas.

(It is important to relate the trance experience to something with which the patient is already familiar.)

SARAH: That's true. You must concentrate.

CK: Yes. It's an activity you cannot force. You actually already know how to develop trance from your own work.

SARAH: I hadn't thought of it like that.

CK: Now, your breathing is a natural process. You breathe in a very particular way. You breathe primarily in one nostril and out the other. In fact, if you ever feel blocked in writing, you might find it useful to alter the hemispheric functioning by lying on your right side and opening up the alternate nostril. Hemispheric functioning is related to nasal dominance so breathing primarily through the left nostril can allow the right hemisphere to produce interesting images and metaphors for your work.

SARAH: (Interrupting) You know I don't really believe that. That is one of the techniques they teach in Yoga. I really think that is just an exercise and the only way to do that is to cover a nostril. I suppose that it is just to make you concentrate, but I don't really believe it.

STAGES IN ACTION

Observe the Hypnotic Dance

Now the patient begins to demonstrate her part of the hypnotic dance. My initial reaction is to want to convince her of the usefulness of this exercise, which is probably how other people react to her.

CK: That really does sound outlandish, hard to believe, even after you read the study done at the University of California, San Diego, (Werntz, D. 1981; Werntz, D. et al., 1983).

SARAH: Well, perhaps it is a learnable skill but I don't know.

Pace the Affective Reality of the Problem

Her response is continued disbelief, and now a shift is made to pacing to reestablish rapport that was disrupted from the previous comments.

CK: Certainly it is good to have a healthy dose of skepticism while you experiment with it.

SARAH: Well, if they have been studying it, maybe it's true. I just think it is a device to center your attention. But, if someone else has done it, well O.K., I'll try it.

CK: Being cautious about new ideas is important when it comes to trying them with yourself. Now, you have come here for hypnotic work today. I wonder if you are wanting to tell me any more right now?

A shift in ideas is important here so the patient can move away from this troubling idea consciously but continue to think about it on her own.

SARAH: Well, I'm perspiring. This fabric I have on is irritating to my skin.

Trapping the Attention

CK: Can you feel the air moving in here?

A disruption of the conscious mind set is utilized at this point to focus her attention away from the symptom.

SARAH: Yes. . . . This has to do with the fact that I overshot the street coming here. They have all that equipment out there. I do the same thing when I write. I perspire. It has to do with the fact that you are working.

CK: Yes, that is hard work. And the perspiration is a signal to you that your body is generating energy . . .

A reframe is used here to continue to disruption of the conscious mind set, but it is not accepted by the patient.

SARAH: (Interrupting) It's also a stress reaction. Oh, well, it happens when I've been writing and concentrating.
CK: As you pay attention to the air flow, you can perhaps feel it on your skin and your face, you can also feel how the air begins to cool that perspiration.

A refocus on what disrupted the conscious mind set before is now accepted by the patient.

SARAH: (Slowing down and beginning to develop trance) Actually yes, that feels very good.

Identify Which Hypnotic Phenomena Are Being Utilized

Now, further eliciting of the patient's ability to dissociate is explored.

CK: Good, and right now, you might begin to contrast how a part of your body feels as the air cools your skin.
SARAH: (Smiles and nods) That's very good.
CK: It's nice to notice a difference . . . in feeling comfort. That's right.
    Your conscious mind is familiar with a variety of topics, since you have lived enough years to develop a healthy dose of skepticism about things in general, and you can wonder about this experience in the back of your conscious mind, while your unconscious can allow you to ready yourself for some new learning. Certainly having a healthy dose of skepticism is important. Otherwise, you might buy something you don't want. As I am talking to you, your conscious mind might want to pay attention to my words, or go off somewhere and make up your own words, or do something else of importance, while your unconscious mind can utilize

my words in a way that seems most appropriate for your
learning and growth. I don't know if you can yet develop
a tingling in your hands, as you did the last time you were
here; maybe it might begin in the right. . . .
SARAH: Not yet. Wait, now it is happening in the left.

She demonstrates how she needs to stay in control of any
change even though the dissociation continues to develop
nicely.

CK: That's right. Your unconscious has selected your left to be
the right hand to have that tingling feeling . . . or just how
that tingling feeling will move up your arms while the other
hand might begin to have a lighter feeling.
SARAH: It is feeling like a heavy warmth.

Determine the Symbolic Meaning of the Problem

Again, the patient demonstrates oppositional behavior to the
suggestions. Permission is now given for her to have her own
response. Further evidence is mounting for the meaning of the
symptom to be a fear of being accepted and a solution to keeping her away from others. In the first session, she had revealed
that she often had an allergic response to her husband's cologne
when they were having sex, and she would need to withdraw
from the experience.

CK: Your unconscious mind has selected a feeling of heavy
warmth, and you can have a particular association with
heavy warmth . . . and your unconscious mind has decided
that it is the right arm and hand to have that light feeling
that can be left right there in that right arm and hand
and that feeling can shift; your conscious mind can be
aware of a variety of things.

Retrieve Resources

Other resources are now explored to eventually help the physical symptom and her interpersonal relating.

CK: Being a physician, you certainly are good with observations. Your unconscious mind operates all the time giving you messages about what to pay attention to, and what to push into the background. Everybody has had the experience of traveling by a familiar place and one day noticing one thing, and some time later traveling by the very same place and forgetting to notice that familiar detail, and really attending to something quite different so that the whole scene changes. It's an unusual experience.

A series of anecdotes to elicit positive hallucination as a resource is used for two reasons. Previously the patient had reported that just the seeing of a particular fabric could begin the symptoms. Also, she became overly focused on other people's responses, followed by a fear response, and she failed to receive any feedback concerning herself. Positive hallucination could be useful for both problems.

SARAH: (Ideomotor movements of the head indicate agreement.)
CK: Noticing what comes into the foreground and what can be put into the background. Most people have the experience that this just happens to them. That your unconscious mind selects those details for you to really notice and some things are important for your own well-being to just not notice. For example traveling in the car, . . . with a child can certainly be an obnoxious experience if that child is making a lot of noise or it can be a pleasurable experience if you focus on the sounds of a happy family and put the obnoxious noise way into the background. Everybody has had the experience of turning up the volume of the radio and turning it down; turning up a hearing device and turning it down [Sarah wears a hearing aid] . . . Most people don't know that they have the ability to turn up their own hearing and turn it down. But being a very astute observer, you already know how to change many different sensations.

Dr. Erickson, a famous hypnotist, told a story of spending an entire night in a boiler factory. When he first went there, the noise was just awful. Through the evening he had the experience of actually being able to tune out that sound and go to sleep. He discovered what you can pay attention to and what you can forget to pay attention to. . . . noticing that those things your unconscious mind brings to your awareness are there for some important reason.

Utilize the Symptom in the Intervention

The entire session has utilized the symptom by suggesting that she have the symptom but have it in a particular way. The symptom is now referred to at multiple levels and expanded upon to change the experience.

Everybody has experienced muscular pain here and there. You certainly know what it means to have an area of irritation . . . noticing it at first and feeling an annoyance and then you can begin to feel the areas of comfort outside the irritation.

Symbolize the Solution

The solution to managing the symptom is offered. The psychodynamic meaning of the symptom was as yet unknown so management was selected as a goal rather than amelioration. It was assumed that the symptom might be operating for a purpose but to a lesser degree.

. . . and then noticing just where the edge of comfort begins around that area like the shoreline of a lake of cool water; . . . focusing your attention on some other area of comfort like you can do when you have a mosquito bite. My father used to teach me as a little girl how to spoof a mosquito bite by lightly rubbing around the edges so the bite thought it was scratched and how that experience then changes. You don't really need to pay attention to every ache and pain, though certainly having pain is important, . . . sometimes an important signal. Your unconscious mind can be the guardian for any difficulty that you need to give attention to. That nice state of comfort can continue in the future while we explore other aspects of trance. Anyone who practices a skill notices that the skill becomes easier the next time, just like going into trance.

The above is a condensation of suggestions that have been given to elicit analgesia. At this point, further attention is paid to alterations in the patient's body, as trance is ratified, and the conscious mind is depotentiated.

Now Sarah was able to experience a feeling of heaviness that moves up the arms. Later she was able to change the feeling into numbness, utilizing anesthesia. As she practiced with this new skill and after about eight sessions, the allergic response that before occurred within five minutes of contact with certain materials did not occur before four hours. Even then, the irritation was much less severe. Sarah remarked, "I feel so much more mastery over this problem." After the symptom reduction, Sarah decided on her own that she wanted to be much less oppositional with people. She told me how she realized that her first response to other people's suggestions or opinions was always to be negative or to criticize them—that she had been oppositional with me. Using the affect bridge, she age regressed to a time when she had that oppositional feeling, and she discovered that underneath there was really a feeling of fearfulness. Surprisingly to her, she remembered being two years old. Her mother had become quite ill and was kept in a room far away from Sarah. She was unable to be with her mother for several months. When she was a little older, she remembered her mother mentioning to her father how Sarah seemed so reluctant to go anywhere or do anything without her. As an adult, Sarah had many fears about being able to drive somewhere new or meet new people, and she became isolated as a consequence. We proceeded with psychotherapy until she was able to retrieve safety and security resources in strange situations. The February Man technique was utilized so that a figure of comfort accompanied her back to the age of two years old to develop a new perspective in the present.

The February Man technique was developed by Erickson (Erickson & Rossi, 1989) as he worked with a young woman who was so lacking in good mothering experiences that she was afraid of being inadequate as a mother herself. Erickson used age regression in a series of therapeutic sessions and placed himself in her past as a kind old friend of her father who guided her through important experiences. The name February Man was derived from Erickson visiting the woman as a little girl on her birthday in February. After treatment, the woman was able to have a baby and mother her children appropriately.

After several sessions using an older woman to accompany her and interpret the traumatic experience she had at age two, Sarah brought me a poem. The title of the piece was "My Father's Back" and she repeated several lines from it.

> I don't know why we go over the old hurts
> Again and again in our minds, the false starts
> and true beginnings
> As if it could tell us of a world we call the past
>   who we are now,
> Or were, or might have been.
>
> *(Hirsch,* 1989, p. 38)

She told me that she no longer felt sad about that time in her past. It was over and completed.

In this chapter we have examined a variety of hypnotic strategies that may be used by the therapist. These are based on trance phenomena that couples may already be using. Any choice of strategy should be based on the individuals in the marriage; the individual and marital developmental stage and the particular idiosyncracies of the patients should be considered. The therapist should ask: Who are these people? What resources do they have? What are they attempting to learn?

Epilogue

Since Freud, the unconscious has been viewed as a seething cauldron of untamed passions and spirits that psychotherapy was designed to tame or vanquish. Milton Erickson was, perhaps, the first to view the unconscious as a reservoir of untapped resources or hidden treasures to be discovered and used positively. Rather than thinking of the unconscious mind as something to be controlled, Erickson discovered from his own life experience that within the unconscious are remarkable abilities or resources with which to master any life situation. These resources may be elicited through trance phenomena, symbol, and metaphorical experience—and they may redirect our own personal paths and spirits toward balance and harmony.

Milton Erickson is not alone in viewing psychotherapy as a process of connecting with the deeper self. Carl Jung, Karen Horney, Carl Rogers, Virginia Satir, and Carl Whitaker also hold this perspective. Erickson described this deeper self as "that vital sense of the 'beingness' of the self . . ." (CP II, p. 345). The object for the therapist is to tap into the unconscious wisdom and clarity and to help the patient see the world the way children often do: simply, precisely, imaginatively, creatively, spontaneously, and with a sense of connectedness to self and other. This alchemical adventure that is shared with another in marriage is the "grace of participation in another's life" (Campbell, 1988, p. 74).

In working with couples the therapist quickly becomes aware of the fact that each partner brings an individual unconscious and a couple unconscious to the situation. The task of the therapist is to align with the unconscious of each, and to appreciate the pain the couple experiences as well as the potential resources available in the unconscious interactional dance.

This volume has explored the use of Ericksonian hypnosis in marital therapy. We have examined the philosophy and ideas of Ericksonian psychotherapy, assessment and hypothesis building, metaphor construction, and strategies for intervention based on an integration of system dynamics and individual developmental issues that are always reflected in each partner's functional and dysfunctional attitudes, emotions, and behaviors. Out of the marital hypnotic dance that takes place between unconscious minds emerges intriguing and curious patterns. The unconscious minds find exquisite ways to dance together to create their own unique experience of intimacy. To see the dance as a potential positive force toward healing is to trust the power of the unconscious that can be evoked and utilized to transform a problem into a solution.

I have been a student of this dance in the marriages of my patients and in my own marriage for many years. However, it was not until Milton Erickson became a focus of my study through his students and family that I found a much more positive and hopeful approach to change. This volume synthesizes and interprets Erickson's approach as it applies to marital therapy. A bridge is built between systemic and developmental theory. Ericksonian hypnosis is incorporated as one major instrument for shifting couples' interactional sequences and their attitudes, behaviors, and emotions.

Purple haze has settled over the city this morning, as my stepson Chris points out to me. The sky is overcast and there is little wind. The purple tint has altered the shape of houses and trees so that surrealistic images come to mind; how fitting as I put finishing touches on this manuscript based on Milton Erickson's work. Purple was his favorite color. Perhaps the Chinese would surmise that the Dragon, the respected and loved guardian of inner treasure, is moving across the land. Perhaps he is.

Certainly, there are unconscious treasures that each of us

utilizes. The object of psychotherapy is to retrieve and use the resources that each person has—to recognize these resources as being pathways to transformation. In this dynamic relational process, both the therapist and the couple will find themselves learning new movements in the hypnotic dance.

Bibliography

Achterberg, J., & Lawlis, F. (1980). *Bridges of the bodymind.* Chicago: IPAT.

Achterberg, J., Simonton, C., & Matthews-Simonton, S. (1976). *Psychology of the exceptional cancer patient: A description of patients who outlive predicted life expectancies.* Unpublished manuscript, Cancer Counseling and Research Center, Ft. Worth, Texas.

Ahsen, A. (1968). *Basic concepts in eidetic psychotherapy.* New York: Branden House.

Ahsen, A. (1978). Eidetics: Neural experimental growth potential for the treatment of accident traumas, debilitating stress conditions, and chronic emotional blocking. *Journal of Mental Imagery, 2,* 1–22.

Ammons, A. R. (1972). Reflective. *Collected poems.* New York: W.W. Norton.

Anderson, J. K. (1988). *Tales of great dragons.* Santa Barbara, CA: Bellerophon Books.

Araoz, D. (1985). *The new hypnosis.* New York: Brunner/Mazel.

Bach, R. (1977). Illusions: *The adventures of a reluctant messiah.* New York: Delacorte Press.

Banyai, E. I., & Hilgard, E. (1976). A comparison of active-alert hypnotic induction with traditional relaxation induction. *Journal of Abnormal Psychology, 85,* 218–224.

Barber, T. X. (1961). Psychological aspects of hypnosis. *Psychological Bulletin, 58,* 390–419.

Barber, T. X. (1984). Changing unchangeable bodily processes by hypnotic suggestions: A new look at hypnosis, cognitions, imagining, and the mind-body problem. *Advances, 1*(2), 7–40.

Bateson, G. (1972). *Steps to an ecology of mind.* New York: Ballantine Books.

Bateson, G. (1978). The birth of a matrix or double bind and epistomology. In Milton Berger (Ed.), *Beyond the double bind: Communication and family systems theories and techniques with schizophrenics* (pp. 39–64). New York: Brunner/Mazel.

Bateson, G. (1979). *Mind and nature.* New York: Bantam Books.

Bateson, M. C. (1972). *Our own metaphor: A personal account of a conference on the effect of conscious purpose on human adaptation.* New York: Knopf.

Baum, L. F. (1900). *The Wizard of Oz.* New York: Grosset & Dunlap Publishers.

Beahrs, J. O. (1982). *Unity and multiplicity: Multilevel consciousness of self in hypnosis, psychiatric disorder, and mental health.* New York: Brunner/Mazel.

Beahrs, J. O. (1988). Hypnosis can not be fully nor reliably excluded from the courtroom. *American Journal of Clinical Hypnosis, 31*(1), 18–27.

Bliss, E. (1980). Multiple personalities: A report of 14 cases with implications for schizophrenia and hysteria. *Archives of General Psychiatry,* 37, 1388–1397.

Bourguigon, E. (1988). Dragons. *Encyclopedia Americana, International Edition.* Danbury, CT: Grolier, Inc.

Bower, G. H. (1981). Mood and memory. *American Psychologist, 36*(2), 129–148.

Bowlby, J. (1973). *Separation: Anxiety and anger.* New York: Basic Books.

Bowlby, J. (1984). Violence in the family as a disorder of the attachment and caregiving systems. *American Journal of Psycho-analysis, 44,* 9–27.

Braun, B. (1984). Toward a theory of multiple personality and other dissociative phenomena. *Psychiatric Clinics of North America,* 7(1), 171–193.

Brown, D., & Fromm, E. (1986). *Hypnotherapy and hypnoanalysis.* Hillsdale, NJ: Lawrence Erlbaum Association, Publisher.

Brown, H. (1921). The fifty-first dragon. Adapted from *The Collected Edition of Haywood Brown* and found in Adventures in Reading. Chicago, IL: Harcourt Brace Jovanovich, Publishers.

Burgess, A. (1974). *Rape: Victims of crisis.* Englewood Cliffs, NJ: Prentice-Hall.

Calof, D. (1989). Adult survivors of incest and child abuse, Part One: The family inside the adult child. *The Newsletter of the London Society for Ericksonian Psychotherapy and Hypnosis,* 2(1), 11.

Campbell, J. (1988). *An open life: In conversation with Michael Toms.* New York: Larson Publications.

Campbell, J. with Bill Moyers. (1988). *The power of myth.* Betty Sue Flowers (Ed.). New York: Doubleday.

Capra, F. (1975). *The tao of physics.* Berkeley: Shambhala.

Cashdan, S. (1988). *Object relations therapy: Using the relationship.* New York: W.W. Norton & Company.

Casteneda, C. (1971). *A separate reality.* New York: Pocket Books.

Cheek, D. (1960). Removal of the subconscious resistance to hypnosis using ideomotor techniques. *American Journal of Clinical Hypnosis, 3*(2), 101–113.

Chessick, R. (1965). Empathy and love in psychotherapy. *American Journal of Psychotherapy, 19,* 205.

Chiba, Y., Chiba, K., Halberg, F., & Cutkomp, L. (1977). Longitudinal evaluation of circadian rhythm characteristics and their circadian modulation in an apparently normal couple. In J. McGovern, M. Smolensky, & A. Reinberg (Eds.), *Chronobiology in allergy and immunology* (pp. 17–35). Springfield, IL: Charles C. Thomas.

Cirlot, J. E. (1971). *A dictionary of symbols (2nd ed.).* Hillsdale, NJ: Lawrence Erlbaum Association Publisher. Philosophical Library.

Combs, A., & Snygg, D. (1959). *Individual behavior: A perceptual approach to behavior (revised edition)*. New York: Harper & Row, Publisher.

Condon, W. S. (1975). Multiple response to sound in dysfunctional children. *Journal of Autism and Childhood Schizophrenia, 5*(1), 37–56.

Condon, W. S., & Sander, L. W. (1974). Neonate movement is synchronized with adult speech: Interactional participation and language acquisition. *Science, 183*, 99–101.

Cooper, L., & Erickson, M. H. (1959). *Time distortion in hypnosis*. New York: Irvington.

Courtois, C. (1988). *Healing the incest wound*. New York: W.W. Norton & Company, Inc.

Cox, M., & Theilgaard, A. (1986). *Mutative metaphors in psychotherapy*. London: Tavistock Publications.

de Saint-Exupery, A. (1943). *The little prince*. New York: Harcourt, Brace & World, Inc.

DeLozier, P. (1982). Attachment theory and child abuse. In C.M. Parkes & J. Stevenson-Hinde (Eds.), *The place of attachment in human behavior* (pp. 95–117). New York: Basic Books.

Delozier, J., & Grinder, J. (1987). *Turtles all the way down: Prerequisites to personal genius*. Bonny Door, CA: Grinder, Delozier and Associates.

Dicks, H. (1967). *Marital tensions: Clinical studies toward a psychological theory of interaction*. New York: Basic Books.

Didion, J. (1979). *The white album*. New York: Simon & Schuster.

Dossey, L. (1982). *Space, time, and medicine*. Boulder: Shambhala.

Eliot, T. S. (1943). The dry salvages. *Four Quartets*. New York: Harcourt, Brace & World Inc.

Eliot, T. S. (1986). Burnt Norton. In *Collected Poems, 1909–1962*. New York: Harcourt, Brace, Jovanovich, Publishers.

Erickson, M. H. (1964). Initial experiments investigating the nature of hypnosis. *American Journal of Clinical Hypnosis, 46*, 152–162.

Erickson, M. H. (1966). The interspersal hypnotic technique for symptom correction and pain control. *American Journal of Clinical Hypnosis, 3*, 198–209.

Erickson, M. H. (1980a). The nature of hypnosis and suggestion. In E.L. Rossi (Ed.), *The Collected Papers of Milton H. Erickson (Vol. I)*. New York: Irvington.

Erickson, M. H. (1980b). Hypnotic alteration of sensory, perceptual, and psychophysiological processes. In E.L. Rossi (Ed.), *The Collected Papers of Milton H. Erickson (Vol. II)*. New York: Irvington.

Erickson, M. H. (1980c). Hypnotic investigation of psychodynamic processes. In E.L. Rossi (Ed.), *The Collected Papers of Milton H. Erickson (Vol. III)*. New York: Irvington.

Erickson, M. H. (1980d). Innovative hypnotherapy. In E.L. Rossi (Ed.), *The Collected Papers of Milton H. Erickson (Vol. IV)*. New York: Irvington.

Erickson, M. H., & Lustig, H. (1975). *The artistry of Milton H. Erickson*. Produced by Milton H. Erickson Foundation, Phoenix, AZ.

Erickson, M. H., & Lustig, H. (1976). *The primer of Ericksonian psychotherapy.* New York: Irvington.

Erickson, M. H., & Rossi, E. (1979). *Hypnotherapy: An exploratory casebook.* New York: Irvington.

Erickson, M. H., & Rossi, E. L. (1980). *Healing in Hypnosis.* New York: Irvington.

Erickson, M. H., & Rossi, E. L. (1981). *Experiencing hypnosis: Therapeutic approaches to altered states.* New York: Irvington.

Erickson, M. H., & Rossi, E. L. (1989). *The February Man.* New York: Brunner/Mazel.

Evans, J. (1987). Mythical and fabulous creatures: A source book and research guide. In Malcolm Smith (Ed.), *Dragons.* New York: Greenwood Press.

Fisher, R. (1971). Arousal: Statebound recall of experience. *Diseases of the Nervous System, 32*(6), 373.

Fossum, M., & Mason, M. (1986). *Facing shame.* New York: W.W. Norton & Company.

Franck, F. (1973). *The Zen of seeing.* New York: Vintage Books.

Frankel, F. H. (1974). Trance capacity and the genesis of phobic behavior. *Archives of General Psychiatry, 31*, 261–263.

Frankel, F. H. (1976). *Hypnosis: Trance as a coping mechanism.* New York/London: Plenum Medical Book Co.

Freud, S. (1895). Project for a scientific psychology. In *The standard edition, Vol 1.* (pp. 281–397). London: Hogarth Press.

Fromm, E. (1980). Values in hypnotherapy, *Psychotherapy: Theory, research, and practice, 17*(4), 425–430.

Frost, R. (1965). The road not taken. *Complete Poems of Robert Frost.* New York: Holt, Rinehart, & Winston.

Garner, L. V. (1988). *Dragons: Villain or victim, a fantasy publication from Gargoyle Printing.* Powell Butte, OR: Fundivision of Artware.

Gilligan, C. (1982). *In a different voice.* Cambridge, MA: Harvard University Press.

Gilligan, S. G. (1987). *Therapeutic trances: The cooperating principle in Ericksonian hypnotherapy.* New York: Brunner/Mazel.

Gilligan, S. G. (1988). Symptom phenomena as trance phenomena. In: J. Zeig & S. Lankton (Eds.), *Developing Ericksonian Therapy: State of the Art.* New York: Brunner/Mazel.

Gloor, P., Olivier, A., Quesney, L., Andermann, F., & Horowitz, S. (1982). The role of the limbic system in experimental phenomena of temporal lobe epilepsy. *Annals of Neurology, 12*, 129–144.

Goolishian, H., & Anderson, H. (1988, October). *Human systems as linguistic systems.* Paper presented at the meeting of the American Association of Marriage and Family Therapists, New Orleans, LA.

Grahame, K. (1983). *The reluctant dragon.* New York: Holt, Rinehart, & Winston. (Originally published in 1898 in a collection of short stories called *Dream Days.*)

Green, A. H. (1978). Self-destructive behavior in battered children. *American Journal of Psychiatry, 135,* 579.

Haley, J. (1963). *Strategies of Psychotherapy.* New York: Grune & Stratton, Inc.

Haley, J. (1973). *Uncommon therapy.* New York: Ballantine Books.

Hawking, S. (1988). *A brief history of time.* New York: Bantam Books.

Heckler, R. (1984). *The anatomy of change.* Boston: Shambhala.

Heller, S., & Steele, T. (1987). *Monsters and magical sticks.* Phoenix, AZ: Falcon Press.

Henry, G., Weingartner, H., & Murphy, D. L. (1973). Influence of affective states and psychoactive drugs on verbal learning and memory. *American Journal of Psychiatry, 130,* 66–71.

Herman, J., & van der Kolk, B. A. (1987). Traumatic antecedents of borderline personality disorder. In B. A. Van der Kolk (Ed.). *Psychological trauma* (pp. 111–126). Washington, DC: American Psychiatric Press.

Hilgard, E. R. (1977). *Divided consciousness: Multiple controls in human thought and action.* New York: John Wiley & Sons.

Hilgard, J. (1972). Evidence for a developmental-interactive theory of hypnotic susceptibility. In E. Fromm & R. Shor (Eds.), *Hypnosis: Research developments and perspectives.* Chicago, IL: Aldine-Atherton.

Hirsch, E. (1989). *Night Parade.* New York: Knopf.

Hoffman, L. (1985). Beyond power and control: Toward a "second order" family systems therapy. *Family Systems Medicine, 3*(4), 381–396.

Holloway, F. A. (1978). State dependent learning and time of day. In Ho, B. H., Richards, D. W., & Chute, D. L. (Eds.), *Drug discrimination and state dependent learning.* London: Academic Press, Inc.

Holman, C. H. (1978). *A handbook to literature (3rd edition).* Indianapolis, IN: Bobbs-Merrill.

Hoorwitz, A. N. (1989). *Hypnotic methods in nonhypnotic therapies.* New York: Irvington.

Horowitz, M. (1983). *Image formation (revised edition).* New York: Jason Aronson, Inc.

Hovland, C. I., Harvey, O. J., Sherif, M. (1957). Assimilation and contrast effects in communication and attitude change. *Journal of Abnormal Social Psychology, 60,* 242–252.

Jacobs, W. (1980). *Higher levels of meaning.* Paper presented at the American Association of Marriage and Family Therapists. San Diego, CA.

Kandel, E., & Schwartz, J. H. (1982). Molecular biology of learning: Modulation of transmitter release. *Science, 218,* 433–443.

Kantor, K., & Lehr, W. (1975). *Inside the family: Toward a theory of family process.* San Francisco: Jossey-Bass Publishers.

Kardiner, A. (1941). *The traumatic neuroses of war.* New York: P. Hoeber.

Kaufman, G. (1980). *Shame, the power of caring.* Cambridge, MA: Schenkman Publishing Co., Inc.

Kelly, G. A. (1963). *A theory of personality: The psychology of personal constructs.* New York: W.W. Norton & Company, Inc.

Kernberg, O. (1979). *Object relations and clinical psychoanalysis*. New York: Jason Aronson.

Kernberg, O. (1984). *Severe personality disorders: Psychotherapeutic strategies*. New Haven: Yale University Press.

Kershaw, C. J. (1986). Therapeutic metaphor in the treatment of childhood asthma. In S. Lankton (Ed.), *Ericksonian Monographs, No. 2: Central themes and principles of Ericksonian therapy*. New York: Brunner/Mazel.

Kinsella, W. P. (1982). *Shoeless Joe*. New York: Ballantine Books.

Korzybski, A. (1933). *Science and sanity: An introduction to non-Aristotelian systems and general semantics*. Lancaster, PA: The Science Press Printing Co.

Kroger, W. S. (1963). *Clinical and experimental hypnosis*. Philadelphia: J. B. Lippincott.

Krugman, S. (1987). Trauma in the family: Perspectives on the intergenerational transmission of violence. In van der Kolk Ed.), *Psychological Trauma*, Washington, DC: American Psychiatric Press.

Lankton, S. (1980). *Practical magic: A translation of basic neurolinguistic programming into clinical psychotherapy*. Cupertino, CA: Meta.

Lankton, S. (1986). Elements and dimensions of an Ericksonian approach. In S. Lankton (Ed.), *Ericksonian monographs, No. 2: Central themes and principals of Ericksonian therapy*. New York: Brunner/Mazel.

Lankton, S., & Lankton, C. (1983). *The answer within*. New York: Brunner/ Mazel.

Lankton, S., & Lankton, C. (1986). *Enchantment and intervention*. New York: Brunner/Mazel.

Lankton, S., & Lankton, C. (1988). *Tales of enchantment*. New York: Brunner/ Mazel.

Lenrow, P. B. (1966). The uses of metaphor is facilitating constructive behavior change. *Journal of Psychotherapy: Theory, Research, and Practice, 3*(4), 145–148.

Leonard, G. (1978). *The silent pulse*. New York: E.P. Dutton.

Lewis, H. (Ed.) (1987). *The role of shame in sympton formation*. Hillsdale, NJ: Lawrence Erlbaum Associates, Publisher.

Lindemann, E. (1944). Symptomatology and management of acute grief. *American Journal of Psychiatry, 101*, 141–148.

Ludwig, A. (1966). Altered states of consciousness. *Archives of General Psychiatry, 15*, 225–234.

Luria, A. R. (1968). *The mind of a mnemonist*. New York: Basic Books.

Luthe, N., & Schultz, J. H. (1969). *Autogenic therapy: Vols 1–6*. New York: Grune and Stratton.

Lynch, M., & Roberts, J. (1982). *Consequences of child abuse*. Orlando, FL: Academic Press.

Main, M., & Weston, D. (1982). Avoidance of the attachment figure in infancy. In C. Parkes & R. Hinde (Eds.), *The place of attachment in human behavior* (pp. 31–59). New York: Basic Books.

Marcuse, F. L. (1959). *Hypnosis: Fact and fictions*. Harmondsworth: Penguin Books.

Masterson, J. (1981). *The narcissistic and borderline disorders.* New York: Brunner/Mazel.

Masterson, J., & Rinsley, D. (1975). The borderline syndrome: The role of the mother in the genesis and psychic structure of the borderline personality. *International Journal of Psycho-Analysis, 56,* 163–177.

Maturano, H. (1984). *Bringing forth of reality: Presentation at construction of realities conference.* Family Therapy Program. University of Calgary Medical School. Calgary, Alberta, Canada.

Maturano, H., & Varela, F. (1987). *Tree of knowledge.* Boston: Shambhala.

McClelland, D. (1984). *Advances,* 5, Spring Issue. Journal of the Institute for the Advancement of Health.

Meissner, W. W. (1988). *Treatment of patients in the borderline spectrum.* New Jersey: Jason Aronson.

Melges, F. (1982). *Time and the inner future: A temporal approach to psychiatric disorders.* New York: John Wiley & Sons.

Mendelson, M. (1974). *Psychoanalytic concepts of depression.* New York: John Wiley & Sons.

Meredith, R., & Fitzgerald, J. (1972). *Structuring your novel: From basic idea to finished manuscript.* New York: Harper & Row, Publishers.

Mittelmann, B. (1948). Complementary neurotic reactions in intimate relationships. *Psychoanalytic Quarterly, 13,* 479–483.

Moyers, W. (1989). *A world of ideas: Conversations with thoughtful men and women about American life today and the ideas shaping our future.* (pp. 345–357). New York: Doubleday.

Murphy, M., & Vogel, J. (1984). *David and perception.* Unpublished manuscript.

Nichols, M. (1987). *The self in the system: Expanding the limits of family therapy.* New York: Brunner/Mazel.

Nye, J., & McCaffrey, A. (1989). *The dragonlover's guide to Pern.* New York: Ballantine Books.

O'Hanlon, W. (1987). *Taproots: Underlying principles of Milton Erickson's therapy and hypnosis.* New York: W.W. Norton & Company, Inc.

Orne, M. T. (1959). The nature of hypnosis: Artifact and essence. *Journal of Abnormal and Social Psychology, 58,* 277–299.

Pearce, J. (1971). *Crack in the cosmic egg: Challenging constructs of mind and reality.* New York: Pocket Books.

Peebles, M. J. (1989). Through a glass darkly: The psychoanalytic use of hypnosis with post-traumatic stress disorder. *International Journal of Clinical and Experimental Hypnosis,* July, *37,* 192–205.

Peebles, M. J., & Fisher, V. (producer), (1987). *Hypnosis in the treatment of post traumatic shock disorder: A case of awareness under surgical anesthesia.* Topeka, KS: Menninger Video Productions.

Perls, F., Hefferline, R., & Goodman, P. (1951). *Gestalt therapy.* New York: Dell Publishing Co.

Piaget, J. (1969). *The mechanism of perceptions* (G. N. Seagrim, Trans.). New York: Basic Books. (Original work published 1961).

Pintauro, J. (1970). *To believe in man.* New York: Harper & Row.

Pribram, K. (1971). *Languages of the brain.* Monterrey, CA: Brooks/Cole Publishing Co.

Pribram, K. (1976). *Freud's project reassessed: Preface to contemporary cognitive theory and neuropsychology.* New York: Basic Books.

Protinsky, H. (1988). Hypnotic strategies in strategic marital therapy. *Journal of Strategic and Systemic Therapies, 7*(4), 29–34.

Ritterman, M. (1983). *Using hypnosis in family therapy.* San Francisco: Jossey-Bass.

Ritterman, M. (1985). Family context symptom induction and therapeutic conterinduction: Breaking the spell of a dysfunctional rapport. In J. Zeig (Ed.), *Ericksonian psychotherapy. Vol. 2: Clinical applications.* New York: Irvington.

Rogers, L., Tenhouten, W., Kaplan, C. D., & Gardiner, M. (1977). Hemispheric specialization of bilingual Hopi Indian children. *International Journal of Neuroscience, 8*, 1–6.

Rossi, E. L. (1986). *The psychobiology of mind-body healing.* New York: W.W. Norton & Company, Inc.

Rossi, E. L., & Cheek, D. (1988). *Mind-body therapy.* New York: W.W. Norton & Company, Inc.

Rowe, D. (1982). *Experience of depression.* New York: John Wiley & Sons.

Samuels, M., & Samuels, N. (1975). *Seeing with the mind's eye.* New York: Random House.

Sanders, B., McRoberts, G., & Tollefson, C. (1989). Childhood stress and dissociation in a college population. *Dissociation, 2*(1), pp. 17–23.

Segal, L. (1986). *The dream of reality.* New York: W.W. Norton & Company, Inc.

Shaffer, P. (1974). *Equus.* New York: Atheneum.

Sherif, M., & Sherif, C. W. (1969). *Social psychology.* New York: Harper & Row, Publishers.

Solomon, M. (1989). *Narcissism and intimacy.* New York: W.W. Norton & Company, Inc.

Sperry, R. (1968). Hemisphere disconnection and unity in conscious awareness. *American Psychologist, 23*, 723–733.

Steiner, G. (1975). *After Babel, aspects of language and translation.* London: Oxford University Press.

Turbayne, C. M. (1962). *The myth of metaphor.* New Haven: Yale University Press.

van der Hart, O. (1983). *Rituals in psychotherapy.* New York: Irvington.

van der Kolk, B. A. (1987). *Psychological trauma.* Washington, DC: American Psychiatric Press.

van der Kolk, B. A., Greenberg, M., Boyd, H., Krystal, J. (1985). Inescapable shock. *Biological Psychiatry, 20*, 314–325.

Wachtel, P. L. (1985). Integrative psychodynamic therapy. In S. Lynn & J. Garske (Eds.), *Contemporary psychotherapies.* Columbus, OH: Charles E. Merrill.

Wachtel, P. L., & Wachtel, E. (1986). *Family dynamics in individual psychotherapy: A guide to clinical strategies.* New York: Guilford Press.

Walker, A. (1983). *In search of our mothers' gardens.* San Diego: Harcourt Brace Jovanovich, Publishers.

Watkins, J. G. (1971). The affect bridge: A hypnotherapeutic technique. *International Journal of Clinical and Experimental Hypnosis, 19,* 21–27.

Watkins, J., & Watkins, H. (1979). Theory and practice of ego state therapy: A short-term therapeutic approach. In H. Grayson (Ed.). *Short term approaches to psychotherapy.* New York: National Institute for the Psychotherapies and Human Sciences Press.

Weiner, H. (1966). External chemical messengers: Emission and reception in man. *New York State Journal of Medicine, 66*(24), 3, 153–170.

Wells, H. G. (1968). *The time machine, the war of the worlds.* Greenwich, CT: Fawcett.

Werntz, D. (1981). *Cerebral hemispheric activity and autonomic nervous function.* Unpublished doctoral dissertation, University of California, San Diego.

Werntz, D., Bickford, R., Bloom, F., & Shannahoff, S. (1983). Alternating cerebral hemispheric activity and lateralization of autonomic nervous function. *Human Neurobiology, 2,* 39–43.

Whitaker, C. (1989). *Dancing with the family.* Seminar sponsored by the M.H. Erickson Institute of Central Texas, Houston, Texas.

Whorf, P. (1969). *Language, thought, and reality.* Cambridge, MA: MIT Press.

Willi, J. (1982). *Couples in collusion.* New York: Jason Aronson.

Winch, R. F. (1958). *Mate selection: Study of complementary needs.* New York: Harper & Row, Publishers.

Wolf, F. A. (1984). *Star wave: Mind, consciousness, and quantum physics.* New York: Macmillan Publishing Co.

Youtz, R., Makous, W. L., Weintraub, D., & Buckhout, R. (1966). Dermooptical. *Science, 152,* 1108–1110.

Zeig, J., (1982) *Symbolic hypnotherapy: A Training video featuring inductions conducted by Milton H. Erickson in 1979.* Produced by The Milton H. Erickson Foundation, Phoenix, AZ.

Zeig, J., (1984) *The process of hypnotic induction: A training video featuring inductions conducted by Milton H. Erickson in 1964.* Produced by The Milton H.Erickson Foundation, Phoenix, AZ.

Zeig, J. (1985). *Experiencing Erickson.* New York: Brunner/Mazel.

Zeig, J. (1990). *Seeding.* In: J. Zeig & S. Gilligan (Eds.) *Brief Therapy: Myths, Methods, and Metaphor.* New York: Brunner/Mazel.

Zinker, J. (1977). *Creative process in Gestalt therapy.* New York: Brunner/Mazel.

Name Index

237

Subject Index